Race, racism and developme

About the author

KALPANA WILSON is a Fellow at the Gender Institute, London School of Economics. Her experiences teaching development studies in British universities, as well as her involvement as an activist around issues of racism and imperialism, led her to pursue the themes of this book. She has also written and researched extensively on agrarian transformation in Bihar in India, women's participation in rural labour movements and the relationships between neoliberalism, gender and concepts of agency.

Race, racism and development

Interrogating history, discourse and practice

KALPANA WILSON

Zed Books

LONDON | NEW YORK

Race, Racism and Development: Interrogating History, Discourse and Practice was first published in 2012 by Zed Books Ltd, 7 Cynthia Street, London N1 9JF, UK and Room 400, 175 Fifth Avenue, New York, NY 10010, USA

www.zedbooks.co.uk

Designed and typeset in Monotype Bembo Book
by illuminati, Grosmont
Index: rohan.indexing@gmail.com
Cover design: www.roguefour.co.uk
Printed by CPI Group (UK) Ltd, Croydon CRO 4YY

Distributed in the USA exclusively by Palgrave Macmillan, a division of St Martin's Press, LLC, 175 Fifth Avenue, New York, NY 10010, USA

A catalogue record for this book is available from the British Library
Library of Congress Cataloging in Publication Data available

ISBN 978 1 84813 511 6 hb
ISBN 978 1 84813 512 3 pb

Contents

Acknowledgements

This book has taken me a long time to write and an even longer time to start writing. Far from being based on a discrete period of research, it has been influenced by so many people, and in such varied contexts, that acknowledgements are perhaps particularly difficult to write. Among those whom I would especially like to thank for reading and commenting on parts of the manuscript and for discussing its themes and sharing their knowledge and ideas with me are Vron Ware, Andrea Cornwall, Nalini Visvanathan, Charles Abugre, Samarendra Das, Sadie Wearing, Jin Haritaworn, Paul Gilroy, Clare Hemmings, Anne Phillips, Sumi Madhok, John Newsinger, Diane Perrons, Ania Plomien, Anandi Ramamurthy, Carolyn Williams, Gwendolyn Beetham, Naaz Rashid, Sachin Gupta, Jeanne Firth and Caitlin Fisher.

My colleagues at the LSE Gender Institute have been unfailingly supportive and encouraging during the period this book has been in the making. I would also like to thank all the students at Birkbeck who took my 'Race', Ethnicity and Development MSc option course from 2004 onwards and whose questions, arguments and insights helped me to clarify and develop my ideas for the book, my colleagues on the Development Studies programme at Birkbeck, and especially Jasmine Gideon for her ongoing support for both the course and the book.

At Zed Books, I benefited from the expertise and patience of my editors Tamsine O'Riordan, who shared my enthusiasm for this project from the outset, and Jakob Horstmann, who helped to keep me writing with his perfectly timed emails!

The book owes a great deal to South Asia Solidarity Group, as a member of which I have been involved in many of the political campaigns referred to in the book, and especially my dear friend Sarbjit Johal, who is continuing to participate in them – and to inspire others – while courageously waging a protracted battle with illness.

This book would never have happened without the taken-for-granted support and enthusiasm of my family – John Wilson, my father, whose passion for and in-depth knowledge of history I have turned to repeatedly, my daughter Ananya Wilson-Bhattacharya with her clarity of vision and her optimism about the future, and of course Dipankar Bhattacharya who always, even across continents, succeeded in convincing me that this book was worth writing, and that I could write it. Finally, my mother, Amrit Wilson, has been beside me every step of the way, and made it possible in uncountable ways – this book has been inspired by the dreams we share.

Introduction

I was in the last stages of completing this book in March 2012 when the 'Kony 2012' video went viral. The video and the responses it generated seemed to highlight many of the questions I had been thinking and writing about over the preceding months. Produced by the US-based NGO Invisible Children, the video was part of a campaign for the arrest of Ugandan Joseph Kony, the leader of the armed group the Lord's Resistance Army, and his trial by the International Criminal Court for crimes against humanity, in particular the abduction of thousands of children as soldiers. The video called for US military intervention in Central Africa to be stepped up in order to 'Stop Kony' and targeted young people in the global North to join a mass movement demanding this action.

Less than three weeks after being uploaded to the Internet, 'Kony 2012' had been viewed by more than 84 million people, and had already generated intense controversy. Many commentators highlighted the fact that the video was heavily oversimplified and referred to a situation which had since changed drastically – Kony was no longer active in Uganda, and, it was argued, resources were more urgently needed to help ex-child soldiers to rebuild their lives than for the mission of capturing him. Perhaps most tellingly, although this was less widely circulated in the mainstream media, far from being reluctant to sustain a military presence in the region as the video suggests, the US administration had ongoing military involvement and significant strategic and economic interests in the area bordering Uganda and the DRC (where Kony had now fled), not least because of the existence of significant oil resources which are already being exploited by North American and British companies.

Meanwhile, other writers focused on the racism implicit in 'Kony 2012', which was seen as reproducing colonial narratives about Africa in which white people are constructed as having a moral obligation to intervene to rescue and 'save' black people from chaos, violence and irrationality. Although the video is ostensibly about children in Uganda, the emotional core of the film is in fact the scene in which the white American film-maker Jason Russell shows his 5-year-old son a photograph of the 'bad guy' Joseph Kony, setting up a highly racialised dichotomy between the 'evil' black man and the innocent white child who, once he understands the all-too-simple problem, can help to 'fix' it.

But these two strands of criticism – of the role of global capital in producing the US military intervention the video supports, and of the role of ideas of 'race' and of racism in shaping the video – remained largely separate. The questions I would like to pose in this context relate to the connections between the two. What is the work that ideas of 'race' do here? Can we understand 'Kony 2012' as not simply reflecting latent racism, but mobilising it, and if so, to what ends? More broadly, how do we understand the ongoing relationship between 'race' and capital on a global scale? How does racism inform and legitimise changing patterns of exploitation, exchange and accumulation? And how do these patterns, in turn, reproduce material inequalities which continue to be explained through a lens of 'race'?

In this book, which in many ways takes these questions as a starting point, I have sought to bring a critical understanding of 'race' and racism into the same frame as 'development', which I conceptualise as including not only the vast array of development organisations and initiatives but the wider processes of economic, social and political change with which these are concerned.

The period when I first began teaching development studies in London more than a decade ago coincided with a phase when anti-racist activists in Britain were rethinking the contours of racism in the changed circumstances of the 'War on Terror'. More than ever, it was felt to be imperative to seek to understand racism as it was experienced and confronted in Britain in the context of imperialism and the changing strategies of global capital. The changes under way had begun well before 9/11, however, with the advent of neoliberal globalisation and, from the 1990s onwards, the rise of new civilisational discourses and the construction of new 'threats', which were racialised in ways both novel and familiar.

With the invasion of Iraq following on rapidly from the occupation of Afghanistan, the tone of apologists for Britain's colonial history became increasingly celebratory. Simultaneously, the notion of 'development' increasingly appeared in public pronouncements in the context of military intervention, combating terrorism, preventing migration and securing populations in the global North, a set of linkages which were to crystallise in the development/security paradigm according to which, as Tony Blair put it, 'the yearning is for order and stability and if it doesn't exist elsewhere, it is unlikely to exist here'.

In a couple of decades, 'development' as it was popularly understood in Britain had acquired a dramatically increased visibility and a whole range of new meanings. These meanings were embodied in the figure of the development worker – almost always the employee of an NGO, but with increasingly dense connections with northern militaries on the one hand and corporates on the other, who appeared in different guises: morally compelled to 'take sides' on the frontline of war zones in Africa, embedded in military intervention to protect human rights in the Middle East, and teaching people everywhere in the global South about civilisational 'values' like democracy, gender equality and entrepreneurialism – and they were meanings which, as I argue in this book, were always, also, implicitly about race. Yet race and racism remained an area of profound silence in development studies, a silence which was all the more weighted by the fact that experiences of learning and teaching were structured by power-laden encounters between academics, the overwhelming majority of whom, still, were white, and a very diverse range of students, many of whom had travelled from countries in the global South to acquire the qualifications which would mark them as having the skills required to work in development.

I argue that the ideas of 'race' and of development have in fact been intimately related from their consolidation in the late eighteenth and nineteenth centuries onwards, but that the relationship between the two has changed significantly in different historical periods. To understand this, I suggest, we need to treat development as not simply encompassing institutions which are avowedly engaged in international development – government departments like DfID or USAID, international organisations like the World Bank, or development NGOs – even though there is so much to be said about 'race' and racism within these institutions. Rather, development should be understood more broadly as incorporating the whole complex of unequal material relationships and processes which structure engagement between the global South and the global North, as well as the primary discursive framework within which these relationships have been constructed for more than sixty years. It is therefore inextricable from the rapidly shifting and mutating operations of global capital, and should be understood in relation to concepts of imperialism, rather than, as in much development discourse, as an alternative which renders these concepts invisible.

In the process of making these connections, three recurring analytical themes have emerged. The first relates to my preoccupation with tracing the relationship between race and capital. I argue that constructions of race and racial hierarchy (explicit or implicit) are reconfigured and redeployed both in response to resistance to capital which threatens to transform radically the distribution of power and resources, and in the context of often related shifts in patterns and strategies of global capital accumulation. This is explored and elaborated, for example, in the context of the uprisings of 1857 in India and the decades that followed; in the context of resistance to neoliberal economic policies and the good governance agenda of the 1990s; and in Britain during the contemporary War on Terror.

The second theme involves exploring what the materiality of race might mean in the context of global structures of capital and processes of accumulation. Questions of the body and embodied experience, the material production of difference, and how these are shaped by racial ideologies, emerge as central from discussion of development policies and interventions such as those relating to (or impacting upon) population control, HIV, famine and malnutrition, and are elaborated further in Chapter 6 in particular.

The third theme relates to the tendency of discourses of development to appropriate and incorporate critical approaches. This has been particularly marked, I argue, since the advent of neoliberalism as the dominant model of development. The means by which elements of both postdevelopment and postcolonial critiques have been, apparently paradoxically, incorporated within neoliberal frameworks is examined at a number of points in the book. In these contexts, I reflect on the implications for the theorisation of race in development and for the politics of transnational solidarity.

Theorising race and development

If 'race' in development is an arena of silence, it is at the same time a theme that precipitates engagement with a very rich variety of work by scholars and activists. In particular, three interrelated and overlapping kinds of analytical work have inspired and informed this book: Marxist theorisation of imperialism, and in particular 'Third World' Marxism or the diverse approaches to revolutionary theory and practice which have been developed in, and with reference to, the global South (this evidently extends beyond the work of the dependency theorists usually cited in histories of development thought); analysis of 'race' and racism as it operates within North American and European social formations, much of it broadly identified with critical race theory; and scholarship which is located within the avowedly diverse and porous analytical field of postcolonial theory.

The emergence and establishment of postcolonial theory has generated a sustained critical focus on discourses of development, the 'representations and institutional practices that structure the relationships between West and Third World' (Kapoor, 2008: xv). The deconstruction of discourses of development and their role in regulating the 'Third World', in particular through processes of construction of the 'other' by way of a series of binary oppositions and strategic silencings, has formed the basis for much contemporary critical work around development. Crucially for thinking about race, it has challenged the construction of development as a neutral, 'technical' field, making it possible to raise questions of power, difference, location and subjectivity. Not surprisingly, then, it is within a postcolonial theoretical framework that the relatively small body of existing work which directly addresses 'race' and racism in development is located.

But the postcolonial approach also leaves unanswered or even unaskable a number of questions which become particularly pressing in the context of the historical and contemporary relations between race and development. For example, precisely what kinds of material arrangements and relationships underpin and are perpetuated by the discourses that postcolonial theorists deconstruct? Is it enough to speak, as much postcolonial theory does, of the overarching category of modernity as the framework within which colonial discourses emerge, or do we need to distinguish the particular economic processes under way in different periods, and, critically, how these change and the implications of these changes? These are particularly salient questions when considering race, because the centrality of the idea of 'race' to Enlightenment thinking cannot be fully understood without foregrounding the enabling relationship between race and capital, and the accumulation from racialised slavery it allowed, which in turn made possible the establishment of European capitalism. Further, as I explore in this book, constructions of race have been repeatedly transformed, reworked or reanimated in the context of both changing strategies of capital accumulation and resistance to them. But because postcolonial approaches tend to regard all conceptions of economic development in poststructuralist terms, as metanarratives of progress, they often neglect the changes in patterns of global capital accumulation reflected in changing models of development, such as the shift from developmentalism to neoliberalism, and their implications for race. This approach also does not encourage us to consider the visions of different kinds of development which often inform resistance to capitalist accumulation processes, so that paradoxically those engaging in this resistance may be silenced in postcolonial literature.

As well as the key influence of Fanon, postcolonial theory has drawn directly and indirectly on the work of Foucault, whose thinking also informs much current critical scholarship in development which is not avowedly postcolonial. Foucauldian concepts of discourse, power/knowledge, disciplinary power and the production of the subject are all ones that I deploy repeatedly in the chapters that follow. At the same time, in incorporating these concepts within a broad framework of Marxist political economy, I also diverge from a Foucauldian perspective in a number of key respects, in particular in relation to Foucault's conceptualisation of power as circulating and pervasive, rather than located, which characterises his later work. This notion of power has often been adopted in ways which, I have argued, preclude a consideration of the sources of power, or examining its relationship to material structures of production, exchange and accumulation in any depth. Further, Foucauldian approaches to development, as I suggest later in the book, have tended to emphasise the regulation, management and containment of populations at the expense of attention to the dynamics of extractive and exploitative processes, thus limiting the possibilities for an exploration of the changing relationship between race and capital.

This is by no means to suggest that postcolonial and Marxist thinking can be distinguished by a simple discursive/material dichotomy, or indeed that they represent mutually exclusive systems of thought. Marx's own engagement with the role of discourse in sustaining power is evident in much of his work but is most fully elaborated in *The German Ideology*, in which he argues with reference to the ruling class that 'insofar ... as they rule as a class and determine the extent and compass of an epoch, it is self-evident that they do this in its whole range, hence among other things rule also as thinkers, as producers of ideas, and regulate the production and distribution of the ideas of their age' (Marx and Engels, 1974: 64)

Nor am I arguing here that postcolonial theorists completely neglect material relations. Although postcolonial theorists have tended to emphasise discursive continuities with the colonial period, as in other work influenced by poststructuralism, notably feminist theory, there has been a significant 'turn' to the material, particularly in relation to the body and space. This is particularly significant for discussions of race, and, as I indicate below, forms one of the elements on which I have drawn in order to explore questions of embodied difference in the context of development.

I have indicated some of the areas where the framework of postcolonial theory has seemed to me to be insufficient to address the questions of race, racism and development, even though many ideas within it are invaluable for such a project. The central aspect of this, however, is the way postcolonial ideas have proved amenable to appropriation within neoliberal approaches to development. As I have suggested, neoliberalism has shown a remarkable capacity to incorporate and transform critical ideas. I explore this in detail in the context of the response to critiques of representations of Third World women and the foregrounding of notions of women's agency and empowerment within development in Chapter 2, and elsewhere I look at how, more broadly, elements of postcolonial ideas about difference and hybridity as well as critiques of Eurocentrism have been incorporated into neoliberal development discourses such as those produced by the World Bank. This is partly made possible, I argue, by the prominence of notions of choice and of freedom within neoliberal discourses that are constructed as emancipatory narratives, primarily in relation to a state that is by definition oppressive. The specific and often fatally constrained and constraining meanings of these terms within this context, I suggest, can only be fully exposed by a political economy critique which not only establishes the shackling of these notions to the institutions of property and the capitalist market, but demonstrates the day-to-day material effects of their operation.

Attempts to theorise 'race' and racism within a Marxist framework have, of course, had to challenge economic reductionist and essentialising interpretations of Marxism, in which lived experiences are seen as determined by the individual's relations to the means of production alone, and a consideration of, for example, racism among the white working class in countries of the global North is viewed as divisive and irrelevant. Yet, as Stuart Hall has argued, historical materialism as a method explicitly rejects this reductionism, allowing us to trace the relationship between racism and capitalism, and explore specific conjunctures of time and space in order to establish how this relationship has evolved in a variety of ways (Hall, 1986). As Hall explains in his exposition of the ideas of Gramsci, this involves 'not simply more detailed historical specification, but – as Marx himself argued – the application of new concepts and further levels of determination in addition to those pertaining to simple exploitative relations between capital and labour' (1986: 7).

Hall has argued for an analytical focus on the social formation rather than the mode of production as the framework within which historical specificities can be explored at a more particular level and the possibility of the articulation of more than one mode of production within a single social formation can be acknowledged (1986). This approach has been important for Marxist-oriented scholarship on race and racism, generating influential concepts such as Omi and Winant's racial formation (1986). But the tendency to treat the social formation as a bounded category for analysis of race, which has characterised some critical race theory in the USA, raises questions about how to address the more extensive scope of imperialism, the contemporary operations of global capital, and neoliberal globalisation, questions which come to the fore in a consideration of race in development.

While remaining attentive to the inherent mutability of racial categories, as well as the ways in which experiences of racialisation are shaped by particular histories, I am concerned here to locate the ideas and the practices of race within processes taking place on a global scale, including not only the history of racialised slavery and European colonialism, but also 'neocolonial' Cold War economic, political and military relationships of power; the consolidation of global capital and of neoliberalism; and the post-Cold War expansion of direct military intervention and the 'War on Terror', all of which have seen the deployment of a variety of concepts and practices of development. Rather than investigating the dynamics of particular racialised societies in the global South (for example, Brazil or South Africa), then, the book focuses attention on the racialised implications of development interventions taking place on a global scale – such as population control, or the good governance agenda, recognising that these cannot be fully grasped without a consideration of how they are experienced, negotiated and contested in a variety of different contexts.

This recognition of imperialism as central to an understanding of race, wherever one is located, brings the book closer to some of the concerns of earlier radical critiques of racism, most notably those present in the later work of W.E.B. Du Bois. At the same time, in focusing on the changing material dynamics of imperialism, and relating it to structures of inequality and multiple struggles for social transformation in the global South, it draws extensively on the work of a wide range of 'Third World' Marxist scholars and activists who have sought to apply and extend Marxist ideas to further these struggles.

All of these strands of thinking, organising and struggling have shaped this book, and in particular the ways in which I attempt to think through the central question of the work race does. The starting point is that race is a social construct rather than a biological fact, a temporally and spatially contingent and mutable system of categorisation, only intelligible in terms of ideas of racial hierarchy. At the same time, as Linda Martín Alcoff puts it, 'race is real': it is lived experience (2001). It shapes material structures of power and distribution of resources, and regulates bodies and spaces. This second aspect is, of course, less acknowledged within dominant discourses about race than the first, because it is much more threatening to existing contemporary structures of power and control of resources.[1]

But the book's focus on the global inequalities that are central to questions of development made me want to look in more depth at the relationship between race and material processes. Contemporary theorising around racialised embodiment has drawn on ideas developed in the context of feminist theory that focused on the indeterminacy of the embodied subject which is repeatedly reproduced in contingent ways. Yet looking at race in relation to global capital complicates this, while further reinforcing the central fact that the differences of race are socially produced, not biological. As I argue in Chapter 6, this perspective highlights how the 'idea of race' legitimized and made possible processes which produced bodies differently in material ways related to access to and control over – or violent denial of – resources, such as for example land, or health care. At the same time, these processes are sites of ongoing contestation and resistance, which also has corporeal implications. In considering embodiment, I suggest that we need to consider not only the discursive production of racialised bodies but equally the racialised material production of bodies. This shift also has a bearing on the apparent contradiction of thinking about the work race does on a global scale, while recognising that for many people in the world race as a category for subject formation may have little meaning.

The emphasis on the global implications of constructions of race and of racism, and specifically on the relationship between global capital and race, requires some explanation. This does not imply that the ever-expanding scale of global capital accumulation has a homogenising effect: rather, as I have argued, capitalism is productive of difference, and this continues to be evident in the context of neoliberalism, which frequently sustains, intensifies and incorporates pre-existing inequalities, such as those of gender, caste or ethnic group. The multiplicity of experiences and relationships in different global locations and the extent of the differences between them cannot be underestimated – and processes of racialised essentialisation such as those which have produced the tropes of the

'Third World woman as victim' have been the focus of some of the most influential postcolonial critiques of development, notably those of Chandra Mohanty (1986) and Gayatri Spivak (1988). But more recently, reflecting on the influence and interpretation of her article 'Under Western Eyes', first published in 1986, Mohanty has called attention to the potentially paralysing effects of an emphasis on difference, which elides analysis of wider transnational structures of capital and therefore limits the possibilities for a radical politics of solidarity that remains attentive to difference (Mohanty, 2003). I would suggest that work which contributes to such a politics must not only engage with the operations of global processes, as I have outlined above, but attempt, at least provisionally, to make links and trace connections transnationally between vastly different historical and spatial contexts. While clearly such an approach has inherent risks of simplification and misrepresentation, I would argue that these risks are outweighed by the potential insights to be gained.

For example, although the empirical focus of the book is on more recent historical periods, I refer to the events of the Haitian Revolution – which overturned the meaning of race as an idea at the very moment when it was being consolidated – drawing upon the extremely rich and varied accounts and analysis of those scholars and writers who have studied it in depth. The Revolution and the questions of race, capital, labour and freedom at its heart have, I suggest, inescapable implications for the central themes of this book. Further, the exclusion of these seminal events from many mainstream accounts of the period only testifies to the enduring effects of racism, and is a process with which there must be no further collusion.

Inevitably perhaps, this book has left me with more questions than it has answered, and many of its conclusions are simultaneously appeals for further engagement, exploration and elaboration. While it is customary to begin with a 'theoretical' chapter which introduces the relevant existing literature and move on to the presentation of empirical material, this book is structured slightly differently, reflecting my commitment to a dialectical and reflexive approach which questions the theory/practice dichotomy that is so ingrained in development, as well as the fact that the book in many ways represents an unfinished journey towards theorising 'race' and racism in the context of development.

The starting point in Chapter 1, then, is an exploration of the historical and conceptual roots of the ideas of development and progress in the emergence of European capitalism, and how they were related to the consolidation of constructions of 'race' in the contexts of slavery and colonialism which made this emergence possible. The chapter goes on to look at how changing patterns of imperial accumulation and multiple forms of resistance to these processes reshaped and reconfigured constructions of 'race' in the nineteenth century, and set the parameters for future development interventions, through a focus on a key moment in this process: the Indian uprisings of 1857 and their protracted aftermath. In Chapter 2, the question of racialised representations and the impact on them of changing strategies of capital accumulation is explored further, in the context of contemporary neoliberal globalisation. This chapter examines changing gendered and racialised visual representations of 'poor women in the global South' by development institutions, looking critically at new racialised constructions of the empowered, agentic entrepreneurial subject through a discussion of three recent publicity campaigns, each belonging to a different strand within the development industry.

The next three chapters examine how 'race' and racism are implicated in particular development policies that have been pursued at specific historical conjunctures. Chapter 3 examines population control policies in the context of the Cold War, the reconfiguring of imperialism after formal colonialism, and the challenge to the existing global distribution of wealth and resources posed by communist movements in the global South, and explores how these were related to the pathologisation of racialised sexualities which mark discourses of population control. Continuing with this theme, Chapter 4 looks at the HIV/AIDS pandemic in sub-Saharan Africa, which has mirrored the trajectory of neoliberal policies introduced in the 1980s, examining how the operation of 'race' and racism have shaped both the pandemic and the changing responses to it. Chapter 5 focuses on the 1990s as a decade in which 'race' was mobilized in new ways which both evoke and extend earlier deployments. It explores this mobilisation in relation to three interlinked processes that spanned the decade: the shift from 'needs-based' to 'rights-based' approaches to humanitarian intervention; the emergence of the good governance agenda; and the reconfiguration of the relationship between development and liberal democracy within dominant discourses. Both this chapter and the one that precedes it highlight the continuing centrality of racialised and pathologising tropes of 'Africa' to development interventions, which not only renders invisible the heterogeneity of the continent and its multiple trajectories and histories, but operates to reinscribe and extend global relationships of inequality and exploitation.

The last three chapters focus directly upon different strands of critical thinking about development and their implications. Building on the earlier chapters, they move towards a possible theorisation of 'race' and racism in development. Chapter 6 discusses recent critical analysis of the development/security paradigm associated with twenty-first-century neoliberal imperialism, and, drawing on feminist, postcolonial and Marxist approaches to the body, looks at the implications for analysing contemporary race and racialisation of bringing questions of embodiment, labour, land and capital accumulation into the frame. Chapter 7 examines racialised constructions within postdevelopment approaches, and, through a reflection on some aspects of an international campaign against bauxite mining in India, considers the extent to which postdevelopment ideas have been selectively appropriated within the neoliberal project, particularly in the context of the activities of NGOs, and explores the implications for practices of transnational political solidarity. It discusses the increasing construction of Northern publics as powerful collective agents with moral and civilisational obligations to intervene in the global South, a process that is evident in the 'Kony 2012' campaign with which we began this discussion. Chapter 8 continues with the theme of appropriation, considering in particular those postcolonial critiques of development which have directly addressed 'race' and racism. The chapter examines the initiative of the British government's Department for International Development (DfID) to involve diasporas in development, along with some wider representations of the role of 'diasporic' subjects in development in the British media, in the context of contemporary reconfigurations of 'race' within Britain, which are both shaped by and in turn affect the multiple trajectories of neoliberal imperialism and the resistance it generates.

CHAPTER I

Race, capital and resistance through the lens of 1857

> You may hang me, or such as me, every day but thousands will rise in my place and your object will never be gained.
>
> Pir Ali, a bookbinder from Patna
> hanged by the British in 1857

This chapter looks at the historical and conceptual roots of the ideas of development and progress in the emergence of European capitalism, and how they were related to the consolidation of constructions of 'race' in the contexts of slavery and colonialism, which made this emergence possible. It will then consider how both changing patterns of imperial accumulation and multiple forms of resistance to these processes reshaped and reconfigured constructions of 'race' in the nineteenth century, setting the parameters for future development interventions, through a focus on one of a number of key moments in this process: the Indian uprisings of 1857 and their aftermath. By looking at the events of 1857 through the lens of some of the debates which surrounded them on their 150th anniversary, we will also reflect on some continuities in the relationships between 'race', capital, and the discourses, structures and practices of development.

Drawing on the extensive critical theorising around race which has informed challenges to racialised power in multiple locations, I treat 'race' as simultaneously a socially constructed, historically contingent and mutable category, and a material reality which shaped and constrained, often fatally, embodied and lived experience, and continues to do so in changing ways. Race, then, cannot be understood simply as a legitimating ideology for capitalist accumulation, or even, in more Foucauldian terms, as a discourse of disciplinary power for categorising subjects and facilitating colonial regulation. It became a system of organising capital accumulation, and as a result its implications were not limited to naming difference and giving it material effects. Racialised capitalist accumulation in the late colonial form it took from the mid-nineteenth century onwards, I suggest, was productive of material and embodied difference on a global scale, most centrally through the systematic dispossession of working people in the global South of the resources needed to sustain human life.

This period saw the consolidation of a global division of labour in which vast regions of the global South became primarily suppliers of raw materials and food grains for European industrial centres. As we will see, everywhere this relationship was established not primarily through the operation of 'free market' processes but through direct interventions by the colonial state marked by violence, coercion and repression. This period saw the decisive divergence in the standards of living of the producing classes in the North and the South which has been called the 'creation of the Third World' (Davis, 2001), and the increasing externalisation of the phenomena of chronic hunger, large-scale destitution and recurrent famine from Europe to its colonies.

As I argue here, these global processes, on the one hand, demanded and were strengthened by the new so-called 'scientific racism' of Social Darwinism with its emphasis on racial hierarchies of evolution. On the other hand, they put in place economic structures which produced and reproduced the embodied difference implied by marked global inequalities. The experience of chronic undernutrition and its accompanying effects on the immune system, for example, shaped subjectivities but was also reproduced through intergenerational processes. These experiences are contingent on a number of interlinked axes of inequality – class and gender in particular – as well as global location. But these embodied differences were in turn racialised, as poverty and destitution were discursively decoupled from colonial processes of appropriation and accumulation, and essentialised as products of the innate inertia and passivity of the colonised, which directly contrasted with European dynamism and industry. Of the many interlinked oppositions that have characterised racial discourse, it was arguably this dichotomy between poverty-stricken apathy and prosperous dynamism which was most intimately related to the development enterprise, and provided its underlying logic.

Michael Cowen and Robert Shenton (1995, 1996) have traced the emergence of the concept of 'development' in Western thought to the rise of industrial capitalism in Europe. In a departure from earlier theories of societal change as cyclical, with capitalism and the possibility of accumulation on an ever-expanding scale had come the idea that there could be constant 'progress'. Development came to be seen as the means through which the bourgeoisie 'entrusted' with it would bring 'order' to this otherwise chaotic and potentially dangerous progress (Cowen and Shenton, 1995: 34); as an idea it was a product of the fear of the powerless by the powerful, and specifically the anxieties among the rising bourgeoisie generated by the 'dangerous classes', the dispossessed who were drawn to the industrialising cities but were yet to be disciplined by capital. For Cowen and Shenton, the notion of 'trusteeship' was central to the idea of intentional development, which implied an 'external authority of development' that would regulate the internal 'immanent' development of capitalist production. They contrast this with Marx's idea of an 'expanded domain of development' whose source is not capital but the potential embodied in human 'capacities to create and imagine if freed from the dictates of production' and which encompassed 'the potential for universal freedom' (Cowen and Shenton, 1996: xii).

However, the notion of constant progress itself was defined in counterpoint to the non-European societies whose resources provided the basis for European capitalism through the processes of slavery and colonialism. Reproducing the racialised binaries of passive/active and emotional/rational, these societies were constructed as stagnant, either lacking history altogether in the case of Africa (Goldberg, 1993;

Mbembe, 2001) or fundamentally corrupt and in permanent 'decline' in the case of the 'Orient' (Said, 1978; Sangari and Vaid, 1989). Only under the direction of benevolent colonial rulers, therefore, could they achieve progress. Thus development had a different though related implication outside Europe, where, rather than regulating and controlling immanent processes, the trustees of development considered themselves responsible for bringing progress itself.

These racialised notions of 'trusteeship' (later to be immortalised as Kipling's 'white man's burden')[1] and the concept of the civilising mission thus deeply influenced the elaboration of 'development' ideas, which in turn were used to legitimise and perpetuate colonial rule, and, particularly in the twentieth century, to counter the demands of anti-colonial movements.

'Race', capital and freedom

The central role of transatlantic slavery and early colonialism, and of the huge transfer of resources to the global North involved in these processes, in creating the conditions for the development of capitalism in Europe has been established in extensive work by political economists. In analysing the impact of the enslavement and transportation of millions of people, the direct appropriation of resources, the extraction of surpluses through taxation, exploitation and unequal trade, and the shifting of resources away from productive activities and enforced deindustrialisation, all of which accompanied European incursions, these writers have also demonstrated the inseparable economic relation between the development of capitalism in the global North and the structures and conditions associated with what are now called 'developing' countries in the global South.[2]

With the restructuring of Western societies associated with the transition to metropolitan industrial capitalism, liberal Enlightenment ideas about freedom, the rights of the individual and universal humanism became increasingly important. As Susan Buck-Morss writes, by the eighteenth century slavery had become the root metaphor of Western political philosophy, connoting everything that was evil about power relations ... Yet this political metaphor began to take root at precisely the time that the economic practice of slavery – the systematic, highly sophisticated capitalist enslavement of non-Europeans as a labor force in the colonies – was increasing quantitatively and intensifying qualitatively to the point that by the mid-eighteenth century it came to underwrite the entire economic system of the West. (2000: 821)

Enlightenment ideas were clearly inconsistent with the dynamics of colonialism – and in particular with the system of transatlantic slavery – on which continuing capital accumulation depended, as they were with the continuation, or consolidation, of patriarchal gender relations within capitalism. Not surprisingly, then, Enlightenment 'universalism' was from the outset based on multiple exclusions, with only the white, property-owning man ultimately defined as capable of 'rational' thought and action and therefore fully human and entitled to rights (Jaggar, 1988; Goldberg, 1993; Eze, 2000), reflecting what Sherene Razack calls the 'paradox of liberalism': 'all human beings are equal and are entitled to equal treatment; those that are not entitled to equality are simply evicted from the category human' (Razack, 2004: 40). In this context, as Paul Gilroy writes, there is a 'need to indict those forms of rationality which have been rendered implausible by their racially exclusive character and further too explore their complicity with terror systematically and rationally practiced as a form of political and economic administration' (Gilroy, 1993: 220).

Influential liberal philosophers such as Locke and Hume were explicitly racist in their writings, defining black people as lacking the capacity for rationality and therefore agency (Goldberg,1993; Eze, 1997, 2000). It was in this period that discourses of 'race' came to be structured around a set of binary oppositions (such as civilisation/savagery, reason/emotion and culture/nature), which characterised Enlightenment definitions of the human (Hall, 1994) and indeed, as we will see, continued to structure discourses of development even much later, when constructions of 'cultural difference' replaced

explicit references to 'race' (Kothari, 2006). These claims by liberal
thinkers were not, however, simply philosophical speculations but
direct interventions into contemporary political debates (Eze, 2000)
and, crucially, responses to the multiple forms of continuous and
sustained resistance by the enslaved people themselves. They sought
to provide a justification for plantation slavery as a form of surplus
accumulation and its institutionalisation in forms such as France's
Code Noir, which applied to black slaves in its colonies (James, 1938)
and 'legalized not only slavery, the treatment of human beings as
moveable property, but the branding, torture, physical mutilation,
and killing of slaves for attempting to defy their inhuman status'
(Buck-Morss, 2000: 380). As this implies, the invention of 'race'
was itself from the outset conditioned by the resistance of those it
sought to exclude from humanity. Plantation slavery, however, can
be understood not as an anomaly of capitalism but as its epitome,
in which race makes possible the full commodification and therefore non-integrity of the body, which is 'fully opened to capital'
(Cherniavsky, 2006: xvii). Revealed here are the interconnections
of liberalism, 'race' and capital in lived experiences, one of the
overarching themes of this book and one to which we will return
in detail, particularly in Chapter 6.

Yet the racialised conceptualisation of notions of freedom and
human rights was from their inception a site of resistance and
contestation. The Haitian Revolution, which began with a massive
uprising by slaves in the French colony of Saint-Domingue in 1791
and culminated in the establishment of the first black republic in
1804,[3] has been called 'unthinkable' within Enlightenment thought
by the Haitian historian Michel-Rolph Trouillot precisely because
it 'challenged the very framework in which proponents and oppo-
nents had examined race, colonialism and slavery in the Americas'
(Trouillot, 1995: 82–3). The engagement of enslaved and colonised
people with the ideas of universal rights associated with the Enlightenment is not, as has often been implied, a process of serial
claims to the extension of these rights, but rather a simultaneous
and redefining engagement which was under way even as such ideas

were being formulated. In the case of Haiti, it was an engagement which drew upon several distinct systems of thought and, most significantly, on the lived experiences of slavery, to reconfigure the meanings of 'freedom', 'property' and 'labour' (James, 1938; Fick, 1990; Trouillot, 1995; Sheller, 2000; Bogues, 2004). As Trouillot argues, 'the claims of the revolution were indeed too radical to be formulated in advance of its deeds. Victorious practice could assert them only after the fact' (1995: 88). That mainstream accounts of this period in world history can still ignore the Haitian Revolution (Trouillot, 1995: 95–107; Shilliam, 2008) testifies to the tenacity of racialised exclusion and erasure.

At the same time, the concept of 'race' as a socially constructed, historically and spatially contingent and mutable system of categorisation has not remained static. This chapter seeks to highlight two aspects of this mutability in particular. First, changing dominant notions of 'race' were both shaped by, and in turn made possible, changing patterns of global capital accumulation during the course of the nineteenth century. Second, ideas about racial hierarchy were deployed in response to multiple forms of anti-colonial resistance, and were themselves altered and reconfigured by such resistance. Both of these processes of change, as this book argues, have continued to be important to an understanding of the continuing presence of 'race' in the period since 1945, when 'development' came to the fore as the pre-eminent framework through which relations between the global North and South are understood.

From this perspective, the chapter will examine the uprisings of 1857 in India (still more widely known in Britain as the 'Indian Mutiny') as one of a number of key moments in the social construction of 'race'. This is not to suggest that other events in other places are not equally significant in this respect. On the contrary, the existence of many such formative moments is central to my argument here. For example, the Morant Bay Rebellion in Jamaica in 1865 and the responses to it can be analysed in similar ways (Gilroy, 1993: 11). Further, these events and the responses they generate are always partially shaped by earlier, and often less visible or smaller-scale, acts of resistance. In India, for example, there were at least seventy-seven separate officially recorded instances of peasant uprisings during British colonial rule, and this does not reflect the extent of more 'day-to-day' forms of resistance to colonial rule.

Undoubtedly, however, the unprecedented scale and social diversity of the 1857 uprisings triggered significant changes in colonial strategies. On the one hand, ideas of racial superiority and the importance of racial segregation, which had already taken hold, were consolidated and institutionalised. Colonial narratives of the 'Mutiny' and its suppression were instrumental in the development of notions of the 'barbaric' colonial subject who must be controlled by force, and in the fixing of the still-fluid category of 'whiteness' in the metropolis. On the other hand, and in direct response to the articulations of syncretic and pan-regional political projects within insurgent discourses, the aftermath of the uprisings saw a sustained attempt to 'reinvent' India as a society insuperably divided along religious, ethnic and caste lines, drawing upon specific and selective interpretations of the region's history, cultures and social practices. The rise of Social Darwinism and the emergence of colonial anthropology as a discipline were to systematise the racialisation of difference through processes of enumeration, measurement and categorisation. Dominant classes and groups whose power had been consolidated by post-1857 policies also became invested in these notions of 'race', with important implications for post-independence politics. These approaches influenced colonial policies in Africa from the last quarter of the nineteenth century onwards, in particular the system of indirect rule and the incorporation and transformation of the institutions of chiefship in the name of protecting 'tradition' (Mamdani, 1996; Cooper and Stoler, 1997). However, it is difficult to grasp fully the implications of these processes without considering the changes in the structure of global capital in this period, which in India meant a shift from the extortion of the East India Company's eighteenth-century taxation and trade to nineteenth-century deindustrialisation and, increasingly, forced cultivation, in order to provide markets and raw materials for Britain's rapidly growing industries.

Remembering 1857

> In 1857 Baba Ram Charan Das (who was a Hindu) and Amir Ali (a Muslim), both leaders of the uprisings, were hanged from the same tree in Faizabad (Uttar Pradesh) by the British. In the years that followed, this tree became a shrine for both Muslims and Hindus to remember and celebrate their resistance. Fearful of this unity, the British administration had the tree cut down.

2007 marked the 150th anniversary of the sustained and widespread uprisings against British rule which spread across much of the northern half of what is now India, Pakistan and Bangladesh, and lasted almost two years. At their centre was a massive mutiny by Indian soldiers (known as *sipahis* or sepoys) in the British East India Company's army: of 139,000 sepoys in the Bengal Army, all but 7, 796 rebelled. But the uprisings were also marked by the breadth of popular participation, which 'simultaneously drew together and cut through multiple religious, caste, and regional identities' (Krishna, 2006). Their commemoration, both in South Asia and in Britain, reflected the multiplicity of readings of the events and the meanings attributed to them by different social forces and actors, and the contemporary reconfigurations of 'race' in the context of the current period of neoliberal imperialism.

For left-oriented organisations in South Asia and Britain which were engaged in ongoing movements against imperialism, war, racism and the religious right, the anniversary was an opportunity to highlight parallels between 1857 and the contemporary conjuncture, and to celebrate and reaffirm the anti-imperialist and supra-communal character of the uprisings. For example, in Britain, the 1857 Committee and South Asia Solidarity Group held a conference entitled '1857/2007: Imperialism, "Race", Resistance' in which the participants focused as much on the urgency of contemporary struggles as on those of 1857.

For the Indian state, however, the commemoration was notably muted: in contrast to the triumphalist rhetoric accompanying economic liberalisation which marked the first decade of the twenty-first century, the neoliberal state's approach to what official Indian historiography had come to term the 'First war of independence' was perhaps inevitably ambivalent rather than celebratory. This reflected the deep contradictions at the heart of India's model of economic growth, involving not only rapidly growing inequality and the marginalisation of significant sections of the population, but also untrammelled and destructive incursions by Indian and foreign-owned global corporates uncomfortably reminiscent of the actions of the East India Company, the 'world's first multinational corporation' (Robins, 2006), which represented British interests in 1857. 2007 itself witnessed continuing struggles against the establishment of Special Economic Zones using the colonial Land Acquisition Act of 1894,[4] where state laws were suspended and corporations could appoint administrators. The months leading up to the anniversary in May 2007 year saw killings by police and paramilitaries of people resisting state-sponsored corporate acquisition of their land in Singur and Nandigram in West Bengal and Kalinganagar in Orissa, while similar movements against displacement and corporate takeover of land continued in many other parts of the country.

Meanwhile the Indian state was deeply implicated in contemporary imperialist projects as a key US ally in the 'War on Terror', into which it had integrated its own long-running war on the people of Kashmir and its ongoing conflict with Pakistan, which further complicated its commemoration of the anti-imperialist resistance of 1857. In fact, only two years earlier Prime Minister Manmohan Singh had affirmed his contribution to the 'rehabilitation' of colonialism associated with the post-Cold War era with a speech at Oxford University in which he hailed the 'beneficial consequences' of British colonial rule, including 'Our notions of the rule of law, of a Constitutional government, of a free press, of a professional civil service, of modern universities and research laboratories. ... Our judiciary, our legal system, our bureaucracy and our police', echoing the sentiments of Gordon Brown (then chancellor in the British government), who had chosen a visit to Tanzania to wax eloquent in praise of British colonialism and its promotion of 'British values'. Further, the previous decade had seen the entrenchment within the institutions of the Indian state of Hindu supremacist notions of citizenship (notions which, as discussed in Chapter 10, are quite consistent with neoliberal imperialism) and the Hindu supremacist project of rewriting India's history as one determined by Hindu–Muslim conflict, a version which, as we will see, is decisively undermined by a focus on 1857.

British official references to the anniversary were also subdued and ambivalent, requiring as they did that events marked inescapably by insurgent and counter-insurgent violence should be described in the language in which the entire colonial encounter between Britain and India is now officially cast – as part of a long-running and mutually beneficial 'close relationship'. The burst of popular histories by British writers that the anniversary produced is perhaps more revealing. These included several reworkings of colonial historiography in which the beleaguered British were once again the heroic subjects (see, for example, David, 2003; Spilsbury, 2007; Fremont-Barnes, 2007). Arguably the book that had the greatest impact, however, was William Dalrymple's *The Last Mughal* (2006), which deals with the siege of Delhi in 1857, and promises to present for the first time 'an Indian perspective' on the siege. In the next section, we consider the ongoing debates which surround the events described in the book and the key questions they raise relating to imperialism, resistance, religion and 'race', and ask why Dalrymple's version of 1857 proved so influential 150 years later.

The remaking of 1857 as a 'clash of rival fundamentalisms'

The Last Mughal focuses exclusively on the experiences of Delhi, the seat of the Mughal dynasty, which had ruled for 330 years. Beginning a few years before the uprising when the Mughal emperor had already been reduced to a puppet ruler by the East India Company officials, his writ extending only as far as the walls of the Red Fort (and 'even there it was circumscribed'), Dalrymple argues that this period nonetheless represented the coming to fruition of a syncretic, tolerant, highly literary culture, which the Mughal court had encouraged among its subjects, both Muslim and Hindu. He then traces the events which unfolded after the first major rebellion of sepoys took place in Meerut and the insurgent forces headed for Delhi to claim the Mughal emperor, Bahadur Shah Zafar II, as their leader, narrating the flight of the British from the city, the siege of Delhi, and the wholesale massacre of Delhi's citizens by the victorious British which followed.

In a departure from earlier historiography, Dalrymple portrays the uprisings as primarily a 'war of religion' between Islam and Christianity. While acknowledging that the 'great majority' of the sepoys were Hindus, he places unprecedented emphasis on the presence in Delhi of 'insurgents [who] described themselves as mujahedin, ghazis and jihadis' and who, towards the end of the siege, came to constitute 'about a quarter of the total fighting force' in the city (2006: 23).

Dalrymple claims to have uncovered Islamic 'jihad' in 1857, pointedly ignoring the work of many established Indian historians who have over the last thirty years documented the religious idioms through which resistance to imperialism was expressed among both Hindus and Muslims of various backgrounds during 1857 (see, for example, Mukherjee, 1984: 147–54; Roy, 1994: 51–3). More generally, the influential Subaltern Studies group has extensively critiqued the failure to engage with the varied forms and idioms of resistance which marks both colonial and nationalist Indian historiography. Elsewhere, an in-depth study by Rajat Kanta Ray (2003) describes how, in the case of 1857, people sharing a syncretic culture but identifying with distinct religions consciously united to fight the British colonizers:

> it was, in their view, a struggle of the Hindus and Muslims against the Nazarenes – not so much because the latter were supposed to be determined to impose the false doctrine of the Trinity, but because the identity of 'the Hindus and Muslims of Hindustan' was being threatened by the moral and material aggrandizement of the arrogant imperial power. (Ray, 2003: 357).

In this case, then, resistance to imperial rule was waged in the name of a single nation, 'Hindustan' (India), and two religions: Islam and Hinduism. As Ray notes, rebel proclamations were issued addressed to 'the Hindus and Muslims of Hindustan',[5] and where the British had been defeated it was announced that 'the two religions govern'.

However, Dalrymple dismisses these more complex understandings of the collective anti-imperialist resistance that pre-dated the emergence of bourgeois nationalism in India in favour of the notion of a 'clash of rival fundamentalisms'. This is all the more striking because it contradicts considerable evidence of his own. For example, Dalrymple refers to the ambiguity and multiple meanings of the term 'jihad' itself, which is used, among others referred to in the book, by a Hindu rebel general to describe the uprising; later, he notes the concerted attempt by the British authorities to reconstruct the uprisings as an exclusively Muslim affair, which began even before they had been completely suppressed. He explains that

> the emperor was put on trial and charged, quite inaccurately, with being behind a Muslim conspiracy to subvert the empire stretching from Mecca and Iran to Delhi's Red Fort. Contrary to evidence that the uprising broke out first among the overwhelmingly Hindu sepoys, the prosecutor argued that 'to Musalman intrigues and Mahommedan conspiracy we may mainly attribute the dreadful calamities of 1857'. (Dalrymple, 2007)

As historian Mubarak Ali explains, this theory was consolidated in the years that followed.

> British historians ... Alfred Layall and William Muir argued that generally the people of India were satisfied by the British rule and those who created trouble against the government were the Muslim elite which had lost its privileges during the course of time ... This view was further strengthened by J.G Brown in his book *The Punjab and Delhi in 1857* (1861) He writes that: 'That the Mohammadan should conspire against the Christians is not to be wondered at-his creed teaches it; the Koran demands it of him...' (Ali, 2007a)[6]

Dalrymple once again prioritises the role of religion when analysing British actions both before and during the uprisings, which he attributes to the growing influence of evangelical Christianity. This allows him both to downplay other changes in the character of imperialism in this period and to romanticise an earlier era of British rule under the East India Company from the mid-eighteenth century onwards.

Dalrymple contrasts his apocalyptic, proto-9/11 view of 1857 with a previous golden age where British officers of the East India Company adopted Indian dress and 'cohabited' with 'Indian Bibis'. Oblivious to questions of race, gender and power, Dalrymple lovingly portrays these 'white Moghuls' with their 'numerous' wives as 'splendidly multicultural' and furthering an idyllic 'fusion of civilisations'. In fact, the distinctions between the 'orientalist' ideas which circulated among these representatives of empire and emerging theories of racial hierarchy were far less rigid than writers like Dalrymple suggest (Kapila, 2007).

Equally significantly, Dalrymple ignores the fact that following the British defeat of Siraj-ud-Daula in the Battle of Plassey[7] in 1757, the British presided over a century of intensive plunder and destruction of India's economy, through the twin weapons of ruthless taxation and coerced trade. Thus, for example, Warren Hastings, one of the 'orientalist' British scholars whom Dalrymple refers to with admiration (and so clearly wishes to emulate), is better known for his achievement as Governor General of Bengal of presiding over an increase in the rate of taxes collected by the East India Company at the height of the 1769–73 famine brought on by the company's policies in Eastern India. This famine killed an estimated 10 million people, one-third of the population of what was then known as Bengal.[8] But in February 1771, the Company's officers in Calcutta could report back to the directors that, 'notwithstanding the great severity of the late famine and the great reduction of people thereby, some increase has been made' in revenue collection (Robins, 2006: 92).

The East India Company's records themselves described the extent of the coercion and violence that continued to be involved in the extraction of revenue, as well as in the appropriation of resources and labour power by the Company in the decades that followed, leading Marx to comment in the context of the 1857 uprisings on 'the universal existence of torture as a financial institution of British India' (Karl Marx, *New York Daily Tribune*, 17 September 1857). The East India Company's trade in Indian textiles, which were in huge demand in Europe, was also carried out through intense coercion: 'From a situation of relative economic independence, Bengal's weavers were forced into a position of near slavery, unable to sell to others and obliged to accept whatever the company's agents (*gomastas*) would offer for their cloth' (Robins, 2006: 77).

The years leading up to 1857, however, saw major changes in the objectives, methods and dominant ideology of imperialism, of which the rise of evangelical Christianity emphasised by Dalrymple was only one element. India was now seen not solely as a source of enormous tax revenues and valuable consumer goods procured by force, but as a market for Britain's own manufacturing industries and, increasingly, a source of raw materials. To serve the needs of the powerful new 'millocracy', the British now set about systematically destroying India's thriving and sophisticated textile industry by imposing high tariffs to prevent exports. This ensured that the British textile industry did not have to face free-market competition. The explanation of contemporary historian Horace Wilson is worth quoting in full:

> It was stated in evidence (in 1813) that the cotton and silk goods of India, up to this period, could be sold for a profit in the British market at a price from 50 to 60 per cent. lower than those fabricated in England. It consequently became necessary to protect the latter by duties of 70 or 80 per cent. on their value, or by positive prohibition. Had this not been the case, had not such prohibitory duties and decrees existed, the mills of Paisley and of Manchester would have been stopped in their outset, and could hardly have been again set in motion, even by the powers of steam. They were created by the sacrifice of the Indian manufactures. Had India been independent, she would have retaliated; would have imposed preventive duties upon British goods, and would thus have preserved her own productive industry from annihilation. This act of self-defence was not permitted her; she was at the mercy of the stranger. British

goods were forced upon her without paying any duty; and the foreign manufacturer employed the arm of political injustice to keep down and ultimately strangle a competitor with whom he could not contend on equal terms. (Wilson and Mill, 1848: 383)

By the 1830s, India's thriving textile industry had been all but destroyed, and by the middle of the century India was importing one-quarter of all British cotton textile exports (Palme Dutt, 1945: 119). Prosperous manufacturing towns like Dhaka (now the capital of Bangladesh), Murshidabad (now in West Bengal in India) and Surat (now in Gujarat in India) were devastated as spinning and weaving ceased and people were forced to move out into the countryside for subsistence. Sir Charles Trevelyan told the parliamentary inquiry of 1840: 'The population of the town of Dacca [Dhaka] has fallen from 150,000 to 30,000 or 40,000 and the jungle and malaria are fast encroaching ... Dacca, which was the Manchester of India, has fallen off from a very flourishing town to a very poor and small one' (cited in Palme Dutt, 1945: 120).

This process of deindustrialisation had important implications for gender relations. As Nirmala Banerjee has documented in the case of Bengal (Banerjee, 1989), it involved households in urban areas in which women had been engaged in occupations like weaving, which gave them relatively greater autonomy within the household, losing their livelihoods and being forced to migrate to the countryside and turn to agriculture, within which women's role was seen as primarily reproductive. Such changes were reinforced in the later part of the nineteenth century by colonial interventions in 'culture' that sought to consolidate gendered notions of femininity and respectability that were consistent with dominant patriarchal constructions in Victorian Britain.

The millions who lost their source of employment as a consequence of the destruction of Indian manufacturing included not only spinners and weavers but potters, smelters and smiths, along with many other artisans and crafts workers. This group formed an important section among those who joined the rebels in 1857 (Habib, 2007). In the decades that followed, Indian cultivators would be forced to grow indigo, cotton and wheat for export to Britain. Such policies required the expansion of areas of direct British rule through the annexation of the territories of their erstwhile Indian allies, and an enhanced colonial state apparatus with much larger numbers of British officials. This 'age of empire' saw the consolidation of the ideology of white superiority, racial segregation and the 'civilising mission'. Further, as Rudrangshu Mukherjee writes, describing the quotidian violence of the pre-1857 period, 'British rule … visibly manifested itself by marking the body of the Indian.… Imperial rule in India could only perpetuate itself by a deployment of terror, a terror that would strike awe in the minds of the ruled' (Mukherjee, 1990: 94).

While Dalrymple notes that by 1850 British army officers had 'become increasingly distant, rude and dismissive' to the men under their command (2006: 136), he ignores the ideology of racial supremacy which underpinned the daily racist abuse and violence faced by the sepoys as well as civilians, identified as a central cause of the uprisings within insurgent discourses. Ray cites an English reconstruction of a speech attributed to Maulvi Sarfraz Ali of Shahjahanpur:

> But you will ask perhaps what have they done to deserve this? I answer: If *suar gadha* ['swine, pig or hog, ass or donkey: very common epithets applied by the Europeans to the natives of India': *footnote in the original*] in the public streets and 'damn your eyes' in the public courts is a form of compliment acceptable to you, they then have deserved well at your hands. Have you never seen a fellow-countryman of yours kicked by the whites, and sometimes the cane laid across his back? Have you ever known them to be addressed other than 'nigger' or '*kala suar*'? These are everyday occurrences. (cited in Ray, 2003: 361)

A contemporary British observer noted that

> the sepoy is [regarded as] an inferior creature. He is sworn at. He is treated roughly. He is spoken of as a 'nigger'. He is addressed as 'suar' or pig.… [the younger British officers] seem to regard it as an excellent joke, as an evidence of spirit and a praiseworthy sense of superiority over the sepoy to treat him as an inferior animal. (cited in Hibbert, 1978: 56)

These accounts of day-to-day racism in this period in India, and in particular the prevalence of the word 'nigger' in racist abuse, strikingly highlight the determining category within which all those who were enslaved and colonised were defined within popular racist discourse, even as ever more complex taxonomies and hierarchies of 'race' were being theorised by European scholars. Both of these understandings, however, were underpinned by the same binary opposition in which all those who were excluded from whiteness were constructed as less than fully human, as the constant references to animals underline.

Unlike most British accounts to date, Dalrymple describes in detail the 'full scale of the viciousness and brutality' of the colonial response to the uprisings, which 'in many cases would today be classified as grisly war crimes' (2006: 14–15). In this he departs from the pattern identified in the British press coverage of the time by Karl Marx (who was a contemporary commentator) and still present in recent historiography, where 'while the cruelties of the English are related as acts of martial vigour, told simply, rapidly, without dwelling in disgusting details, the outrages of the natives, shocking as they are, are still deliberately exaggerated' (Marx, 1959: 74–5, cited in Newsinger, 2006: 74; for a recent example of this genre, see David, 2003).

Yet, despite this, Dalrymple seems unable to comprehend fully the nature of colonial violence or its ubiquity. Thus, referring to the mass rape of Indian women following the fall of Delhi, he comments that, 'believing that the British women in Delhi had been sexually assaulted at the outbreak – a rumour that subsequently proved quite false.... British officers did little to stop their men from raping the women of Delhi' (2006: 462–3). In the absence of an analysis of racism he cannot understand why the 'quite false' allegations of rape of British women by Indian men were so effective and so widespread at the time, and how such allegations have been a central instrument in the operation of colonial and racialised power, regulation and violence in many different contexts. Nor can he acknowledge that, with or without such allegations, the rape of colonised women by coloniser men has been a central aspect of colonial violence. Perhaps it is not surprising, then, that Dalrymple ultimately conforms to the dominant version of events: that British atrocities were carried out specifically as 'retribution' for the massacre of British women and children at Kanpur. In reality, the terror had already been unleashed in the countryside by Colonel James Neill, whose troops – burning villages, hanging and shooting men and young boys, and raping women – massacred thousands of men, women and children well before the Kanpur killings.

While Dalrymple enthuses about the 'street-level nature' of the documentation he has unearthed relating to 'ordinary citizens of Delhi', in fact the overwhelming majority of his book, where it is not revisiting the oft-cited accounts of various British officers and civilians in Delhi, presents the perspective of the Mughal elite of the city. Dalrymple makes no attempt to portray the sepoys, who formed the core of the uprisings, in anything but the terms in which they were viewed by the Mughal elite: as 'boorish and violent peasants from Bihar and eastern Uttar Pradesh' (2006: 17). He ignores some of the most significant processes that took place during the uprisings, such as the formation of the semi-republican Sepoy Councils by the rebels, which in practice made the decisions about how and by whom the areas captured from the British would be governed.[9]

Mubarak Ali describes the situation in Delhi after the arrival of the rebel forces:

> The rebels used the king for their interest and issued orders with his seal and signature for the maintenance of peace and order in the city.... real authority was vested into different councils whose task was to keep law and order, collect revenue, get loans from the moneylenders, and organize the army for war. (Ali, 2007b)

By ignoring these aspects of 1857, Dalrymple is able to sidestep the key question of whether the uprisings, while demanding the restoration of the pre-colonial rulers (and constructing the British as rebels against the legitimate authority of these rulers), were actually in the processes of constructing a new order. This view, which clearly undermines Dalrymple's thesis of a religious war or 'clash of fundamentalisms', is put forward by, among others, Ray, who argues, quoting from the rebels' proclamations, that

> the idea of popular authority embodied in the joint rule of the two religions ('the two religions govern') and the act of exercise of power of the elected council of the sepoys ('the command belongs to the sipahi bahadur') amounted together to an unprecedented expression of the power derived in 1857 from the people's will, and there was no question of reconstituting it entirely in the manner of the past. (Ray, 2003: 359; see also Krishna, 2006; Habib, 2007)

Dalrymple's representation of the events of 1857 is ultimately, as with much historiography, more revealing of the particular moment of its writing than of the moment it seeks to describe. As the US establishment pursued its 'War on Terror' and tried to persuade us to view contemporary events through the distorted lens of the 'clash of civilisations', Dalrymple, with his insistence that economic trans-formations are of no relevance to the lives of 'ordinary individuals', and his dogged emphasis on solely religious motivations, appears to be attempting to remake history in the same image. Meanwhile, for many others, the real parallels between 1857 and the contemporary world lay not in a clash between militant Islam and Christianity, but in a struggle between an aggressively expansionist imperialism and people's resistance expressed in a multiplicity of forms.

Reinventing India after 1857

The new global division of labour and the racialisation of hunger

In the aftermath of the uprisings, the British, in addition to acquir-ing huge tracts of land for military cantonments for their massively increased military presence,[10] intensified their policy of promoting cash-crop production – particularly wheat and cotton – for export to Britain. As in the Permanent Settlement for Bengal at the end of the previous century, the colonial state intervened to redefine the relationship between those who directly cultivated and the land, which became private property. Whereas in Eastern India this had consolidated the zamindars as a class of landowners who would be intermediaries between the colonial state and the cultivators, in Central India peasant cultivators were made directly responsible for paying taxes, with the result that moneylenders became increasingly powerful. But whereas earlier the main objective was the collection of revenue itself, what was now even more important was that taxation, and the accompanying debt, could be a coercive instrument to ensure the shift from subsistence to cash-crop cultivation. The Lancashire cotton mill owners 'wielded extraordinary power over the reshaping of the Indian economy in the wake of the Mutiny' (Davis, 2001: 312–13) and, with domestic manufacture destroyed by the influx of British-made cotton textiles, peasant households who cultivated cotton and the growing number who depended on agricultural labour for survival found themselves at the mercy of 'Lancashire's lopsided monopsony' (314). In North India, the emphasis was on expanding the production of wheat for export, once again linked to the demands of British industrial capital, in this case for cheap food for the metropolis, which would allow workers' wages to be kept low (Patnaik, 2006).

By the 1870s, this policy, which came in the wake of the devastating violence of the British response to the uprisings, in which countless villages were wiped out, had led to widespread severe famine. Many of the parts of Northern and Central India which were key areas of resistance in 1857 had by the 1870s become 'epicenters of mass mortality' (Davis, 2001: 312) in these British-made famines.[11] But the terms of their integration into global markets meant not only periodic famines but chronic impoverishment and hunger. In the last half of the nineteenth century, real per capita income in India is estimated to have declined by more than 50 per cent (311).[12]

As Mike Davis (2001) has cogently argued, with an increasing proportion of the agricultural populations outside Europe being incorporated into world markets on these lethal terms, famines became increasingly frequent, in India, China, Brazil and elsewhere. By the end of the century and the rapid expansion of competing European empires on the continent, famine proliferated in parts of Africa, where not only the effects of forced cultivation and the diversion of labour from food production but forced labour in mines and on plantations, military conscription and requisitioning also led in some cases to a long-term decline in populations (Arnold, 1988).

The contrast with the situation in an earlier phase of the colonial era could not be more marked. As historian David Arnold writes evocatively, 'in the first centuries of Western expansionism the world beyond Europe's shores represented a world of riches … still hungry, miserable and desolated by plague, early modern Europe hungered for a world wealthier and more splendid than its cold and shivering self' (Arnold, 1988: 119). Notwithstanding the already circulating fantasies of savages, heathens and cannibals, first-hand European accounts of non-European civilisations in this period emphasised the wealth of cities and courts and the skill and craftsmanship they encountered. Further, as historian Prasannan Parthasarathi points out, the changes that took place in the seventeenth and eighteenth centuries were by no means unique to Europe:

> The expansion of markets, the extension of money use, the growth of commercial manufactures and the rise of more bureaucratized state forms were found not only in Europe, but also in South and South-East Asia, China and West Africa. By 1700, these changes had progressed very far in several parts of South Asia … with the development of sophisticated financial networks, a thriving export trade in cotton cloth, a vibrant internal commerce in cotton and yarn, foodstuffs and metal goods, and a diffusion of coinage to even the lowest strata of society. (Parthasarathi, 1998: 158; see also Pomeranz, 2000)

At the time of the French Revolution, 'the largest manufacturing districts in the world were still the Yangzi Delta and Bengal, with Lingan (modern Guandong and Guanxi) and coastal Madras not far behind' (Davis, 2001: 292). But there is considerable evidence too that the standards of living of the working people were higher outside Europe. For example, comparing the real wages of weavers, spinners and agricultural labourers in South India and Britain, Parthasarathi has concluded that 'there is compelling evidence that South Indian labourers had higher earnings than their British counterparts in the eighteenth century and lived lives of greater financial security' (Parthasarathi, 1998: 82). By 1900, by contrast, average household income in Britain was estimated to be twenty-one times higher than in India according to calculations by economic historian R.C. Dutt (cited in Davis, 2001: 292). As Davis writes, 'By the end of Victoria's reign … the inequality of nations was as profound as the inequality of classes. Humanity had been irrevocably divided' (Davis, 2001: 16).

Thus, whereas the colonies remained a source of immense surpluses for European capitalism, and continued to underwrite metropolitan economies (Patnaik, 2006),[13] peasants, agricultural labourers and other direct producers of this wealth were increasingly impoverished. This became central to racialised constructions from the nineteenth century onwards:

> overlooking the possibility that they, by the very manner of
> their intervention and rule, might have caused or contributed to
> others' sickness and hunger, Europeans instead saw the famines
> they encountered in different parts of the world as a sign of the
> inferiority of the inhabitants and of their apathy in the face of an
> adversary over which Europe had long since triumphed. Just as trade
> and technology became the twin panaceas of the Victorian age, so
> hunger became an imperial stereotype of non-European peoples.
> (Arnold, 1988: 131)

The geographical exception to this of course was Ireland, whose famine was also, however, a characteristically colonial one. Not surprisingly, Irish people too were constructed as 'racially' inferior in the 'scientific' racism of the nineteenth century.

This racialisation of the ideas of poverty and hunger, its association with notions of apathy and passivity, and the contrasting conflation of a recently consolidated whiteness with the capitalist virtues of dynamism and enterprise have underpinned and legitimized the 'trusteeship' inherent in the development project ever since. These binaries have been extensively critiqued in postcolonial feminist thought in particular. But if we are to resist the current dominant development 'solution' of simply bestowing a form of neoliberal agency upon Third World subjects whose newly discovered entrepreneurialism is now celebrated (an approach I examine in detail in Chapter 2), we must also retain a political economy focus on the material relations and processes which reproduced stark inequalities in access and entitlements to food and nutrition globally, as well as the contemporary continuities and changes in these relations and processes.

In a similar vein, this was the period when (as Arnold implies above) industrial and technological skills became particularly significant among the attributes exclusively associated with whiteness in racial discourse. Again, the rural/urban and industrial/agrarian dichotomies are among core racialised binaries which continue to underpin development discourse. Yet, as we saw in the case of India, this emerges precisely at the point when Indian manufacturing had been decisively undermined, its erstwhile skilled workers swelling the ranks of the rural poor, and a global division of labour was being consolidated in which India's role would be that of a supplier of raw materials, primarily agricultural products. Racialised constructions of Indians as poor, hungry and mired since time immemorial in unchanging villages naturalised this arrangement, but equally they perpetuated it, legitimising, for example, the colonial state's active attempts to thwart the emergence of Indian industrial capital later.

Redefining culture

After 1857 administrative power was formally transferred from the East India Company to the Crown. This was accompanied by a marked shift in the approach of the colonial state to notions of indigenous culture. In response to what were constructed as the 'causes' of the uprisings, the 1858 Queen's Proclamation stated that the government would 'abstain from all interference with religious belief or worship' and pay 'due regard … to the ancient rights, usages and customs of India'. While avowedly reacting to the religious idioms used during the uprisings, this response sought to render invisible the underlying issues of power and exploitation which had animated the uprisings and which challenged the very basis of colonial rule.

The late-nineteeth-century colonial state in India thus adopted a strategy of reinforcing or even creating 'ancient customs' which consolidated and extended structures of unequal power within communities and facilitated colonial control. This was the period when 'culture' came to be decisively redefined as static and scriptural, with the living culture that informed and was shaped by anti-colonial resistance in a variety of forms being labelled 'deviant', 'immoral', 'inauthentic' and 'degenerate'. As noted earlier, this was linked to the rise to hegemonic status of colonial notions of gendered morality and respectability and the increased policing of women, in particular, who challenged them. The banning in 1910 of a new edition of the *Radhika Santwanam*, a poem by the eighteenth-century Telegu woman poet Muddupalani which celebrated women's sexuality, by the British authorities on the grounds that it 'would endanger the moral health of their Indian subjects' is one striking example of this (Tharu and Lalita, 1993: 201). Equally significant, as Tharu and Lalita point out, is the adoption of these norms by dominant groups in India and their pervasiveness within later nationalist discourses.

This approach to culture and 'tradition' as a potential support structure for colonial authority was also consistent with the policy of indirect rule adopted after 1857. As Palme-Dutt explains, 'an abrupt end was made of the system of annexation of the Indian States into British India. Henceforth the remaining Princes were zealously preserved in possession of their puppet powers as allied "sovereign rulers"' (Palme-Dutt, 1947: 306). But, even more generally, unequal relations of production and structures of power, particularly in agriculture, were sought to be extended and reinforced. This was to be developed further in what was in many ways the very different context of the colonisation of Africa in the last quarter of the nineteenth century. As Mahmood Mamdani explains,

> Britain, more than any other power, keenly glimpsed authoritarian possibilities in culture. Not simply content with salvaging every authoritarian tendency from the heterogeneous historical flow

that was pre-colonial Africa, Britain creatively sculpted tradition and custom as and when the need arose. In this endeavour, other European powers followed it. (Mamdani, 1996: 49)[14]

Social Darwinism and the racialisation of difference in India

As we have suggested, the unprecedented scale and, in particular, the social diversity of those who participated in the uprisings catalysed a number of interrelated changes in colonial constructions and material practices of 'race'. First, ideas of racial superiority and the necessity of racial segregation, which as we have seen had already taken hold, were consolidated and institutionalised. The remarkable proliferation of colonial narratives of the 'Mutiny' and its suppression, in the form of military and civilian memoirs, popular illustrations, paintings, novels and stories, was instrumental in constructions of the 'barbaric' colonial subject needing to be controlled by force, in the gradual expansion and fixing of the still-fluid category of 'whiteness' in the metropolis to include the working class, and in the establishment of imperial nationalism as a hegemonic discourse of 'Britishness'. These representations of 1857, within which the production for the first time of a large number of novels that 'hinged on the rape of English women by Indian men' 'performed specific ideological work' (Paxton: 1992: 6), illustrate not only that constructions of race are intimately bound to notions of gender and sexuality, but that the reworking and consolidation of ideas about gender and sexuality in the context of colonialism and capitalism was inextricable from emerging definitions of 'whiteness' and exclusions from it.[15] That these processes continue and are continuously reconfigured by both changing patterns of accumulation and resistance is evident from a comparison with the discourses surrounding the current 'War on Terror'.

Second, in a reverse process to the consolidation and reinforcing of overarching notions of Britishness and whiteness, the aftermath of the uprisings saw a sustained attempt to 'reinvent' India as a society insuperably divided along religious, ethnic and caste lines. This drew upon specific and selective interpretations of the region's history, cultures and social practices, and emerged in direct response to the elaborations of concepts such as 'Hindustan' which informed the uprisings. As Lieutenant Colonel John Coke, then Commandant of Moradabad, famously wrote soon after the uprisings had been defeated, 'Our endeavour should be to uphold in full force the (for us fortunate) separation which exists between the different religions and races, not to endeavour to amalgate them. *Divide et impera* should be the principle of Indian government' (cited in Palme Dutt, 1947: 456). Historians began in earnest the project of reconstructing Indian history as one of oppression of Hindus by alien Muslim rulers (Krishna, 2006).

But it was the rise of Social Darwinism after the publication of Darwin's *The Origin of Species* in 1859 and the emergence of colonial anthropology as a discipline which were to systematise the theorisation of difference in India and, crucially, its racialisation, through processes of enumeration, measurement and categorisation. Although the preoccupation with constructing a 'scientific' basis for racial hierarchies was already, as indicated earlier, widespread,[16] Social Darwinists gave these attempts a new legitimacy by appropriating the concept of evolution to construct a 'pseudo-science' in which different 'races' were assigned characteristics that were claimed to reflect their different stages of evolution. Those lower down the scale were literally infantilised: as Herbert Spencer, whom Stephen Jay Gould has called the 'apostle' of Social Darwinism, opined, 'the intellectual traits of the uncivilised ... are traits recurring in the children of the civilised' (Spencer, 1895, cited in Gould, 1981: 117).

Clearly, this was particularly significant in its potential for reinforcing and extending the idea of 'trusteeship' at the heart of development. Thus British sociologist Benjamin Kidd wrote in *The Control of the Tropics* (1898), in which he argued for further colonial expansion into Africa, 'We are dealing with peoples who represent the same stage in the history of the development of the race that the child does in the history of the development of the individual. The tropics will not, therefore, be developed by the natives themselves' (Kidd, 1898, cited in Gould, 1981: 118).

Equally significant, however, was the use of Social Darwinist ideas to racialise difference within colonized societies. After their failure to predict the uprisings of 1857, colonial administrators felt impelled to 'know' more about Indian society, and the process of enumerating and categorising the people gained momentum and resources. The impact of this process for the meaning of caste in India has been analysed extensively. Regionally distinct communities were brought together as belonging to the same caste; caste was defined as an immutable hierarchy, where previously interrelations between castes had changed as a result of political and economic transformations. The sources for caste classifications were based on ancient scriptures and consultations with Brahman officials – consolidating the elite Brahman perceptions of social status. These interventions in turn reshaped identity, particularly as caste became a basis for making claims on the state, in ways which had lasting implications for Indian society and politics (Dirks, 2001). But, as has been pointed out, the anthropologists and colonial officers who set about measuring skulls and enumerating populations were also intervening in debates about 'race' (Bayly, 1995; Bates, 1995) Differences between communities were increasingly defined as 'racial' differences. The caste system, now represented as a 'racial' hierarchy in which 'fair-skinned Aryans' ruled over inferior others, could therefore be mobilised as evidence of the inevitability and fitness of British colonial rule in India and elsewhere. This process culminated in the 1901 census, which 'ranked' castes by status, and involved ethnographic surveys carried out by anthropologist H.H. Risley using 'anthropometric' methods. As Nicholas Dirks writes, 'Risley directed the full apparatus of colonial power to the task of using India to prove the truth of racial difference' (Dirks, 2001: 226). Powerful groups within India also engaged with and incorporated these ideas. Sumit Guha suggests that

> while Indian participation in the process of gathering colonial knowledge was coeval with British rule itself, the nature of the information regime was changing through the later nineteenth century ... The new anthropological enterprise may have been seen as an opportunity to enhance one's own status in an

emerging knowledge system. ... Racial ethnography was thus being appropriated by the indigenous elites to justify South Asian hierarchy on the one hand, and to assert parity with the European upper classes on the other. (Guha, 1998: 424)

More specifically, these racialised colonial understandings also formed the basis from which Hindu supremacist ideologies emerged (see Chapter 8).

In conclusion, through a discussion of a particular historical moment and its aftermath, I have sought in this chapter to highlight the overlapping trajectories of ideas about 'race' and 'development' in relation to changing patterns of global capital accumulation in the nineteenth century. I have indicated the contours of an approach to analysing 'race' and racism on which I will elaborate in the chapters that follow, an approach that simultaneously considers 'race' as a socially constructed, historically contingent and mutable category, but one that not only marks difference, but, as a system for organising capital accumulation, produces material difference and shapes and constrains embodied and lived experience in multiple ways. Further, I have suggested that we should understand development as a product of the interconnections between liberalism, 'race' and capital, and the ways these have been and continue to be reconfigured in response to varied forms of resistance.

CHAPTER 2

The gift of agency: gender and race in development representations

In this chapter, I elaborate the ideas discussed in historical context in the previous chapter, which highlight and seek to map further the relationships between 'race', capital, liberalism and resistance, and look specifically at changing visual representations of women in the global South produced by development institutions. The last two decades have seen policies promoting the use of 'positive', active images of 'poor women in developing countries' adopted by international NGOs, donor governments, the World Bank and other development actors. I suggest here that this has been the consequence of several closely interrelated factors: first, widespread critiques of earlier representations of 'Third World women' as a homogenous category of 'passive victims'; second, the appropriation – and transformation – within neoliberal discourses of development from the 1990s onwards of concepts of participation, empowerment and agency; and third, changes in the role of development NGOs in the same period. I argue that these new images contribute to and extend, rather than challenge, racialised regimes of representation.

Through a discussion of three recent publicity campaigns, the chapter examines the specific and gendered ways in which these more recent visual productions are racialised, exploring, in particular, parallels and continuities between representations of women workers in late-colonial enterprises and today's images of micro-entrepreneurship within the framework of neoliberal globalisation. Like their colonial predecessors, I argue, contemporary representations obscure relations of oppression and exploitation, and work to render collective challenges to the neoliberal model invisible.

Race, gender, development

As we have seen, the historical and conceptual roots of the idea of development are intimately related to the consolidation of constructions of 'race' in the periods of slavery and colonialism, and within Enlightenment thought. In the post-1945 era, as the binary oppositions of race went 'underground' within dominant discourses, they were mapped onto those of development/underdevelopment (Kothari, 2006). Modernisation theory was structured around a series of differences – urban/rural, modern/traditional, productive/ unproductive – which reproduced both the hierarchies of 'race' and the gendered dichotomy between the public and the private. 'Third World women' were associated with the 'backward', unproductive element and targeted by development initiatives focusing on their reproductive roles, notably population policies. Early Women in Development (WID) interventions encouraged a shift of emphasis from reproductive to productive activities, but the racialised violence of population control policies, which, as we will see in Chapter 3, drew on the pathologisation of the sexuality of women in the global South, was only challenged when feminist movements in these countries began to organise against it.

Theories and practices of development have thus not only been racialised, but have been gendered in ways which are inextricable from questions of 'race'. Historically, black and colonised women's experiences of sexual violence, exploitation and dispossession, and the reshaping of gender and class relations *within* colonised societies in ways which intensified women's subordination,[1] testify to this. But these experiences and the resistance they generated were made invisible in colonial discourses: when colonised women did appear, it was frequently in the context of their perceived need to be rescued from 'their' men and/or 'backward' societies (Mani, 1987): in Spivak's memorable phrase, 'white men saving brown women from brown men' (Spivak, 1988).

White women were also implicated in this infantilisation, for example through the relationship between missionary women and the women in colonised societies whom they sought to 'save' (Abu-Lughod, 2002). The continuities with this colonial discourse evident in 'white feminist' approaches in the 1970s and 1980s were highlighted by black and Third World feminists (hooks, 1982; Carby, 1982). These continuities were particularly striking within discourses of development (Mohanty, 1986). Socialist feminists from the South had questioned the WID approach – which was rooted in neoclassical economics and liberal feminism – but racialised power relations inherent within the 'development project' itself, in which people in the global South are the 'objects' of development for overwhelmingly white 'experts' (White, 2006), continued to shape gender and development theory and practice.

Neoliberalism and women's agency

Partly in response to these critiques, notably Chandra Mohanty's powerful dissection of 'the construction in Western feminist discourse of '"third world women" as implicit victims of particular socio-economic systems' (Mohanty, 1986: 338), gender and development theorists have in the last two decades increasingly highlighted women's agency. Women in the global South are no longer invariably seen as passive victims; there is an increased focus on women's ability to make decisions and choices under given circumstances. But, rather than challenging the racialised power relationships inherent in development, this focus on agency has decisively shifted attention away from both material structures of power and gendered ideologies (Wilson, 2007).

Much recent GAD literature has been concerned with constructing a rational self-interested basis for what are described as women's 'choices' to conform to gendered expectations, or to collude in the oppression of other women. Liberal theory's individual exercising 'free will' reappears here, albeit acting within the material constraints imposed by patriarchal power. For example, it is argued that 'women may sacrifice their immediate welfare for future security; this would be perfectly in keeping with self-interested behaviour and need not imply a gap between women's "objective" well-being and their perception of their well-being' (Agarwal, 1994: 434–5). Analysis of the role of gendered constructions and ideologies has been actively delegitimised by suggesting that such a focus attributes 'false consciousness' to women. Further, the use of the concept of 'agency' in these texts frequently has the effect of reassuring us that women do in fact exercise choice in situations where structural constraints mean that women are simply 'choosing' survival. Thus, for example, it is argued that analysis of systematic gender bias in nutrition levels within households in South Asian societies ignores women's agency by failing to take account of their strategies of tasting the food while preparing it and eating leftovers (Jackson, 1998); or that women victims of wartime rape exercise agency by choosing to remain silent about their experiences because to speak out would endanger their own lives (Kelly, 2000; Parpart, 2010).

These analyses were increasingly incorporated into broader post-structuralist critiques of totalising 'metanarratives' in development (Marchand and Parpart, 1995). While poststructuralists' rejection of the idea of the coherent and bounded autonomous subject apparently distances them from liberal theory, in practice their suspicion of structural concerns and materialist analysis has led to a certain convergence, which, I would suggest, has been particularly evident on the terrain of development, and contributed to the marginalisation of questions of oppression and exploitation. Further, the conflation of all possible understandings of development under the rubric of metanarratives of progress in much post-structuralist inflected work has precluded both a cogent critique of neoliberalism and a recognition of the often quite coherent, although contested and changing, visions of development underpinning the movements that oppose it, thus colluding in rendering these movements invisible. As a result, poststructuralist and postcolonial approaches have proved amenable to appropriation and incorporation within neoliberal development discourses. In the case of agency, somewhat paradoxically, concerns with the construction of the subject and the representation of difference have been incorporated alongside liberal definitions of the 'rational individual exercising free will' in what has come to be the dominant approach to agency within gender and development discourses.

In line with this, ideas of difference are mobilized in recent GAD work to argue that concepts of emancipation are always external impositions, with women in 'developing' countries invariably being more concerned with notions of 'security', 'responsibility' and 'respect'. For example, Judy El-Bushra suggests that 'exploitation is a price they are willing to pay for the public acknowledgement that they make important contributions to society, and for the removal of doubt about the security of their marital and other relationships'. (El-Bushra 2000: 83). Increasingly widespread generalisations of this type thus construct desire for structural change as not only irrelevant, but culturally alien in these contexts.

In sum, 'agency' is now cited in development discourse almost exclusively in the context of strategies for survival rather than transformation, and in the context of the individual, rather than the collective. These approaches are consistent with, and indeed have contributed to, the elaboration of neoliberal models of development based on the further intensification of the labour of women in low-income households as a buffer against the ravages of economic reforms.

Underpinning this version of agency is the construction of women in the global South as 'more efficient' neoliberal subjects than their male counterparts. Reference to evidence that women work harder, and expend fewer resources (including time) on themselves, and that women's income will therefore have a far greater impact on children's well-being has become routine in this context. What is rarely acknowledged however, is that these well-documented gender disparities in the use of income and resources stem from specific patriarchal structures, institutions and ideologies (notably the gendered division of responsibility for children, and the various constructions of 'good' mothers/daughters/daughters-in-law as those who 'make sacrifices' for their families). Furthermore, when women have engaged in collective struggles with a transformative agenda, it is often precisely those gendered inequalities which make women 'more efficient' neoliberal subjects – such as the assumption that children are solely the responsibility of women, the acute scarcity of time not spent working; the notions of respectability and reputation which are used to control women, and the ubiquitous threat of violence – which are challenged.[3] This makes it particularly ironic that women's greater 'efficiency' – as workers, creditors or entrepreneurs – should be so frequently cited and even celebrated by feminists working within GAD frameworks.

The moralistic overtones of the development literature's oft-cited contrasts between women's 'good' spending (on food, children's clothes, etc.) and men's 'bad' spending (on alcohol, cigarettes, entertainment etc.) (Kabeer, 1995: 104) are distinct echoes of the Victorian discourses of the 'deserving' and 'undeserving' poor, and, like them, are also deeply racialised in their reinscription of essentialised constructions of men in the global South as inherently 'lazy', irresponsible and preoccupied with sensual pleasure. These tropes of racialised masculinity have been strategically mobilised at a number of historical moments: as Ann Whitehead notes, 'ideas of men as lazy have a long history in European discourses about rural sub-Saharan Africa, occurring wherever rural men resisted colonial labour regimes and coercive forms of rural development, as ... the debate about the colonial government's encouragement of coerced labour for settler enterprises in Kenya in 1919 suggests' (Whitehead, 2001: 42). Currently, these ideas are being reiterated to reproduce the contrasting notion of the 'poor woman in the global South' as a reliable, industrious entrepreneurial subject whose labour can and should be further extended and intensified.

There are signs that approaches involving the further 'feminisation of responsibility' for survival (Chant, 2006) will become even more significant in the period of global recession and crisis. The instrumentalisation of poor women is perhaps epitomised by the World Bank's slogan 'Gender Equality as Smart Economics'.[3] But this represents a much wider consensus across development institutions, including the vast majority of NGOs. Central to this consensus has been the remarkable rise of microfinance models, with their emphasis on women as better borrowers as well as better providers, and a claim to be able simultaneously to resolve problems of poverty as well as gender inequality, even as they integrate women more deeply into global circuits of capital (Kalpana, 2008; Maclean, 2010).

As a result of this consensus, while the concept of agency is regularly mobilised in the construction of poor women in the South as 'enterprising' subjects with limitless capacity to 'cope', movements which run counter to the neoliberal model, demanding the redistribution of resources, challenging the operation of markets, or confronting the violence of the 'democratic' neoliberal state, are rendered invisible.

The neoliberal discourse of agency, however, combines with, rather than displaces, those civilisational discourses which continue to construct 'Third World women' as victims to be saved. This is particularly marked in the context of the 'War on Terror' and specifically the ongoing occupation of Afghanistan, in which the colonial trope of the silently oppressed 'veiled' Muslim woman has been mobilised centrally in the legitimating discourse of imperialist war (Abu Lughod, 2002). Here too, increasingly, the 'salvation' of these women is cast as simultaneously releasing – or bestowing – individual agency defined in precisely the terms outlined above. Thus Women for Women International, a US-based NGO which 'supports women in war-torn regions', offers a number of snapshots of their work with Afghan women on its website, of which the following is typical:

> Zia Gul is a 27 year old mother of four children.... Zia Gul was uneducated and a housewife but through WFWI was offered the unique opportunity to learn about women rights, health, business, and the rights of children from WWI training programs. WWI introduced Zia Gul to Safi Apparel Corporation and now Zia Gul is busy as a tailor, earning 65 dollars a month. Zia Gul is happy to now economically support her family. ...She hopes that WWI will expand their activities so more women can be helped. Zia Gul thanks Women for Women International and says 'Allah keeps Women for Women International successful so that more and more women of Afghanistan can be helped in the right way.' (Women for Women International, 2011)

The seamless combination of racialised civilisational discourse and missionary zeal for 'helping women in the right way' with the neoliberal celebration of women's exploitation-as-agency is all too evident here. But, as this chapter argues, this is not in fact a question of completely new representations, but of the rediscovery, reworking and redeployment of earlier colonial representations for a new phase of imperialism and changing strategies of global capital accumulation.

In the remainder of this chapter, we will explore in more detail how these processes affect the visual images that are currently being produced and circulated by development institutions. First, we need to consider how relationships between representation, knowledge and power are elaborated in the production of visual materials by these institutions.

Thinking about representation in development

The reading of individual images depends on an accumulation of meanings: one image implicitly refers to a series of others, or has its meaning altered by being read in the context of others, in a process that establishes what Stuart Hall has described as 'regimes of representation' of difference (Hall, 1997).

As Edward Said has seminally argued, the work of representation and specifically the construction of the 'other', who is paradoxically both entirely 'knowable' and irreducibly alien, was central to the process of reproducing colonial power. Orientalism involved

> dealing with the Orient ... by making statements about it, authorizing views of it, describing it, by teaching it, settling it, ruling over it: in short Orientalism as a Western style for dominating, restructuring and having authority over the Orient. (Said, 1978: 3)

Postcolonial writers identify a contradiction in the colonial project's 'civilising mission' and the need to establish the colonized as perpetually 'other', which Homi Bhabha describes as the 'ironic compromise of mimicry' (1994: 86). As Baaz puts it, the civilising mission

> constituted and legitimised the 'white man's burden'. Western civilization was presented as the universal terminus of evolution, which the colonized should repeat, copy and internalize. At the same time, continued colonial domination was dependent on the opposite idea, namely that the colonized should remain different. (Baaz, 2005: 45)

As we will see, this insight has a particular bearing on a study of the contemporary visual representations produced by development institutions.

Constructions of the 'Other' in colonial discourses have underpinned conceptualisations of the 'self'. As Said writes, 'Orientalism is never far from ... the idea of Europe, a collective notion identifying "us" Europeans as against all "those" non-Europeans' (Said, 1978: 7). This notion is elaborated within the context of a critique of gender and development by Mohanty, who emphasises that 'images constructed from adding the "third world difference" to "sexual difference" are predicated upon (and hence obviously bring into sharper focus) assumptions about Western women as secular, liberated and having control over their own lives' (Mohanty, 1986: 353).

In examining visual representations in development, we need to ask, then, how these representations construct not only their subjects but also their intended consumers. Of particular relevance to this discussion is Ann Stoler's analysis of the construction of the desiring subject within colonial discourses of sexuality (Stoler, 1995). Stoler suggests that, rather than conceive of these discourses in a Freudian sense as repressing pre-existing desires, we should understand them as productive of these desires: 'The management of European sexuality in the colonies was a class and gender-specific project that animated a range of longings as much as it was a consequence of them' (Stoler, 1995: 176). What desires – licit and illicit – are being produced within the consumer of the 'positive images' of women in the global South?

Much contemporary writing on race, gender and representation, like Stoler's, has drawn extensively on Foucault's influential concept of power/knowledge, which suggests that 'there is no power relation without the correlative constitution of a field of knowledge, nor any knowledge that does not presuppose and constitute at the same time power relations' (Foucault, 1979: 27). Foucault's notion of power as productive of knowledge and discourse and as constructing consent is often contrasted with a conceptualisation of power as repressive and coercive attributed to Marxist thought (Stoler, 1995: 22). However, as Stuart Hall among others has pointed out, there are significant overlaps between Foucault's concept of power and Gramsci's notion of hegemony as involving both coercion and consent, and his identification of power in multiple locations (Hall, 1997: 261). Gramsci's work is in turn rooted in Marx's concept of ideology, taking as its starting point that

> the class which is the ruling *material* force of society, is at the same time its ruling *intellectual* force.... For each new class which puts itself in the place of one ruling before it, is compelled, merely in order to carry through its aim, to represent its interest as the common interest of all the members of society, that is, expressed in ideal form: it has to give its ideas the form of universality, and represent them as the only rational, universally valid ones. (Marx and Engels, 1974: 64–6)

More significant divergences between the approaches, perhaps, are to be found in questions of the location of power. Postcolonial theorists have tended to adopt Foucault's conceptualisation of power as circulating and pervasive, which characterizes his later work, in ways that have militated against identifying and examining specific sources of power, or considering its relationship to material structures of production, exchange and accumulation in any depth.

In order to engage with these differences productively, I seek here to incorporate insights from postcolonial work on the construction of knowledge and representation within a Marxist understanding of 'dominant material relationships' and of the processes of exploitation and accumulation underpinning capitalism and imperialism, in order to explore the implications of current gendered and racialised representations in development. Whereas postcolonial theorists have tended to focus on discursive continuities with the colonial period, this approach involves an emphasis on how historical continuities as well as changes in material structures sustain these representations and lend them continued meaning and legitimacy. What is required here, then, is not only a consideration of how changing eighteenth- and nineteenth-century patterns of capital accumulation shaped racialised regimes of representation[4] but also a recognition of the specificities of contemporary relations and structures which characterise capitalism at the current historical juncture, and how these sustain, reanimate or rework particular constructions of the racialised 'other'. In particular I will be exploring the implications of the rise of neoliberal globalisation – and the accompanying shift in the focus of development policy from the 'developmental state' to the market – for these constructions.

Dominant representations are simultaneously (re)shaped by changing configurations of power, and by the resistance of those who are represented. As we saw in the previous chapter, the emergence and consolidation of racialised categories occurred partially in response to sustained and diverse forms of resistance by those who were dispossessed, enslaved and exploited in colonial processes. Similarly, I suggest that currently multiple forms of resistance to the onslaught of neoliberal globalisation are contributing to a reworking of racialised representations, through simultaneous processes of appropriation and invisibilisation.

NGOs and changing representations

The ongoing debate among development institutions (and NGOs in particular) regarding the use of images is often traced back to the period following the Ethiopian Famine of 1984–85. This period can be characterised as the high-water mark of the tide of charity images which objectified and dehumanised people in 'Third World' countries, portraying them as helpless, starving, passive victims (almost always children and occasionally women) waiting end-lessly to be saved by the generosity of the white, Western donor, images whose racist paternalism has been extensively critiqued (Coulter, 1989; Benthall, 1993). If the scale of this was facilitated by the increasingly symbiotic relationship between NGOs and the media (Benthall, 1993; de Waal, 1997), epitomised by Band Aid and its descendants, the period also saw the beginning of a massive increase in the role of NGOs as a consequence of a series of interlinked changes associated with neoliberal economic reforms. The privatisation of aid, the substitution of NGOs for the state in social provision, and the reconfiguration, within the framework of the liberal democracy/liberalised economy dyad, of 'civil society' as an arena for donor intervention and direction all contributed to a new and expanded role for development NGOs from the 1990s onwards (Duffield, 2001; Chandler, 2006; Ferguson and Gupta, 2002; Hearn, 2007).

Nandita Dogra identifies a link between the growing concern with images – and the shift from what are perceived as 'negative' to 'positive' representations – to NGOs' increasing emphasis on education and advocacy in the 1990s (Dogra, 2007). I argue further that it is the incorporation of NGOs into the structures of 'an emerging system of transnational governmentality' (Ferguson and Gupta, 2002: 990) which has primarily informed the new types of representations produced by them.

In 1989, the Practical Guidelines adopted by the General Assembly of European NGOs in its 'Code of Conduct on Images and Messages Relating to the Third World' (since contracted to 'Code of Conduct on Images and Messages') states that

> The image of our Third World partners as dependent, poor and powerless is most often applied to women who are invariably portrayed as dependent victims, or worse still, simply do not figure in the picture. An improvement in the images used in educational material on the Third World evidently requires a positive change in the images projected of Southern women. (General Assembly of European NGOs, 1989)

There are clearly major questions around the extent to which the recommendation for 'positive change' in the Guidelines – and the more general ones referring to preserving dignity and avoiding discrimination – have in fact been followed in the intervening period. Structural aspects of the relationship between Northern-based international NGOs and people in the South who are portrayed in the images they produce make adherence to the 'Code of Conduct' in many respects a contradiction in terms. It is hardly surprising that a number of major NGOs continued to use, for example, photographs of lone vulnerable children in the South extensively in their publicity.[5] But my focus here is on a new set of images. What are the implications of the kinds of 'positive' images of women which are produced? How is another recommendation which comes earlier in the Guidelines – 'People's ability to *take responsibility for themselves* must be highlighted' – interpreted? In what ways are these images gendered and racialised?

In the following sections, I examine images and text produced by three recent publicity campaigns, each belonging to a different strand within the development industry. First, I will discuss the 'Oxfam Unwrapped' campaign in which one of the biggest international NGOs targets the general public in the UK for purpose-specific donations. Second, I look at the 'Girl Effect' campaign run by the Nike Foundation, a body set up by the corporate giant in 2003 specifically to fund projects involving adolescent girls in the global South. Third, I consider a commercial advertising campaign run by Divine Chocolate, a leading fair trade brand in the UK, to market its products.

'Add to basket': exoticising the deserving poor

In 1992, a special issue of the *New Internationalist* marking 'Changing Charity: 50 years of Oxfam' stated confidently that

> Aid agencies now are very conscious of the photographs they use. They try to choose pictures that show how active their partners in the South are in the process of their own development. The aim is

to present the whole person rather than just the aspect of them that the Western public might want or expect to see. Often they show a person working and will always try to give their name. (*New Internationalist*, 1992)

Oxfam's 'Oxfam Unwrapped' campaign was launched in 2004 in the UK. One of the pioneering schemes of charity gift-giving, the campaign encourages people to give purpose-specific donations to Oxfam in the names of friends and family members as an alternative to gifts. The 'gifts' range 'from schoolbooks to safe water and toilets to training a teacher' as well as the well-known goats. By December 2008, it had sold 'almost 3 million gifts', raising a total of 'more than 50 million pounds' (Oxfam, 2008). Here I look in detail at the campaign's Winter 2007 catalogue in order to consider further the implications of the use of 'positive' images.

The catalogue is divided into several sections, each illustrating the benefits of a particular type of 'gift'. The single largest section, 'working wonders', refers to support for small-scale enterprise: combined with 'gifts that grow', which refers specifically to agricultural production, this section comprises ten pages at the beginning of the 45-page catalogue, which includes shorter sections relating to other Oxfam activities. The people whose photographs appear in this section are overwhelmingly women. Those few images (three out of nineteen) which do show men are all relatively unobtrusive by virtue of their small size and/or the fact that the men's faces are not clearly visible. By contrast, the photographs of women are larger, clearer, and evidently intended to engage the viewer. All are depicted working, and notably only a small number of the women are identified by name or even located geographically in the text. They are photographed surrounded by vegetation, agricultural produce or handicrafts, the natural tones emphasised by their brightly coloured clothing. The most prominent image on the first page shows two Masai women[6] wearing large, elaborate necklaces and earrings pouring seeds into a sack. Most strikingly, the women in this picture and a majority (nine out of fifteen) of the others are looking away from the camera at the task they are doing, but at the same time smiling broadly.

The reader of the catalogue is thus constructed as a consuming subject on several interlinked levels: first, as a viewer sampling multiple images of the 'exoticised', racialised bodies and 'natural' surroundings of the women; second, as a (potential) donor deriving gratification from observing (unobserved) the effects of his/her generosity; and third, as a consumer in the North not only enjoying the undervalued product of the labour applied by 'poor women in the South' but using their leisure time to share vicariously the pleasure that these women are portrayed as deriving from their own labour. (A similar consuming experience can be gained online at the Oxfam Unwrapped website; see, for example, www.oxfam. org.uk/shop/oxfam-unwrapped-gardeners, where the first of these constructions of the consumer is enhanced by the juxtaposition of 'Add to Basket' icons with each smiling photograph).

A browse through these pages creates, through a process of repetition and accumulation of images, an overwhelming sense of 'the South' as a single, though endlessly diverse, place where 'poor women' are constantly, diligently and happily engaged in small-scale but productive labour for the market. Not only does the process of 'othering' continue, but the construction of these women as hyper-industrious 'entrepreneurs' ('active ... in the process of their own development') is incorporated in this process.

This is not so much a new development as a rediscovery and reformulation of an earlier narrative: that of late colonial enterprises which were based on the acute exploitation of largely female labour. In her analysis of British advertising in the colonial period, Anandi Ramamurthy (2003) has demonstrated how tea advertising in the 1920s worked to provide legitimacy for the continuation of colonial rule in the context of growing demands for independence, using images of the Indian woman tea picker, who was not only represented as 'alluring and sensual, but through her apparent contentment and productivity within an ordered environment symbolically affirmed the need for empire' (Ramamurthy, 2003: 126). These images were also read in the context of discourses of the 'work ethic', individual responsibility and the 'deserving' and 'undeserving' poor, which were deployed to extract ever greater surpluses from the working class in Britain and, via missionaries in particular, from its colonial subjects.

Regimes of representation work to evoke these continuities. Thus on the Cafédirect website we find a quotation from 'Mugisha Pauson: Tea picker. Mpanga, Uganda': 'I like my work – I pick tea and put it in my basket. Believe it or not, I can smell the good quality tea leaves. Cafédirect has helped our community by giving us a fair price, so now I pick the tea with a big smile' (http://brewing. cafedirect.co.uk/what-we-grow). This text and the accompanying smiling photograph, which have also been used on tea packaging, contain all the same elements as the colonial advertisements described by Ramamurthy: labour and order producing contentment and a good-quality product for the European consumer, and an explicit recognition of the benevolent role of the white man/company in making this possible.[7]

Perhaps the only factor which makes this stand out among contemporary development images of work is that Mugisha is a man. Like the Oxfam images, however, his portrayal is racialised in specifically gendered ways. Its construction of the naively happy, close-to-nature yet deliberately desexualized black man references a recurring trope which has been analysed extensively.[8]

In the absence, then, of any problematisation of the current global order, the 'positivity' of contemporary development images, from which any contradictions appear to have been elided, implicitly confirms neoliberal narratives in which the 'empowerment' of 'developing world' women via the market is the 'solution'. In a reworking of colonial representations, relations of oppression and exploitation are thus obscured, or reconfigured as 'obstacles' which can be overcome through hard work and a helping hand from the Northern donor/consumer.

Like the image of the cycling Bangladeshi health worker 'Elizabeth' used in a 1990 Christian Aid campaign discussed by Lidchi (1999), each of the women in the Oxfam catalogue is constituted 'not as the object of development – helpless and despairing', but as 'the image of an empowered "participating .... hardworking, industrious and self-determined" subject' (Lidchi, 1999: 99). However, whereas, as Lidchi notes, there is an ambiguity in the status of 'Elizabeth', who can be viewed as a 'conscientious worker' mediating between the viewer/donor and the 'poorest of the poor' beneficiaries of her services, in the more recent images it is the beneficiaries themselves, assumed to be working – as rational economic agents – only for themselves and their children, who are represented as 'empowered subjects'. Just as all remaining barriers to global capital have been removed in the interim, similarly it seems any intermediaries who might imply a lingering role for the state have been erased from the picture, allowing direct access for the viewer/consumer/donor to the hardworking 'developing world' woman within the framework of neoliberal globalisation.

'Invest in a girl'

The Nike Foundation is a body established by the Nike corporation in 2003 specifically to fund projects involving adolescent girls in developing countries.[9] Set up in partnership with the Population Council and the International Centre for Research on Women, the Foundation has gone on to establish partnerships with the World Bank and the UK Department for International Development (DfID). The Foundation's stated aim is to apply business and specifically 'branding' skills to the project; in line with this, all but one of its core staff were recruited from Nike Corporate.

Here I consider two short videos produced by the Nike Foundation for online circulation. The first, *I Dare You* (www.youtube.com/watch?v=-Vq2mfF8puE), produced in 2006, explicitly challenges what are assumed to be the viewer's perceptions of girl children and young women in the global South as victims and objects of pity, deploying the notion of the 'gaze' with a voice-over which states: 'I dare you to look at me without pity, fatigue, dismissal.... I dare you to rethink what it means to look at a girl.' This is counterposed with a series of shots of girl children (some clearly much younger than the target group of the campaign) silently returning the viewer's gaze with a sense of expectancy. The message here, then, is clearly not that women are already acting to change the conditions of their lives, but that they have the potential to be the individual instruments of change if only 'we' – the intended viewers – recognise it and give it shape and direction.

This is made clearer in the second part of the video, which is marked by a shift in tone as the disembodied adult woman's voice – clearly marked by its inflections as African – goes on to tell us that a girl is 'not a burden, not an object, but the answer'. A series of statistics relating to the impact of girls' education on population increase, the prevalence of HIV, malnutrition and economic growth are now superimposed on a series of shots of girl children and women working alone (carrying water, digging soil) in various rural landscapes. The use of these scenes of gendered labour is ambiguous: on the one hand, the focus is on the desirability of girls' education (implying an alternative to the child labour we see), but, on the other, there is an emphasis on 'developing world' women and girls' gendered propensity for hard work and altruism as the reason why girls' education is worthwhile and an effective means of development.

The latter is made most explicit in the final statistic we are presented with: 'when an educated girl earns income she reinvests 90% of it in her family, compared to 35% for a boy'. Thus in the course of two and a half minutes the video moves swiftly from the appropriation and mobilisation of critiques of racialised constructions of the perpetually victimised 'Third World woman' to their apparent resolution in the constitution, through benevolent Western intervention, of the new figure of the Third World woman as instrument of neoliberal development, whose gendered subjectivity continues to make her self-sacrificing, even though her education (presumably) has now taught her to regard the performance of gendered familial obligations as an 'investment'.

The second video, *The Girl Effect* (www.youtube.com/watch?v= WIvmE4_KMNw), produced in 2008, marked the project's launch of the Girl Effect 'brand' and the removal of all reference to the Nike Foundation. This video is notable, particularly in the context of development publicity, for its complete exclusion of images or speech, being based solely on an extremely pared down and simplified textual narrative in which individual capitalised words flash on an empty screen (in contrast to the earlier video, no statistics are cited here). This, along with the complete absence of any markers of place or culture, would appear to avoid some of the more obvious forms of objectification and exoticisation. In fact (continuing one of the themes of the *I Dare You* video), there is a challenge to these processes implied in the invitation here to 'imagine a girl living in poverty, no, go ahead, really, imagine her'. Yet paradoxically, as a result of its generality, it is also free to mobilise intertextual associations to deploy racialised tropes (familiar to the viewer from more explicit photographic images and texts used by NGOs and the media) quite extensively. Thus in the central sequence in the video, the word GIRL appears in the middle of a white screen and soon several tiny versions of the word FLIES are 'buzzing' around her. The word BABY appears. A second later the word HUSBAND in very large letters falls on top of her, followed in quick succession by the appearance of HUNGER and HIV. This memorable chain of effects also serves to locate the causes of suffering (HUNGER and HIV) firmly and solely at the level of the local, the cultural (i.e. early marriage) and the individual, and in particular in the person (or concept) of the oppressive HUSBAND.

Two further aspects of *The Girl Effect* that are facilitated by its format are worth noting here. First, the role of the viewer as the powerful initiator of change, as responsible for releasing and directing the entrepreneurial agency, not in this case of individuals but of the '600 million girls in the developing world', is reaffirmed particularly strikingly here – the viewer is invited to 'pretend that you can fix this' and, as if at the click of a mouse, the GIRL's 'burdens' (FLIES, HUSBAND, BABY...) fall away and the process of turning her into a microfinance entrepreneur, who in turn banishes her community's poverty and generates global STABILITY, begins.

Second, the video is marked by the speed with which the text appears and disappears and these processes of change are conveyed. I would suggest that this has significant effects in terms of the construction of both the object of scrutiny (the GIRL who represents 600 million) as well as the viewing subject. While the speed is clearly intended to identify the video with mainstream popular cyberculture, it also serves to suggest that the potential viewer has very little time to 'waste' and wants quick and visible 'results', implicitly contrasting the Nike Foundation's 'business' ethos with earlier development initiatives presumed to be slower-acting and less 'efficient', and by extension highlighting the compatibility of the present approach with contemporary market-led globalisation. But it also works to construct the 'developing world' GIRL as an 'investment' whose gendered propensity for labour can be instrumentalised to the point where her very life is speeded up: no sooner do we 'put her in a school uniform' than we see her 'get a loan to buy a cow' and 'use the profits to help her family'. This is perhaps made clearest in the video's penultimate slogan: 'Invest in a girl', we are urged, 'and she will do the rest'.

Since the videos discussed here were produced (several others have followed), the focus on adolescent girls in the global South as the 'solution' to the 'problem' of development has been adopted and promoted much more widely by international development institutions. In 2007, UNICEF, UNIFEM and the WHO established the UN Interagency Task Force on adolescent girls. In 2008 the World Bank founded its Adolescent Girl Initiative, aimed at improving girls' and young women's economic opportunities. In 2010 the UK government announced that it would focus its development aid on girls and women (Gill and Koffman, 2013). As Rosalind Gill and Ofra Koffman point out, a striking aspect of this phenomenon has been the way in which 'girls' in the global North are directly addressed by campaigns such as the Girl Effect or the UN Foundation's *Girl Up* campaign launched in 2010. 'Via an extensive range of social media campaigns, "roadshows" and merchandising promotions, girls in affluent societies, particularly the US, are hailed variously as the allies and saviours of their Southern "sisters", using discourses of girl power and popular feminism.' These campaigns reinforce postfeminist notions that women in the global North are free from gender discrimination: 'First World girls are invited to endorse feminism but only in relation to the South. They themselves are seen as being the most empowered, socially connected and educated girls in history' (Gill and Koffman, 2013). This interpellation also, I suggest, further highlights the ways in which contemporary constructions of agency within development are racialised, with the capacity for collective and transformative, rather than entrepreneurial, agency being displaced onto apparently homogenous publics in the global North (and young people in particular), who are increasingly invited by development institutions using the language of 'revolution' to mobilise around agendas that are consistent with the needs of global capital. This is explored further in Chapter 7.

'Race', gender and guilt

Divine chocolate is a leading Fair Trade brand in the UK. It promotes an understanding of 'fair trade' to which the notion of 'empowerment' of women is central.[10] In 2006 Divine launched a series of full-page magazine advertisements, in each of which a different woman is photographed against a background of lush vegetation, holding up a piece of chocolate between her fingertips. On one level, these advertisements move away from the contemporary patterns of development images, as well as disrupting some of the conventions of mainstream advertising. This would appear to be in line with Divine's model of co-operative ownership of the company by farmers, which involves a critique of the 'unfair' operation of global markets while claiming to be able to engage with them beneficially through 'radical mainstream', 'alternative high street' marketing. In each of these advertisements the woman appears at first glance to be a professional model, but the accompanying text belies our expectations by informing us that she is a member of the Kuapa Kokoo Co-operative in Ghana. While a farmer, however, she is not depicted working. She wears African dress, but the photography and pose emphasise mainstream notions of fashion and 'glamour' rather than, as in the Oxfam images, tradition and authenticity. One reaction that this is intended to generate in the (mainly female and fairly affluent) target audience is clearly of empathy, as co-inhabitants of a post-feminist world where pleasure derives from spending one's own earnings on one's own commodification.

But the implications of these images and how they operate can only be fully grasped through a reading which engages with processes of intertextuality and places them in a historical context.

A feature of contemporary development representations of work and production in the South, which is particularly explicit in the Divine advertisements, is the conflation of the worker/producer with her product. In her analysis of advertising by fair trade coffee company Cafédirect, Wright (2004: 671) argues that while photographic images of producers 'could ... be understood as a deliberate attempt to undermine commodity fetishism, to make part of the potential consumer's relationship with the product, coffee, also a relationship with the coffee producer(s)', in fact these images are constructed 'in ways that render them commodities in their own right', and the viewer is 'invited to consume (metaphorically) the very body of the coffee producer' (676).

Once again, there are very clear continuities with colonial representations. The Divine advertisements recall a long history of explicitly racist advertising by European cocoa companies in which the African producers were represented as inseparable from their produce and their skin colour was associated with chocolate (Ramamurthy, 2003: 63–91). Unlike these earlier images, however, these advertisements sexualise this association through their focus on the figure of the beautiful African woman, who is pictured languidly casting a sidelong glance at the viewer.

Leaving aside the question of whether such objectification can be considered empowering, we need to ask whether a sexualised image of an African woman being used in the context of global trade – to sell a product to consumers in Britain – can ever be dehistoricised. In fact a closer look suggests that Divine does not quite wish us to forget the past: while the colours of the image are intense and hyper-real, they are framed by sepia-tinted text in a nineteenth-century-style font. The whole history of plunder, slavery, sexual violence and colonialism is in fact very much present, and is underlined by the slogan of one of the advertisements, 'a not-so-guilty pleasure'. This slogan works on several levels, referring to the 'guilty pleasure' of consuming chocolate which undermines the gendered regime of the body; and the 'guilt' of ongoing exploitative trade relations (and, by extension, of slavery and colonialism) borne by the white British consumer which is supposedly mitigated by Fair Trade practices. If these two meanings are explicit, implicitly there is also the 'guilty pleasure' of enjoying the image itself: guilt associated with the desire it produces for the racialised 'other' in the form of the African woman, which is partially absolved through the viewer's recognition of the image as representing an 'empowered' participant in global markets.

Conclusion

As we have seen, contemporary 'positive' visual representations of women in the South produced by development institutions are rooted in a notion of 'agency' consistent with – and necessary for – neoliberal capitalism.

While earlier representations remain pervasive, critiques of the essentialisation of people in the South – and women in particular – as passively suffering victims have been widely interpreted as an imperative to represent these women as universally enterprising, productive and happy. These 'positive' images are consistent with the current neoliberal development consensus which, as we have seen, portrays an intensification of labour applied by women in the South as the 'solution' to poverty as well as gender inequality. They operate in the same way as the images of 'contented and productive' women workers in colonial enterprises used in British advertising in the late nineteenth and early twentieth centuries: to reassure the viewer of the legitimacy and justice of existing relationships and structures. These connections and continuities are evident in a regime of representation in which the bodies of 'poor' women in the global South continue to be exoticised and racialised even as the construction of these women as hyper-industrious entrepreneurial agents is incorporated in this process.

Significantly, agency as it is portrayed here is not only limited to the 'rational self-interested' individual but is further constrained in the context of the power relations which structure these visual encounters: agency, like empowerment, is projected as a gift to be granted by the consumer of the images – and potential donor – implicitly reaffirming the civilising mission. Thus the notion of victims to be saved that these images supposedly challenge is not in fact eradicated but reworked. This interdependency between constructions of poor women in the South as both objects of transformation and redemption and potential entrepreneurial subjects in fact echoes the structure of colonial discourses of salvation, which simultaneously infantilised its objects and imposed a moral responsibility for self-improvement on them. Mirroring representations of women workers in ordered colonial enterprises, these 'new' images imply that, through the intervention of development institutions, women in the South can be both 'rescued' from oppressive and 'backward' societies and 'civilised' through subjection to the discipline of global markets. Like their colonial predecessors, today's images work to silence or obscure multiple forms of resistance to contemporary imperialism.

CHAPTER 3

Population control,
the Cold War and racialising reproduction

People eating, people washing, people sleeping. People visiting,
arguing, and screaming. People thrusting their hands through the
taxi window, begging. People defecating and urinating. People
clinging to buses. People herding animals. People, people, people,
people.

Paul R. Ehrlich, *The Population Bomb* (1968)

a large part of the world that is poor and coloured and potentially
hostile

Cold War military strategist Thomas Schelling
describing Asia (testimony to the House
Foreign Affairs Committee, 27 January 1966)

This chapter examines the emergence and elaboration of one of the
most significant and sustained interventions to have taken place
within the framework of development: population control. It examines these policies and initiatives in the context of the Cold
War, the reconfiguring of imperialism after formal colonialism,
and the challenge to the existing global distribution of wealth and
resources posed by communist movements in the global South, and
explores how these were related to the pathologisation of racialised
sexualities that mark the discourses, institutions and practices of
population control.

Many recent discussions of the population control policies that
were a key element of development interventions from the 1950s
onwards have highlighted the centrality of eugenicist concepts
of 'race' and their intimate and sustained relationship with neo-
Malthusian theories about population, resources and the environment

in shaping population control initiatives over the course of the twentieth century. The overlapping and intertwined histories of eugenics and population control have been traced rigorously and in detail by a number of writers (see, for example, Mass, 1976; Ross, 1998; Connelly, 2008), often in part through tracing the careers of key individuals such as birth control pioneer Margaret Sanger, US demographers Kingsley Davis and Frank Notestein, and investment banker and cold warrior General William Draper.

The aims of this chapter, however, are somewhat different. First, I look at how racism and racialised constructions – which were both much more established and entrenched and more amorphous and heterogeneous than the ideas about 'race purity' promoted by crusading eugenicist individuals – informed population policies and practices and made it possible for them to continue and reach a peak even after explicitly eugenicist ideas had been marginalised.

Second, I seek to bring the extensive theoretical work on questions of 'race', racism and sexuality – much though not all of which has been elaborated within a postcolonial framework – to bear on population control policies. Surprisingly, despite the extent to which population control policies focused on and, as I suggest, pathologised the sexual activities of women and men in the global South, there has been very little discussion of how this related to constructions of 'race' in which portrayals of sexuality were central, or, indeed, of the continuities and parallels with colonial attempts to regulate and control sex and reproduction. As Laura Briggs, whose work on Puerto Rico is a valuable exception, argues, there is a need to 'think about ideologies of family, sexuality, and reproduction as animating imperial and racial projects' in this context (Briggs, 2002: 16).

Third, I seek to incorporate this focus into a framework which positions Malthusian approaches as central to strategies of accumulation, and of countering resistance, by capital (Ross, 1998), highlighting why in particular population control became such a key development policy during the Cold War era. I argue that Malthusian–eugenicist ideas underpinned not only specific policies but the development project itself in important ways. This emphasis on the relationship between 'race' and capital implies a departure from dominant postcolonial understandings of the pathologisation of the sexuality of racialised others. It favours the kind of historically specific and materially grounded treatment of ideas about 'race' for which Magubane has argued in the context of discussion of the case of Sarah Baartman, when she proposes 'an alternative way of understanding the construction of Black women in colonial discourse', and argues that 'social relations, rather than psychological dispositions, determine how bodies are seen and perceived' (Magubane, 2001: 816).

Malthus, population and poverty

While Thomas Malthus's name has become synonymous with theories of 'overpopulation', his primary legacy, as Ross suggests, has been to provide 'an enduring argument for the prevention of social and economic change' (Ross, 1998: 6) by suggesting that the poverty associated with capitalist development is an inevitable consequence of population increase, rather than of the logic of capital accumulation. Thus Malthusianism has not only shaped population control policies, but has influenced many key theories and practices of development similarly based upon the assumption that poverty stems from the behaviour of the poor, which, as discussed in the previous chapter, then becomes a target for intervention.

Malthus's ideas, put forward in the first edition of *An Essay on the Principle of Population* (1798), emerged against a backdrop of the upheaval associated with the Industrial Revolution in England. The displacement of the poor from the land through the Enclosure Acts and other measures in favour of agrarian capitalism had led to a visible unsettled population wandering the countryside seeking work and converging in the rapidly growing cities. The last years of the eighteenth century saw waves of bread 'riots' in which stocks of food were seized and sold at prices the people considered reasonable (Morton, 1938: 331; Thompson, 1982), Luddite disturbances in which workers destroyed labour-displacing machinery, and strikes (Morton,

1938: 355). The reverberations of the French Revolution less than a decade earlier were being felt across Europe. Evidently, the same fears of the nascent working class, of the 'mob' and of potential social transformation, which were soon to produce the first calls for 'development' to create 'order' out of 'chaos' (Cowen and Shenton, 1995: 34), also animated the more pessimistic Malthus.

But for his contemporaries among the English bourgeoisie, Malthus made an important and valuable contribution in the argument he provided against the continuation of the Poor Laws, which represented a form – albeit an extremely meagre one – of state provision for the destitute. Population among the poor, Malthus warned, would increase unchecked and outstrip natural resources unless natural 'checks' like disease and starvation were allowed to alleviate this pressure. The Poor Laws, which provided for parish relief, paid for by local taxation, were obstructing these processes.[1] Malthus was a supporter of the system of workhouses, universally implemented in 1834 by the notorious Poor Law Commission, whose brutality and effectiveness in discouraging even the most destitute from seeking state support has been extensively recorded (Morton, 1938: 386).

As Ross points out, Malthus (unlike those who were later to adopt his arguments) did not in fact advocate that poor people be encouraged in their attempts to control their fertility – not only did he suggest that such practices were morally wrong, but he argued that continued poverty was necessary to force the labouring classes to seek work (Ross, 1998: 4–6). The whole focus of his argument was to demonstrate that poverty was the result of the fecklessness of the poor themselves, and that capital should bear no responsibility for alleviating it.

Malthus, 'race' and colonialism

While such debates over the accountability of capital took place in England, both labour power and resources continued to be appropriated on a vast scale through the Atlantic slave trade and the plunder of the East India Company in Asia, generating countless forms of resistance. As we have noted, slavery and colonialism fuelled the Industrial Revolution, but increasingly powerful ideologies of 'race' were to legitimise and structure the continuation of these processes of superexploitation even as conditions for the English working class began to improve.

Malthus himself was appointed to the first professorship in political economy at the East India College at Haileybury, where he passed on his ideas to new generations of colonial officials. But his own references to non-European civilisations are rarely cited. In fact, his *Essay on the Principle of Population* includes a full exposition of the ideology of racialised global hierarchies emerging at the time. Malthus

> identified a progression from the 'savages' of South America, Australia and Africa to the more developed civilizations of Turkey, India and China, and on ... via Greece and Rome, to the Western Europe of his own day. What for Malthus marked out the successive stages of this ascent from primitiveness to civilization was a transition from indolence to industry, from privation to property, from hunger to relative freedom from want.... Only Europe and especially Britain (the Irish aberration aside), stood out in his account as possessing the prudence and foresight to limit population by voluntary means. (Arnold, 1988: 128–9)

European references to the notion of overpopulation in Asia in this period were also framed by orientalist imaginaries, which once again contrasted dynamic Europeans with passive and unproductive 'others' bound by static traditions. Thus French cleric and Sanskrit scholar J.A. Dubois travelled around India as a missionary in the late eighteenth and early nineteenth centuries and produced what was for many years considered the definitive European work on Indian culture. Despite acknowledging the destruction of the Indian weaving industry by the British and the impoverishment that resulted, Abbé Dubois wrote:

> Of these causes [of miscry] the chief one is the rapid increase of population.... Some modern political economists have held that a progressive increase in the population is one of the most unequivocal signs of a country's prosperity and wealth. In Europe this argument may be logical enough, but I do not think that it can be applied to

India; in fact, I am persuaded that as the population increases, so in proportion do want and misery. For this theory of the economists to hold good in all respects the resources and industries of the inhabitants ought to develop rather rapidly; but in a country where the inhabitants are notoriously apathetic and indolent, where customs and institutions are so many insurmountable barriers against a better order of things, and where it is more or less a sacred duty to let things as they are, I have every reason to believe that a considerable increase in the population should be looked upon as a calamity rather than as a blessing. (Dubois, 1905, cited in Rao, 1994: PE45)

Malthusian concerns about overpopulation in England declined during the course of the nineteenth century with the beginnings of a demographic transition to lower birth rates[2] as well as mass emigration of the poor as part of the colonial project. While the 'investigations' that characterized the second half of the century continued to portray the problems of the poor as caused largely by their own lack of morals and irresponsibility – including having too many children – and highlighted this as a cause of overcrowding in urban slums, the application of the notion of overpopulation on a macroeconomic scale had decisively shifted to the global South.

It was in the later part of the nineteenth century, when the cumulative effects of deindustrialisation, grinding taxation, forced cultivation of cash crops, and other forms of integration into world markets combined with El Niño crop failures to produce a series of devastating famines across much of the global South, that Malthusian ideas came into their own in shaping colonial responses to famine. As Mike Davis powerfully demonstrates in his classic 'political ecology of famine' *Late Victorian Holocausts*,

we are not dealing ... with 'lands of famine' becalmed in stagnant backwaters of world history, but with the fate of tropical humanity at the precise moment (1870–1914) when its labor and products were being dynamically conscripted into a London-centered world economy. Millions died, not outside the 'modern world system', but in the very process of being forcibly incorporated into its economic and political structures. (Davis, 2001: 9)

In the famines that resulted, colonial officials like Lord Lytton, the viceroy during the Indian famine of 1876–79, in which up to 10.3 million people are estimated to have died, invoked Malthusian principles to justify their refusal to prevent these deaths. In a debate on the government's conduct during the catastrophe, finance minister Sir Evelyn Baring (later Lord Cromer) stated: 'every benevolent attempt made to mitigate the effects of famine and defective sanitation serves but to enhance the evils resulting from overpopulation' (cited in Davis, 2001: 32). Sir Richard Temple, appointed by Lytton to ensure that India continued to produce immense revenues for Britain and its imperial war in Afghanistan even at the height of the famine, implemented the notorious 'Temple wage' in relief camps, which combined with hard labour could only lead to slow death by starvation. Temple 'became to Indian history ... the personification of free market economics as a mask for colonial genocide' (Davis, 2001: 37).

One of Davis's key arguments is that the 'Third World' was 'shaped most decisively in the last quarter of the nineteenth century, when the great non-European peasantries were integrated into the world economy'. This late colonial period of rapid global polarisation was, as we have seen, also marked by the consolidation of the idea of 'whiteness' (Ware, 1992; McClintock; 1995) and the fuller incorporation of the working class poor of European origin within this category (Gould, 1981; Roediger, 1999). The notion of an entirely different, peculiarly intractable colonial poverty, both more extreme and more acceptable to its victims, became ingrained in the common-sense binaries of race by the end of the nineteenth century, reinforced by racialised representations in appeals in news-papers, in books and through lantern-slide lectures, drawings and photographs of the very real 'holocausts' that were taking place across much of the global South.[3] As Arnold suggests, 'the apparent contrast between European dynamism and "native"' apathy already established in the imperial mind and the sense of Western power and superiority which famine in the Third World was increasingly coming to signify were thereby further reinforced' (Arnold, 1988: 135). Henceforth, acute poverty in British cities would be described

– and pathologised – through comparisons with the South, particularly Africa (Magubane, 2004). This construction of naturalised and racialised poverty and destitution is one of the key themes through which 'race' has been inscribed in, and essential to, the development project from its inception.

Racism, 'science' and birth control

The Social Darwinist 'scientific racism' of this period also laid the foundations for the eugenicist ideas which were to impact so heavily on the emergence of the concept of population control in the early twentieth century. The term 'eugenics' was coined in 1883 by Francis Galton, a cousin of Charles Darwin, whose book *Hereditary Genius* claimed that intelligence was inherited and who 'advocated the regulation of marriage and family size according to hereditary endowments of parents' (Gould, 1981: 75). The eugenicists argued that inequality in capitalist society was a natural expression of processes of 'survival of the fittest'. They believed that human 'stock' could be improved by weeding out the 'unfit' (to be found among the poor and destitute) and encouraging the 'gifted' (to be found among the affluent groups) to 'breed' (Gordon, 1976).

The career of American birth control pioneer Margaret Sanger, and her remarkable transformation from feminist and socialist sympathiser to confirmed eugenicist, who famously declared in 1919 'more children from the fit, less from the unfit – that is the chief issue of birth control', have been described in detail elsewhere (Gordon, 1976; Mass, 1976; Davis, 1982; Hartmann, 1995). Ross argues that Sanger's shifting allegiance reflected a wider change after 1917, when, in the context of the Russian Revolution and witch-hunts against the left, 'the birth control movement quickly moved to distance itself from its socialist allies, shifting towards the eugenics camp and becoming more closely associated with establishment interests. … Sanger more than anyone epitomised this general transformation …, in situating birth control within the institutional and ideological framework of capitalism' (Ross, 1998: 68–9).

Yet, as Angela Davis has highlighted, feminist birth control activists in the USA had begun to incorporate eugenicist ideas even earlier, in response to the spread of the idea of 'race suicide' to describe the falling birth rate among US-born white women. The notion of 'race suicide' was promoted notably by President Theodore Roosevelt in 1906 against a background of 'accelerating racist ideology and of great waves of race riots and lynchings', as well as Roosevelt's attempts to muster public support for the recent US seizure of the Philippines, 'the country's most recent imperialist venture' (Davis, 1982: 209). Davis describes how

> birth control advocates either acquiesced to or supported the new ·
> arguments invoking birth control as a means of preventing the
> proliferation of the 'lower classes' and as an antidote to race suicide.
> Race suicide could be prevented by the introduction of birth control
> among Black people, immigrants and the poor in general ... More
> and more, it was assumed within birth control circles that poor
> women, Black and immigrant alike, had a 'moral obligation to
> restrict the size of their families.' What was demanded as a 'right'
> for the privileged came to be interpreted as a 'duty' for the poor.
> (Davis, 1982: 210)

The Birth Control Federation of America was formed in 1939. At its 1940 Annual Conference, Henry Pratt Fairchild, former president of the American Eugenics Society, commented:

> One of the outstanding features of the present conference is the
> practically universal acceptance of the fact that these two great
> movements, eugenics and birth control, have now come to such a
> thorough understanding and have drawn so close together as to be
> almost indistinguishable. (cited in Mass, 1976: 33)

Underlining this integration of birth control and eugenics within a racial supremacist ideology, the Birth Control Federation planned a 'Negro Project'. In the Federation's words,

> The mass of Negroes, particularly in the South, still breed
> carelessly and disastrously, with the result that the increase among
> Negroes, even more than among whites, is from that portion of the

population least fit, and least able to rear children properly. (cited in Davis, 1982: 214)

Along with birth control, eugenicists demanded sterilisation of those deemed 'unfit' to reproduce. By 1932 at least twenty-six US states had passed compulsory sterilisation laws and thousands of people had already been sterilized (Mass, 1977: 67). In Britain, the Ministry of Health established a National Birth Control Council in 1930, which became, in 1931, the National Birth Control Association. This included a number of prominent British eugenicists, notably Julian Huxley (Rao, 1994: PE47).

If this demonstrates the extent to which eugenicist ideas had become institutionalized within state structures, increasingly the eugenicist/birth control movement was also funded and promoted by corporate capital. Linda Gordon suggests that 'in no academic field was the coalition between corporate capital and scholars developed more fully than in eugenics' (Gordon, 1976). As we will see, after the Second World War and with the formation of the International Planned Parenthood Foundation (IPPF) in 1948, this corporate support was to become instrumental in the promotion of racialised population control policies.

Eugenicist birth control advocates focused considerable attention on poor white communities right up until World War II; but this too was understood and expressed in 'racial' terms. The way recent migrants to the USA from Italy and elsewhere in Europe were categorised racially in the early twentieth century was relatively unstable: Guy Irving Burch, director of the American Eugenics Society in the 1920s and one time leader of the American Birth Control League, supported birth control to 'prevent the American people being replaced by alien or negro stock, whether it be by immigration or by overly high birth rates among others in this country' (Mass, 1976: 29).

There was also the underlying assumption that eugenicist selective 'breeding' among white people was crucial to ensuring the continuation of white supremacy. This was particularly clear in the targeting of 'poor white' women for birth control in South Africa (Klausen, 2004), although racialised anxieties later reversed these policies and led to a shift in state policy to targeting the fertility of black women (Klausen, 2004: 153).[4] For Britain, the continuation of the colonial project was also argued to require a strong white 'race' by those like birth control activist Marie Stopes whose 'imperial dreams for birth control were reflected in her firmly pro-imperialist sentiments generally' (Klausen, 2004: 81). As Connelly notes,

> When birth rates began to fall among the European peoples in the first decades of the twentieth century – at the same time fears of degeneration became pervasive – increasing the size and 'quality' of nations provided both the rationale and the human resources to renew colonial expansion. (Connelly, 2008: 378)

But, as we have seen, the notion of 'overpopulation' in the global South was also already entrenched and established, and from this period it came to be portrayed as not only an explanation for poverty and a way of ignoring the role of colonial exploitation in creating it, but as a threat to the West. For American economist Joseph Spengler, writing in 1932, 'The steady decline in the birth rate threatens Western civilization both from within and without…. A thinning of ranks may expose the social superstructure of non-growing nations to the onslaught or the overflow of the swarming people' (cited in Mass 1976: 34). With anti-colonial resistance intensifying, fear increasingly permeated the discourse of overpopulation in the South, and this was reflected in a subtle change in the racialised representation of non-white populations: whereas earlier the emphasis had been on 'apathy', 'indolence' and 'fatalism', tropes which were used to justify colonial inaction in the face of famine and starvation, these same populations now began to be more often portrayed as ominously hyperactive, incessantly 'swarming', 'teeming' and 'seething'. These ideas would soon be mobilised to call for direct interventions to limit these populations.

Increasingly, colonial governments focused on population growth as a problem:

> Concern about population increase had now spread far beyond India. In 1939, a Royal Commission insisted that reducing birth rates was 'the most pressing need of the West Indian colonies.' ... The West India Royal Commission observed that high fertility was a phenomenon 'throughout the whole tropical and sub-tropical world,' and that its 'sharp contrast' to the trend among Europeans ... was 'of the most profound importance, with far-reaching implications.' (Connelly, 2008: 113)

This was despite the fact that birth rates were in fact low in many parts of the 'tropical' world – for example, in most of Africa. Not only this, but some regions of sub-Saharan Africa had experienced dramatic depopulation resulting from the devastating effects of colonial rule in the previous four decades. Thus Arnold estimates that 'the population of French Equatorial Africa, put at 15 million in 1900, had fallen to 10 million by 1914, and sank still further to 3 million by the census of 1921. Famine and related diseases were important causes of this immense human wastage. The population was worn out and worn away by forced labour, by military requisitioning and conscription, and by the interruption to family life caused by periods of prolonged and enforced separation' (Arnold, 1988: 124–5).

In many other colonized regions such as South and Southeast Asia and the Caribbean, birth rates were high but population growth was undermined by extremely high infant mortality rates under colonial rule. Public health measures outside of European settlements and army barracks had been almost non-existent, and colonial policies such as the spread of irrigation in India to facilitate cash-crop cultivation for the world market had hugely increased the incidence of malaria and water-borne diseases (Whitcombe, 1995).

The racialised fears about population growth that were increasingly being expressed in the 1930s and 1940s reflected a recognition that a decline in mortality rates was inevitable as policies to improve public health were finally implemented under pressure from anti-colonial movements in these countries. This focus on population growth as a 'problem' coincided with colonial powers, again largely in response to growing demands for independence, increasingly casting colonial policy in the terms of 'development' and 'modernisation'.

But it was after World War II, when 'development' was officially anointed as the new relation governing interactions between colonizers and ex-colonies, and the Cold War was fully under way, that the 'population bomb' in the global South became a major focus and population control emerged as a central thrust of development policies. The manner in which eugenicists rapidly incorporated their organisations into the new and respectable cause of international population control in the post-war period has been well documented. Eugenics, with its promotion of compulsory sterilisation for the 'unfit' and ideas of 'racial purity', had been a key influence on Nazi ideology and Hitler's 'Final Solution', and states and institutions now sought to distance themselves from it. Prominent eugenicists were explicit about plans to repackage their ideas: in 1956 a meeting of the British Eugenics Society resolved

> that the society should pursue eugenic ends, by less obvious means, that is by a policy of crypto-eugenics. The Society's activities in crypto-eugenics should be pursued vigorously, and specifically that the Society should increase its monetary support to the Family Planning Association and the International Planned Parenthood Federation. (Rao, 1994: PE46)

But committed eugenicists were only one – albeit highly influential – element in the powerful alliance that drove population control policies in an era of the Cold War, decolonisation and revolution. As we will see, a number of historical conjunctures shaped these policies. Furthermore, 'race' and racism structured and facilitated these policies in fundamental ways which did not necessarily depend on the involvement of individual eugenicists: once again it was the changing relationship of 'race' with capital, and the emergence of new challenges to capital accumulation in the form of anti-imperialist struggles in the global South, which animated the gendered and racialised violence of population control policy and practice.

The Cold War and population control

The period of the Cold War – which coincided with the era of developmentalism – was one in which racial supremacist ideas, while often expressed less explicitly than before in official discourse at the international level, continued to shape development interventions. Not only was the Cold War being fought in defence of capital, states and economic and political systems which were themselves racialised, but most Cold War conflicts were fought in the global South in the context of a new phase of imperialism, and racism was deeply implicated in anti-communist discourses, which were at times indistinguishable from the colonial discourses that had preceded them. Moreover, while mainstream development chronologies imply that the emergence of developmentalism marked the end of the colonial era, this was not the case even in a formal sense. The 1950s and 1960s were marked by independence struggles which were bitterly resisted by the colonial powers, such as those in Malaya, Indochina, Algeria and Kenya, and by the rapid spread of left-led anti-imperialist nationalist movements. The ideologies of racial superiority which underpinned population control were thus central to its effectiveness as an ideological and practical weapon of the Cold War.

Meanwhile racism within the USA and European countries was also changing. In the United States, African-American, Latina and Native American women were increasingly targeted for population control. As the INCITE! Women of Color Against Violence activist network argues,

> the state's increased interest in limiting the growth of people of color in the US coincided with the expansion of post-World War II welfare provisions that have allowed many people of color to leave exploitative jobs. As a result, the growing unemployment rate among people of color means that non-white America is no longer simply a reservoir of cheap labor; it is considered 'surplus' populations. (INCITE!, 2010)

And the questions of population and immigration once again became linked in dominant discourses, this time in Western European contexts, where immigration from the ex-colonies to meet the need for low-paid workers was accompanied by the emergence of new forms and expressions of racism. In France, as early as 1952 the head of the National Population Commission was articulating this ideology, warning that if France and Algeria remained 'communicating vessels' then 'there will no longer be any possibility of planning a pro-family and pro-natalist policy in France: in the future millions of Muslims will come to fill our empty spaces' (cited in Connelly, 2008: 121). In Europe too, it was black and ethnic minority women who were targeted for sterilisation and untested and dangerous long-acting contraceptives.

Cold War population control policies epitomized the way Malthusian discourse combines fear of a potential threat to the established order and existing distribution of resources with an explicit counter to critiques of economic and social institutions, pathologising the behaviour of the poor as the cause of their own poverty. In the wake of the Chinese revolution, images of Asia's 'teeming hordes' were incorporated seamlessly into the construction of the communist 'threat': population control was seen as a material weapon against the spread of discontent which 'breeds' communist ideas, while simultaneously acting as an ideological weapon against the critique of capitalism offered by communism.[5] With the Cuban Revolution following a decade later, the fear of losing access to raw materials from the Third World increasingly became central in shaping Cold War policies. The strategy of increasing profits by outsourcing manufacturing to low-paid women workers in the global South (which implied orchestrating demographic changes, and in particular a reduction in women's fertility to facilitate their entry into the labour market) was also pioneered in Puerto Rico in the 1950s, where 'Operation Bootstrap' was accompanied by highly coercive population control measures (Mass, 1976, 1977; Briggs, 2002). Whereas contraception for 'birth control' and eugenic sterilisation had been differentiated in the earlier period (although often advocated by the same groups), now sterilisation came to be used as a key method of population control. In Puerto Rico, by 1955, 16.5 per cent of women of childbearing age had been sterilized (Mass, 1977: 71).

The constitution of population control as a Cold War political and economic weapon is reflected in the transformation in the field of demography described by Mohan Rao – a primarily descriptive social science discipline dedicated to observing long-term historical changes in population patterns rapidly came to be viewed in the 1950s as a technical, policy-oriented 'science' (Rao, 1994: PE47). The idea of a demographic transition in which a fall in infant mortality rates along with industrialisation led in the long term to people choosing to have fewer children was rejected by US demographers on the basis that 'rapid modernization might not lead to fertility decline before it led to a threatening level of social and political instability' (Ross, 1998: 92). Reflecting the change in dominant representations of racialised populations described earlier, Robert McNamara, President Kennedy's Secretary of Defense and soon to be president of the World Bank, described development as turning 'traditionally listless areas of the world into seething cauldrons of change' (93). Instead of waiting for this to happen, demographers like Kingsley Davis argued for intensive and large-scale population programmes to be made central to US aid.

In 1958, the Eisenhower administration established the Committee to Study the US Military Assistance Program, chaired by General W.H. Draper Jr. Describing the composition of the Draper Committee and the corporate, political and military affiliations of its members, Ross comments that they were 'collectively... the supreme embodiment of the major forces that directed US foreign policy' (Ross, 1998: 100). The Draper Committee recommended that the US government finance population research 'as part of its own Mutual Security Programme' and that assistance be given to those 'developing countries who establish programmes to check population growth' (Mass, 1976: 41).

In 1966, President Johnson announced that for the first time population control would receive federal funding. In 1969, the US government set up the United Nations Fund for Population Activities (UNFPA), and the World Health Organization established a Special Fund for Research Development and Research Training in Human

Reproduction (Wilson, 1994: 2201). This was alongside ongoing investment by corporate capital in population control, both directly and via the Rockefeller and Ford Foundations. Thus the funding for the IPPF

> initially came from the Hugh Moore Fund and Rockefeller Foundation. Soon it attracted funding from DuPont Chemicals, Standard Oil and Shell. On the board of IPPF sit representatives of DuPont, US Sugar Corporation, General Motors, Chase Manhattan Bank, Newmont Mining, International Nickel, Marconi RCA, Xerox and Gulf Oil, a veritable Who's Who of America's corporate and finance capital. (Rao, 1994: PE49)

The perceived relationship between population control and the interests of US corporate capital were set out clearly in National Security Study Memorandum 200: Implications of Worldwide Population Growth for U.S. Security and Overseas Interests (NSSM200), completed in 1974 by the United States National Security Council under the direction of Henry Kissinger. It outlines the US government's major concerns: first, the radicalisation of the global South to a point where 'younger people – who are more prevalent in high fertility populations – can more readily be persuaded to attack such targets as multinational corporations'; second, that certain Third World countries might 'advocate a better distribution of the world's wealth'; third, that 'in the absence of slow or zero population growth, concessions to foreign companies are likely to be expropriated or subject to arbitrary intervention. Whether through government action, labour conflicts, sabotage, civil disturbance, the smooth flow of needed materials will be jeopardised' (cited in Wilson, 1994: 2201).

Despite the preoccupation with numbers in population control discourses, Kingsley Davis's 'teeming millions' of Asia (Connelly, 2008: 123), McNamara's 'seething cauldrons of change' or Paul Ehrlich's terror-inspiring 'people, people, people, people!' (Ehrlich, 1968: 1) are clearly far from disembodied statistics. Not only is population control by definition concerned with regulating sexual and reproductive activities, but, like earlier colonial projects of enumeration and measurement, is marked by an overwhelming preoccupation with racialised notions of 'deviant' sexuality.[6] As Laura Briggs puts it, 'Third World women's sexual behavior was rendered dangerous and unreasonable, the cause of poverty and hence of communism, and needed to be made known, managed and regulated' (Briggs, 2002: 117).

Attempts to regulate sexuality in the interests of imperialism have a long history with a plethora of colonial discourses, laws and practices, including those relating to marriage, children of mixed race, prostitution and sexually transmitted infections (Briggs, 2002; see also Arnold, 1988; Stoler, 1995, 2002; Sangari and Vaid, 1989; Razack, 1998). Dominant constructions of 'race' in the colonial period were themselves infused with ideas about the different and dangerous sexuality of racialised 'others'.

A 1951 report, *Reproduction Patterns of Aymara and Quechua Speaking People*, by Dr Richard Patch, a US anthropologist and foreign policy adviser concerned with developing population control programmes for the Peruvian and Bolivian governments, is a particularly explicit example of the pathologisation of racialised sexualities which characterized population control discourses, policies and practices.

Patch's report, having assumed that the region is being held back from development by overpopulation (Bolivia had one of the lowest population densities in Latin America), goes on to reproduce three well-established racialised tropes of deviant sexuality to explain Latin America's 'incredible rate of fertility'. These are first, the 'primitive' and 'bestial' approach to sex of the indigenous people: Patch like his colonial predecessors uses his anthropologist's status to both titillate and scandalise his (in this case US policymaking) readers with his descriptions of 'semipublic couplings ... in the aftermath of a frantic fiesta, usually religious in nature' when participants are 'driven by drink and desire behind the church and into the underbrush' (Patch, 1951, cited in Mass, 1976: 226). Second, recycling well-worn constructions of racialised hypermasculinity, Patch focuses on 'machismo' as a major aspect of Latin American culture, with particular reference, again, to the indigenous peasantry: 'the ideal macho is a man who flaunts his maleness, excelling in sexual activity, either heterosexual or homosexual, and is unworried, pugnacious and violent' (225).[7] Third, he identifies Peruvian and Bolivian women of all classes as 'passive' and dominated by men (as we have seen, this too is a long-established trope and has been reproduced repeatedly within development discourses in almost every context of the global South). As Mass notes, the attitudes inherent in the report were 'not atypical of those expressed in traditional social science circles, congressional committees and the demography and birth control fields' (225).

These racialised constructions are less fully elaborated but equally evident in the oft-cited passage from Paul Ehrlich's sensationalist and influential *The Population Bomb* (Ehrlich, 1968) in which he explains how, having long 'understood the population explosion intellectually', he came to 'understand it emotionally'

> one stinking hot night in Delhi a few years ago. My wife and daughter and I were returning to our hotel in an ancient taxi. ... As we crawled through the city, we encountered a crowded slum area. The temperature was well over 100, and the air was a haze of dust and smoke. The streets seemed alive with people. People eating, people washing, people sleeping. People visiting, arguing, and screaming. People thrusting their hands through the taxi window, begging. People defecating and urinating. People clinging to buses. People herding animals. People, people, people, people. (Ehrlich, 1968: 1)

This remarkable if faintly ridiculous passage has all the elements of the colonial narratives it recalls – the sensual intensity of the 'stinking hot night' which terrifies, repels and fascinates; the threat made more vivid by the fact that the white male protagonist undertaking this dangerous journey must not only preserve himself but protect his 'wife and daughter'; the contempt for 'primitive' others portrayed publicly 'defecating', 'urinating' and 'begging', inseparable from a voyeuristic gaze which fetishises the physical, describing them 'screaming', 'thrusting' and 'clinging' – as Ehrlich adds 'it seemed that anything could happen' (Ehrlich, 1968: 1).

Ehrlich implicitly acknowledges his debt to colonial writers when he concludes self-deprecatingly that 'Old India hands will laugh at our reaction' (Ehrlich, 1968: 1). In fact, he was following in the footsteps of birth control activists of the colonial era: as Connelly points out, 'India under the Raj remained open to inspection and instruction', and 'innumerable Americans and Europeans therefore traveled to India, witnessed "overpopulation" firsthand, and returned ashen-faced, suitably appalled, to tell others of their experience' (Connelly, 2008: 89).

In fact *The Population Bomb* does not focus exclusively on population control in the global South, although it recommends the USA cutting off food aid to countries that are beyond redemption in a process Ehrlich refers to as 'triage' (Ehrlich, 1968). Unlike the US foreign policy makers to whom its doomsday scenarios provided intellectual fuel, Ehrlich rejected eugenicist ideas and wanted population control applied to white middle-class Americans too. But the fact that the book opens with this passage demonstrates how deeply the 'fears' that population discourses sought to mobilise remained rooted in constructions of racial difference. The 'people' who so terrified Ehrlich that night were clearly identified by markers of race and class as those whose fertility needed to be controlled. But, equally powerfully, the passage constructs its readers as those who, like the small, beleaguered white American nuclear family in the taxi, are under threat, and who, therefore, have both a right and a duty to act to control the population of others.

How do we understand this fear which has been so central to population control discourses? On one level, postcolonial analysis, which, building on Fanon's *Black Skin, White Masks* (1967), puts forward the idea of fear of the 'other' as inextricable from the projection of illicit desires onto the body of the other, seems particularly apposite in considering the pathologisation of racialised bodies and sexualities implied in these constructions of 'extraordinary' or 'incredible' fertility.

However, much postcolonial work on 'race' has tended not to question the Freudian assumption that 'desires' for the gendered and racialised other are 'natural' (and located within the white male subject), and it is only the repressive response to these desires that needs to be problematised. As we noted in Chapter 2, Ann Stoler argues that such desires themselves need to be understood as produced by colonial discourses rather than inherent within the subject (Stoler, 1995: 176).

Zine Magubane also provides a critique of psychoanalytical approaches to the construction of the deviant 'other' in her discussion of the 'recommodification' of Sarah Baartman (the so-called 'Hottentot Venus') by poststructural theorists, who, she writes, have 'placed her outside history' (Magubane, 2001: 818).[8] Magubane challenges the assumptions in this work that 'Europeans' fears of the "unique and observable" physical differences of racial and sexual "others" was the primary impetus for the construction and synthesis of images of deviance' and that 'ideas about Blackness remained relatively static and unchanged throughout the nineteenth century' (817). She argues for the importance of locating constructions of 'race' at the specific historical junctures when they appear, and examining their relation to changing political and economic structures.

In the context of population control, this would involve, for example, paying attention to the particular political and economic reasons why deeply rooted constructions of deviant sexuality in Latin America were consolidated and mobilized around population control interventions in Bolivia by the US government at just this moment in the early 1950s, despite continuing low population density. An approach informed by political economy can similarly help us begin to understand why, having been largely ignored by the population control establishment during the Cold War, sub-Saharan Africa became a key target for population control in the 1990s (see Chapter 5).

While there are elements of fear underlying population control interventions, they cannot be understood simply in terms of the psychological repression – or indeed the discursive production – of desire for racialised others. If poor women in the global South and their children are objects of fear to those who formulate these interventions, it can be argued that this is not because they deviate from constructed norms, but because they may seek to transform the existing distribution of power and resources, and disrupt global processes of capital accumulation. As this chapter has argued, fears associated with 'unchecked' population growth have been articulated explicitly at specific historical moments of potential radical transformation, from the Industrial Revolution in Britain to the anti-colonial resistance of the nineteenth century to the revolutionary Third World nationalism of the Cold War years. But equally, these fears are expressed and perpetuated, and unequal relations are sustained and reproduced, through the pathologisation of those whose exploitation is central to these relations, a process in which racialised constructions of 'excessive' fertility and 'abnormal' sexuality have been central.

Population control as racialised violence

Acknowledging the centrality of constructions of 'race' to population control discourse and practice helps us to understand how the violence of population control against women in the global South and against black and ethnic minority women in the North (Davis, 1982; Robertson, 1997; INCITE, 2010) was sustained and perpetuated. Those targeted as 'acceptors' were not simply devalued as members of poor and powerless groups whose potential suffering as individuals could be outweighed by the benefits to 'humanity' of reducing their fertility: racism dehumanized them.

The notion of fetishism, in which the dominant gaze reduces a person to their body, which in turn is reduced to sexual organs, is particularly relevant in this context. Fanon famously described how 'the Negro is eclipsed. He is turned into a penis' (Fanon, 1967a: 170). Population control discourse reduces 'Third World' women to their reproductive organs, and specifically their wombs, pathologised as 'excessively reproductive' and requiring intervention.

Population control in the 1970s and 1980s became one of the key markers of the deep fissures along lines drawn by 'race', class and imperialism within the women's movement. The slogan 'a woman's right to choose' was mobilized around abortion rights by overwhelmingly white middle-class organisations in Europe and North America, rendering invisible the experiences of women of colour, who were often the target of forced sterilisation or compulsory use of unsafe contraceptives. Eugenicist ideas have continued to shape policies such as the use of Norplant (a hormonal implant contraceptive whose effect lasts for five years) in the USA, which targeted black, migrant and Native American women, and women with disabilities. In a number of states, black women convicted of drug-abuse- or child-abuse-related crimes were required by judges to have Norplant implanted, making particularly explicit the ways in which such contraceptives can be used 'as a tool to control women and discipline them' (Srinivas and Kanakamala, 1992: 1531).

Women in the global South were both denied access to contraceptive methods that were safe and that they could control, and subjected to the acute violence of population control policies in which targets were set by the international development institutions, including the World Bank. Forcible and coercive sterilisation of urban and rural poor women took place on a massive scale – in Bangladesh sterilisation was in many cases made a condition for food relief (Hartmann and Standing, 1985; Akhter, 1992). In India, when central and state governments were unable to meet impossibly high targets, local administrations set targets for sterilisations for non-health personnel like teachers and forest officers. An investigation revealed that in Puranpur in Pilibhit district, Uttar Pradesh, 'in December 1993, 80 per cent of these employees had their salaries stopped for non-achievement of targets. In 1994 they kidnapped large numbers of women from neighbouring Nepal, forced them onto buses and then drove them to dingy warehouses to be forcibly sterilized' (Wilson, 1994).

Population control programmes also created the conditions for large-scale testing of contraceptives on women in the global South, with minimal or no information being given to the participants in these tests (Mass, 1976; Hartmann, 1995). Where contraceptives were indeed found to have serious side effects, this did not discourage their promotion in the global South as part of population control

programmes. In fact for pharmaceuticals companies, these programmes have provided massive opportunities for 'dumping' drugs
which have been banned in the global North having been found to
be unsafe. Injectable and implantable hormonal contraceptives such
as Depo-Provera (Akhter, 1992; Hartmann, 1995), Norplant (Wilson,
1994) and Net-Oen (Nair, 1989) have been particularly favoured
by the population establishment because they are long-acting: it
is argued that in contrast to other methods such as the pill or the
diaphragm, the woman does not have to 'remember' to take it or
to insert it herself. This clearly perpetuates racialised constructions
of these women as inherently less able to act responsibly (a similar
racist argument has been used to deny people in Africa access to
anti-retroviral treatment for HIV – see Chapter 4). Even more
significantly perhaps, while claiming to give the woman greater
'choice' and control over her own fertility (as she no longer has to
directly confront potential opposition to contraception from male
sexual partners) these methods actually shift control over her body
to health professionals and population-control institutions – the effect
of injectables is non-reversible and removing implants is a complex
process which health professionals often refuse to perform when
requested to do so by women experiencing some of the debilitating
side effects of these drugs (Wangari, 2002). And in the context of the
undermining of already limited health services in many countries
since the introduction of structural adjustment policies in the 1980s,
the follow-up services required by those using these contraceptives
are rarely available.

In fact, until the 1990s 'population control' was clearly distinguished from the notion of the right of individuals to control
their fertility. For example, in 1984 the UNFPA's representative in
Dhaka, Walter Holzhausen, wrote a letter to key officials in the
World Bank, USAID and other institutions criticising the notion
of 'voluntarism' in 'family planning' programmes in Bangladesh.
The coercive sterilisations already taking place in the country were
clearly not enough for Holzhausen, who wanted the government
and donors to espouse compulsion openly:

as I see it, voluntarism is based on the idea that couples should have the right – the basic human right – to determine the number of their children. But what is a human right in one country may not be a human right in another. If couples in Bangladesh decide to have a big family they endanger the well-being of their compatriots and threaten the very existence of the next generations of Bangladeshis. Thus having a large family in Bangladesh is anti-social and contrary to the common weal and, hence, a matter that deserves drastic Government intervention. (in Hartmann and Standing, 1985: 38)

In the 1990s, however, and particularly after the United Nations International Conference on Population and Development held in Cairo in 1994, population policies began increasingly to be articulated in the terms of reproductive rights and 'choices'. This shift came in response to the demands of feminist movements which had been opposing coercive population control interventions, but has been analysed as part of the strategic appropriation of feminist critiques within neoliberal development discourses, a process that was discussed in the previous chapter. The discursive emphasis on reproductive rights in development has been incorporated into neoliberal policies, which have further intensified inequality and further constrained women's choices on many different levels. It has also been accompanied by the incorporation of new concerns and 'threats' into the agenda of population control, which has remained despite the successive shifts in funding patterns associated with the attacks of the Christian right on reproductive rights under Republican administrations in the USA. In particular, population growth in the global South is being linked to climate change, once again shifting attention from the role of corporate capital and the fact that industrialized countries, with only 20 per cent of the world's population, are responsible for 80 per cent of the accumulated carbon dioxide in the atmosphere, while 'the few countries in the world where population growth rates remain high, such as those in sub-Saharan Africa, have among the lowest carbon emissions per capita on the planet' (Hartmann, 2009). Related to this is an intensified emphasis on population control as a counter to migration from the global South to the global North.[9]

Redeploying the Cold War fears about 'young populations' and the related 'youth bulge' theory of security threats developed by the CIA in the 1980s,[10] population growth is now also linked to terrorism, embodied in the racialised and gendered constructions of the 'angry young men' it produces and the 'veiled young women' who in the future will produce yet more 'dangerous' children (Hendrixon, 2004). As Anne Hendrixon writes, 'The implied dual threat – of explosive violence and explosive fertility – provides a racial- and gender-based rationale for continued US military intervention and US-promoted population control initiatives in other countries, particularly in the South. It also justifies government surveillance of Muslims and Arabs within US borders' (Hendrixon, 2004).

Racialised population control initiatives thus fit in neatly with the twenty-first-century development/security paradigm, in which development interventions in the global South, now framed in the discourse of 'rights' and 'choice', are simultaneously projected as necessary for the 'security' of populations in the global North. It is in the context of this discourse, for example, that the British government's minister for international development Stephen O'Brien vows bravely that 'we will not shy away from talking about population – about global population growth and its impacts', adding without irony that 'we are proud to be giving more women the choices they crave', while announcing a joint initiative with the pharmaceuticals corporation Merck to promote their long-lasting implant Implanon to '14.5 million of the poorest women between now and 2015' (O'Brien, 2011). Implanon was discontinued in the UK in 2010 because trained medical personnel were finding it too difficult to insert correctly, as well as over fears about its safety (bbc.co.uk, 5 January 2011).

As we have seen, constructions of 'race' and racialised sexualities, in particular, have been central to the promotion of population policies at a global level, through the interventions of international institutions, donor governments and corporate capital. But these constructions have also articulated with spatially contingent structures and relations of power within the countries and regions where these policies have been adopted and implemented. In particular, relations of gender and class, which have been recast by successive encounters with colonial and imperial capital, have shaped experiences of population control interventions – among, for example, poor rural women, predominantly from lower castes, who have been the main target of these interventions in India. (It is notable that the only example of large-scale coercive population control policies primarily targeting men's bodies, the notorious 'sterilisation campaign' orchestrated during India's emergency of 1975–77 in which men were rounded up and taken to camps for vasectomies, is widely cited as one of the main reasons for the historic electoral defeat of the Congress Party in 1977.)

Furthermore, in many cases population control policies have also been adapted and refined at the level of the nation-state by dominant racialised constructions of different ethnic groups within them – for example, in the targeting of indigenous women for forced sterilisation on a massive scale in Peru in the 1990s, a policy which received favourable reports from the UNFPA and the World Bank (Schmidt, 1998). Elsewhere, discourses about minority populations, while not articulated in terms of 'race', mirror the structure of racialised discourses: for example, in the claims by the Hindu right in India about differential population growth among the Muslim minority, which have been mobilized in the orchestration of genocidal violence against Muslim communities.

The experience of China's 'one-child policy' implemented in 1979 provides a significant example of coercive population control, and raises key issues about how such policies contribute to the phenomenon of 'missing girls' in the context of particular forms of patriarchal gender relations (as in India, son-preference has led to a significant gender imbalance in the population). A detailed discussion of this is beyond the scope of this chapter. However, it is worth noting two points here: first, at the height of the Cold War population control discourse and policy that we have discussed here, China still considered its population as a resource rather than a liability for development. Second, it is widely accepted that China's population growth began to slow down in the mid-1960s and fell rapidly in the 1970s, in response to wider social and economic changes such as improved standards of living, universal health care and women's participation in the labour force, before the post-1978 economic reforms that accompanied the introduction of the one-child policy.

Conclusion

This chapter has examined one of the most extensive, most lavishly funded and most sustained development interventions of the last half-century, and has looked at the ways in which ideas about 'race' and racism have been central both to its conceptualisation and to its implementation. I have argued that the intertwined ideas of Malthusianism and eugenics not only provided the environment from which concepts of population control historically emerged, but continued to shape population control discourse, policy and practice throughout the Cold War period and beyond.

But an analysis of these approaches in isolation is insufficient for an understanding of the extent to which population control has drawn upon, elaborated and reproduced constructions of racialised sexualities. These focus in particular on 'Third World women', who were identified as 'excessively reproductive' and whose sexual behaviour was constituted as a threat to the existing order. They reanimate and mobilise a repertoire of racialised representations which is much more entrenched and embedded in common-sense ideologies than explicitly eugenicist theories. An approach that traces the specific historical, economic and political moments in which the discourses of population control emerged suggests that the anxieties that were articulated in these terms are not primarily rooted in fears of – or desire for – the 'other', however. Rather, they express materially grounded apprehensions about the possibility that oppressed majorities would succeed in carrying out radical redistributions of power and resources. In the following chapter, we will explore some of these themes further, in the context of contemporary interventions in the HIV/AIDS pandemic.

CHAPTER 4

Pathologising racialised sexualities in the HIV/AIDS pandemic

Africans don't know what Western time is. … And if you say, one o'clock in the afternoon, they do not know what you are talking about. They know morning, they know noon, they know evening, they know the darkness of the night.

> Andrew Natsios, USAID (2001),
> explaining the US government's failure
> to support antiretroviral programmes

the ultimate expression of imperial sovereignty [which] seems to reside, to a large extent, in the power and the capacity to dictate who may live and who must die.

> Achille Mbembe (2002)

in America today, AIDS remains suffused with race, with race and place, and of course irrevocably with the sexual attributes imputed to people of other races and places.

> Phillip Alcabes (2006a)

'Race', gender and imperialism have been central to the interrelated processes of structuring the AIDS pandemic, constructing and representing it, and determining global responses to it. Building on the previous chapter, where we looked at population control policies, this chapter seeks to explain how what Jean Comaroff calls the 'colonial ideologies that have tied life, even at its most bioscientific, to racialized sexuality' (Comaroff, 2007: 214) have shaped and legitimised the interventions of development institutions in relation to the pandemic. Further, it considers how the racialised Malthusianism whose historical trajectory was described in the previous chapter has underwritten the actions of international financial institutions and transnational corporations which deliberately failed to prevent the deaths of millions of people in sub-Saharan Africa.

In line with the themes of the book, this chapter focuses in particular on development organisations, policies and discourses, rather than attempting to engage with the entirety of the vast body of epidemiological and biomedical literature on HIV/AIDS. It also has a specific focus on sub-Saharan Africa, not only because of the disproportionate burden of infection and mortality rates borne by people who live in the continent – in 2009, 68 per cent of people living with HIV were in this region, while approximately 72 per cent of AIDS-related deaths of adults and children took place there (UNAIDS, 2010) – but also because, as we will see, particular colonial constructions of 'Africa' in general and 'African sexuality' in particular have played a significant role in shaping their experiences of the virus.

It is not my intention to engage with the assertion, made in one section of the literature that links racism and AIDS, that there is no single, or unique, AIDS virus, and that in this sense the virus itself is a racist construction. Rather, this chapter is based on the position that it is precisely in order to reach a full understanding of the global significance of the HIV/AIDS pandemic that we must consider the ways in which 'race' and racism have been central to its emergence and development. Further, following the lead of commentators like Sitze (2004), Comaroff (2007) and Wang (2008), it suggests that it is only possible to frame a constructive response to what has been called 'AIDS denialism' by situating it within the framework of historical and contemporary racism and imperialism.

'Race' and neoliberalism in the structure of the AIDS pandemic

Much of this chapter is devoted to discussing how dominant explanations of the HIV/AIDS pandemic in Africa have been explicitly or implicitly founded on notions of 'race' and of the exceptionalism of

'African' sexuality in particular, and how this has shifted attention from the real causes of the pandemic, with devastating effects.

Before we begin to look at this, however, I would like to suggest that 'race' does, in fact, have a key place in our understanding of HIV/AIDS in sub-Saharan Africa – in so far as the conditions for a pandemic on this scale have been shaped by the history and contemporary manifestations of imperialist intervention in the region. These interventions, as we have seen in the preceding chapters, have not simply been contiguous in their geographies with differences constructed as 'racial': rather, they have both catalysed and been sustained by constructions of 'race' and, more specifically, 'Africa' as the 'dark continent' and its inhabitants as 'savage', 'uncivilised' 'childlike' and naturally given to excess of all kinds.

While the role of these tropes in legitimising and sustaining the notorious late-colonial 'Scramble' and the systematic devastation that ensued goes almost without saying, they also, as we discuss in the following chapter, continue to have a strong presence in the discourse of neoliberal development interventions such as economic liberalisation and governance reforms.

In this sense, then, we would suggest that the racialised structures of imperialism have significantly determined the spatial shape of the global pandemic. This impact takes two broad forms: first, that relating directly to the body, and the factors which determine the differential vulnerability of different people to the transmission of HIV. These factors themselves, relating broadly to the effects of malnutrition and the prevalence of co-infections, are contingent upon relations of political economy and power, complicating models which seek to separate the 'biological' from the 'social' . In other words, they highlight the vulnerability to HIV transmission of bodies already bearing the scars of incorporation on highly unequal terms into the circuits of global capital, and its multiple articulations with local inequalities. This is an example of how 'race', while not itself constitutive of difference, is centrally implicated in the material production of embodied difference.

Second, and this has received far more attention for reasons outlined below, there are explicitly social factors which relate to the differential prevalence of situations in which transmission becomes possible. Dominant discourses on HIV/AIDS have, as we will see, since the emergence of the virus attempted to incorporate these differences into behavioural models (with or without an emphasis on 'culture') focusing on the 'problem of African sexuality' (Packard and Epstein, 1991: 776). More critical approaches, notably that developed by Paul Farmer in the context of Haiti (Farmer et al., 1996; Farmer, 2005), use the concept of 'structural violence', which takes account of 'the interactive or synergistic effects of social factors such as poverty and economic exploitation, gender power, sexual oppression, racism, and social exclusion' in generating the dynamic of the epidemics (Parker, 2001: 169). It is this understanding that I adopt in this chapter, with a particular focus on the overarching framework of racialised imperialism.

Since the late 1980s, a number of studies have suggested that, as with other infectious diseases, the weakening of the immune system, which is prevalent when people are living in conditions of acute poverty, is likely to reduce resistance to the transmission of HIV. They cite nutritional deficiencies as well as parasitic infections and the presence of immunosuppressant conditions such as tuberculosis and malaria as causes of this weakened immunity (Stillwaggon, 2002, 2006; Packard and Epstein 1991; Quinn et al., 1987). However, despite the reiteration of the significance of these phenomena in studies spanning two decades, this has remained an under-researched area, with these studies repeatedly concluding with calls for further investigation to establish more fully the relationship between these factors and resistance to HIV infection. This leads us to consider again the ways in which knowledge about HIV/AIDS is constructed: which questions are asked and, more specifically, which research is funded and promoted. As we will see, HIV/AIDS policy has focused heavily on identifying 'risk groups' and, subsequently, 'risk behaviours', and there has been relatively little emphasis on factors which might make the *same* behaviour substantially more dangerous for people whose immune systems are already compromised by the conditions of their lives.[1]

If racialised imperialism has been inscribed on the bodies of many people living in sub-Saharan African countries, making them more vulnerable to transmission of HIV, it has had no less drastic an impact on social relations which produce the conditions in which transmission is more likely to occur. Of particular significance here is the articulation between imperialist processes of capital accumulation and dynamic local gender relations. As we have noted, the reconfiguring of unequal gender relations in which the most oppressive elements were frequently reinforced was a recurring feature of colonial interventions in multiple contexts. But incorporation into global markets and interpolation into other globalised processes continues to shape and constrain gender relations, and other relationships marked by power, at a local level. The effects of the imposition of neoliberal economic policies on the continent, whose chronology corresponds closely to the emergence and rapid development of the HIV/AIDS crisis, are central to an understanding of the role of 'structural violence' in the spread of the virus (Basu, 2003).

The impact of the structural adjustment policies imposed by the international financial institutions in the 1980s has been extensively documented.

> As wages plunged, unemployment soared and poverty deepened, social sector funding shrank or remained constant but insufficient to meet escalating needs. Such safety nets as were in place were usually inadequate and were developed late in the process. Households survived by drastically cutting consumption, substituting market-purchased goods and services with reproductive labour, overwhelmingly provided by women. (Molyneux, 2008: 779)

Privatisation led to large-scale unemployment, particularly among women, for whom the state has been the main source of formal employment, particularly in sub-Saharan Africa. Teachers, health workers and civil servants lost their livelihoods. Removing subsidies and price controls, along with enforced currency devaluation, led to increased prices of food and other necessities. Agrarian crises created by the opening up of agriculture to world markets triggered escalating indebtedness and rural unemployment. In sub-Saharan Africa, in particular, access to land for poor farmers, many of whom are women, has been undermined by policies promoting private property in land.

These changes led to deepening poverty and malnutrition (see, for example, Cornia et al., 1987), which, as we have seen, has been suggested to be a direct cause of increased vulnerability to transmission. 'Rolling back the state' also meant the drastic cutting of health services. In Zambia, for example, real per capita expenditure on health fell by 16 per cent in just two years in the mid-1980s (Elson, 1991). A survey of real health expenditures in twelve sub-Saharan African countries undertaking some adjustment during the 1980s

> indicated an average real per capita decline of close to 20 per cent.... Ghana spent $10 per capita in 1976 but a mere $6 in the period 1995–2000; Côte d'Ivoire dropped from $9 to $6; Zambia from $14 to $11; Nigeria from nearly $3 to $1.81; Liberia actually spent $7 per capita in 1976 compared to $1.50 in the most recent period. (Stein, 2008, cited in Rowden, 2011: 155)

Insistence by the IMF and the World Bank on the introduction of user fees had particularly serious effects on the spread of HIV, for example by discouraging attendance at STD clinics in the early 1990s. As Rick Rowden argues,

> [the] neoliberal idea that individual 'health consumers' who rationally base every purchasing decision on how best to optimize their cost efficiency, ought to 'purchase' health services only when they have begun to show symptoms – and not before – was more than just a convenient cost-cutting measure, it was precisely the kind of lethal reasoning that arguably has contributed to weakening the public health response to the HIV/AIDS crisis, thus making the epidemic far worse than it otherwise needed to be. (Rowden, 2011: 148)

The drastic decline in funding for health services has also increased the use of unsterilised injections and the failure to screen blood before transfusions, which has been identified as a neglected source of HIV infection in sub-Saharan Africa (Oppong and Kalipeni, 2004; Packard and Epstein, 1991).

But it has also been suggested that the gendered effects of these neoliberal reforms have led to an increase in commercial sex work as a means of survival for women in particular, and more broadly to greater prevalence of what HIV/AIDS experts like to refer to as 'transactional sex' (raising the question of the usefulness of a distinction between 'transactional' and 'non-transactional' sex in any context of gender inequality), which facilitates the spread of the virus. An example of 'risk behaviour' that is frequently cited in the literature on HIV/AIDS in sub-Saharan Africa is that of young women, particularly school students, who risk infection with the virus by much older 'sugar daddies' who pay their school fees and costs or help to support their families (Luke, 2005). While anthropologists have been busy seeking the cultural roots of these 'intergenerational' relationships (Kalipeni et al., 2004) and governments like Uganda's have received funds for large-scale publicity campaigns condemning such relationships (Jolly, 2006) there is little mainstream acknowledgement that neoliberal privatisation of education and undermining of social provision underpin and perpetuate these strategies for survival.

The destruction of agrarian livelihoods, as a result of the liberalisation of markets and the subsequent drop in primary commodity prices, has led to large-scale migration, which has also been associated with more people being exposed to the virus. The separation of households through forced migration is not a new process in the context of sub-Saharan Africa. As we have seen, forcible conscription and transportation of men for work in mines, on plantations and as porters were intrinsic to colonial economies, and had devastating effects in earlier periods, contributing to famine and population decline. More recently, the prevalence of HIV was identified in regions which had long been constructed as 'labour reserves' for the mines of Southern Africa, as the virus circulated in the mining settlements among sex workers and the migrant mineworkers who were their clients, and was transmitted to the wives of miners when they returned home (Packard and Epstein, 1991; Basu, 2003; Crush, 2010). Currently, however, it seems that the forcible separation from partners, displacement and daily confrontation with possible death that characterise the experiences of migrant mineworkers (Basu, 2003; Campbell, 2004) have become a much more generalized feature of life under neoliberalism for many people in the global South.[2]

The wars and conflicts which affected a number of countries in sub-Saharan Africa in the 1990s resulted partially from the economic crises gripping the region in the wake of neoliberal reforms. As has been well documented, these conflicts were fuelled, extended and deepened by transnational capital's drive to control valuable resources such as diamonds, columbite-tantalite (coltan) and oil. As elsewhere, armed conflict has been inseparable from escalating sexual violence against women as well as (although this has been far less widely acknowledged) against men. Forced sex has been shown to be more likely to result in the transmission of HIV. Further, the collapse of livelihoods and communities in the wake of conflict often leads to greater dependence on sex work for survival.[3] Parallels with the development of HIV/AIDS epidemics in this context have been drawn with the post-World War II situation, where 'in the absence of penicillin, the war-ravaged Europe of the late 1940s would have been devastated by epidemics of syphilis and gonorrhea' (Katz, 2003: 3).

However, since the 1990s, it has been increasingly widely accepted that higher levels of 'risky' sexual behaviour cannot in themselves possibly explain the far more rapid spread of the virus in sub-Saharan Africa in comparison to other regions and the much higher levels of HIV prevalence. As Eileen Stillwaggon argues, with rates of HIV in Africa that were 25 to 100 times those in the rest of the world, for behaviour to be a credible explanation would require 'epic rates' of partner change (Stillwaggon, 2003: 811). As Stillwaggon notes, since 1995 both the World Health Organization and UNAIDS have published reports which 'subjected the behavioural hypothesis to testing and found little empirical support for the notion that African levels of HIV could be explained chiefly by behavioural factors' (811).

But even if it is accepted that behaviour cannot be the cause of the epidemic in Africa, as long as strategies for combating it are focused on prevention through behaviour modification, racialised constructions of 'uniquely African' sexual behaviour are likely to continue to be reproduced. And, as we will see, even in the wake of the development of anti-retroviral treatment in the 1990s, prevention through behaviour modification has remained the dominant response to HIV and AIDS in the global South, with ongoing struggles over access to treatment.

Indeed any other response is currently severely constrained by the neoliberal framework of public health policies imposed on the global South since the early 1980s, since, as Rick Rowden points out, most countries experiencing acute epidemics have had their health facilities, and particularly trained health staff, systematically depleted (Rowden, 2011). As we discuss later in this chapter, the idea of 'race', with its devaluation of certain lives in relation to others, plays a central role in making possible the perpetuation of this lethal combination of policy-driven circumstances and the deliberate failure to save lives on an unimaginable scale.

'Race' in the representation of HIV/AIDS

To bring sex and sexuality into development has been the stated aim of a number of recent initiatives. This approach sees sexuality as something which has been neglected or excluded by mainstream development discourse and practice: 'consigned to being treated as a health issue, or disregarded altogether as a "luxury"' (Cornwall and Jolly, 2006: 1). But, as we have seen in the previous chapter, an exploration of the way notions of 'race' shape development highlights the presence of sex and sexuality running through development discourses from their inception, in terms of both the reproduction and reinscription of tropes of deviant and dangerous racialised sexualities, and interventions to regulate and control sexualities in order to further the interests of global capital in the name of development and global security.

As Cornwall and Jolly suggest, 'the AIDS epidemic may have forced open spaces for sexuality to gain greater prominence within the strategies of development agencies, but even in this context sex itself only comes into focus as a 'risk' in representations of sex and sexuality which are 'persistently negative [and] profoundly normative' (2006: 1).

In fact, the epidemic has led to an eruption of submerged racialised tropes of sexuality within development discourse, as HIV/AIDS was 'deflected onto Africa as primal other, Africa as an icon of dangerous desire, Africa as the projection of a self never fully tamable' (Comaroff, 2007: 197). As Eileen Stillwaggon writes,

> persistent notions of racial difference suffused the social science literature on AIDS in Africa, especially in the first fifteen years of the epidemic. No one used the word 'race', but it entered into the discourse as 'culture'. HIV prevalence is attributed to cultural characteristics that are said to be common to 700 million people from hundreds of language/ethnic groups. This supposedly homogeneous cultural zone is coincident in its boundaries with a region identified in the Western view with blackness. (Stillwaggon, 2003: 811–12)

These 'cultural characteristics' were, of course, primarily related to sexuality and reproduction, and centred upon the reproduction of stereotypes of Africans as hypersexual: while the early literature provided sensationalised descriptions of 'exotic' and deviant, uniquely African sexual practices (Patton, 1990) – there was a similar wave of hysteria surrounding Haitians in the context of AIDS (Farmer, 2006) – the underlying and more durable theme was an emphasis on African 'promiscuity' as the cause of the spread of the virus. As late as 1999, despite the earlier WHO and UNAIDS reports discrediting behavioural explanations, the United Nations Population Fund published an AIDS Update in which the largest of several text boxes was entitled 'Promiscuity, and the Primacy of Cultural Factors: A Lethal Mixture in Africa' (UNFPA, 1999, cited in Stillwaggon, 2003: 826).

Signs of this deviant and dangerous sexuality were sought not only in behaviour but on the bodies of African people. Cindy Patton graphically describes how in the mid-1980s, when researchers were promoting the idea that a prevalence of genital ulcers led to greater potential for transmission from women to men in an African context in comparison to Europe and North America, 'conference visual aids … were never complete without pictures of diseased genitals – projected six to eight feet high – to get over the point that the equipment of men and women in Africa is "different"' (Patton, 1990: 35). There are inescapable reminders here of the nineteenth-century exhibiting of Sarah Baartman, and the history of interwoven constructions of 'race', sexuality and disease (Gilman, 1985). As Patton points out, 'what remained unspoken here was that those differences occur, not at the level of sexual, but of medical practice – at the level, that is, of the availability of STD health care services' (Patton, 1990: 35). This essentialisation has a markedly gendered character. As Ugandan feminist scholar Josephine Ahikire notes,

> the notion of the female face of HIV/AIDS has over time carried within it different constructions of the female subject. While some of the interpretations stem from grounded social and biomedical analysis, others – and often the most dominant – are based on construction of the female as a problem, invariably making HIV/ AIDS a female disease. (Ahikire, 2008: 30)

Like earlier colonial interventions, the response to HIV and AIDS in Africa involved processes of knowledge construction in which social scientists, and anthropologists in particular, had a key role. According to Packard and Epstein,

> anthropologists found themselves being asked to dig through the ethnographic record on African cultures in order to identify possible patterns of behavior which might facilitate HIV transmission …. From the broad array of data on African sexual practices imbedded in the ethnographic record of Africa, data which reveal a wide range of patterns and extreme variation with regard to sexual permissiveness, were drawn only those cases which were possible 'risk behaviors'. (Packard and Epstein, 1991: 775)

They cite an article which 'was circulated in advance to the 300 or so participants who attended a USAID/NIAID sponsored conference on "Anthropological Perspectives on AIDS," presumably because the organizers viewed it as a model of the type of data they hoped would be presented at the conference':

> Although generalizations are difficult, most traditional African societies are promiscuous by Western standards. Promiscuity occurs both premaritally and postmaritally. For instance, in the Lese of Zaire, there is a period following puberty and before marriage when sexual relations between young men and a number of women is virtually sanctioned by the society. (Packard and Epstein, 1991: 775)

Somewhat contradictorily, some of these same anthropologists constructed the 'problem' of African sexuality in terms not of generalized 'promiscuity' but of 'urbanisation'. Thus

> the image of the 'detribalized African', the bane of colonial urban authorities, and a central image in earlier discussions of black susceptibility to TB and syphilis, an image that was fairly well excised from social science discussions in the 1970s, was being resurrected to explain the frequency of heterosexual transmission of HIV in Africa in the 1980s. (Packard and Epstein, 1991: 775)

The fears running through development discourse, which posited 'progress' as both necessary and containing within it the danger of disorder and disruption of the racialised global order, thus found a new focus in the spectre of AIDS.

Whereas Packard and Epstein's account positions anthropologists as essentially passive, called upon to 'dig through' an apparently neutral 'ethnographic record', anthropologists had long been deeply implicated in the construction of knowledge as a means of the exercise of power and the control and regulation of bodies. The 'ethnographic record of Africa' is thus better read as testimony to the day-to-day operation of colonial power through processes of categorisation, enumeration and regulation, as well as the basis on which anthropologists played a central role in providing 'evidence' claiming to prove the existence of 'race' as a scientific category.

Not surprisingly this role of generating ethnographic knowledge to sustain and legitimise imperial interventions has continued, with anthropologists being mobilized during the Cold War (Bilgin and Morton, 2002; Price, 2003) and currently in the context of the War on Terror (Price, 2011). It is in this context, I argue, that we can usefully understand the role of ethnographic research on 'cultural factors' in relation to the transmission of HIV.

While the language has changed, with the continuing emphasis on people learning to behave differently as the central strategy for addressing HIV/AIDS, the preoccupation with the identification and targeting of culturally sanctioned sexual excess has persisted. In recent years, as we have seen, the hypothesis that higher rates of risky sexual behaviour could in themselves explain the higher levels of prevalence of HIV in Africa has been discredited. In fact studies found that 'rates of risky behaviours are considerably higher in affluent and middle-income countries with low HIV prevalence, including early initiation of sex, number of sexual partners, and pre-marital and extramarital sexual relations' (Sawers and Stillwaggon, 2010: 1). But, rather than leading researchers to look at factors other than behavioural ones, this has led to a shift from claims about general 'promiscuity' to the current emphasis on 'multiple concurrent partnerships' (defined as long-term overlapping partnerships) as a 'cultural' practice prevalent in east and southern Africa which explains the far more rapid spread of HIV in the region (Halperin and Epstein, 2004; Epstein, 2007; Mah and Halperin, 2010).

Once again, it has been argued that this hypothesis is based on a number of empirically problematic assumptions, including that people in such partnerships would have sex with each of their partners every day, and that multiple concurrent partnerships are equally common among men and women (see, for example, Lurie and Rosenthal, 2009; for a summary of the debate, see Sawers and Stillwaggon, 2010). Despite this, however, the 'multiple concurrent partnerships' hypothesis remains popular, in part because it moves away from the explicit racism of the 'promiscuity' approach, but retains the preoccupation with African 'culture' and continues to indicate a focus on prevention through behaviour change. And tellingly, even though some within mainstream policymaking are questioning the effectiveness of behaviour change models, they are doing so precisely on the basis that behaviour is determined by 'culture', and 'culture' cannot be easily changed (World Bank/USAID 2010).

Thus the construction of African exceptionalism continues to shape approaches, so that in the literature on HIV a sentence like 'both women and men in Africa are subject to intense social pressure to conform' (Daniel, 2007) becomes an expert's explanatory statement of Africa's difference, rather than a truism which could be applied to any continent. Not surprisingly perhaps, then, the behaviour change literature can take on a tone strongly reminiscent of colonial missionaries' reports of their conversions:

> When people begin to make explicit the link between their own behaviour and the HIV epidemic, a revelation can occur, as reported by the United Nations Development Programme (UNDP) in Ethiopia: 'In the night, Ana Dentamo wakes up in excitement, he's had a sudden insight: "I *am* the medicine", he keeps repeating to himself. "The disease does not jump up and attack me unless I myself give a way for it to attack." From now on he knows how he can protect himself and his family from infection.' (Daniel, 2007)

Racialised masculinities and heteronormativity in representations of HIV in Africa

As with the trajectory of the virus itself, the implications of 'race' and racism for representations of HIV cannot be understood outside the framework of gender. As we saw in the context of population control policies, development interventions relating to sexuality and reproduction were already predicated on gendered and racialised constructions of 'women' in the global South as simultaneously passive and potentially dangerous. Debates surrounding how to address the HIV/AIDS pandemic emerged, however, in an era when questions of unequal gender relations had become an important theme in development discourse and practice. The construction of the essentialised 'Third World woman' as victim of an oppressive culture and needing to be saved, which itself has a long colonial genealogy, and has been extensively critiqued, was clearly present in dominant representations of the dynamics of the spread of HIV in Africa. As I have suggested in Chapter 2, elements of these critiques have been incorporated in ways which are consistent with neoliberal models and continue to produce racialised representations of 'poor women in the global South', now recast as entrepreneurial 'agents'. But in the case of HIV/AIDS, complementary constructions of an essentialised 'African' masculinity have also come to the fore.

The last decade has seen a growing focus on men and masculinities in Gender and Development, a process in which the questions raised by the HIV/AIDS epidemic have played a significant role (Cornwall et al., 2011: 1). However, as Andrea Cornwall argues, 'engaging men in the project of development has come to be about addressing the need to transform masculinity by changing cultural or social norms that guide men's behavior rather than addressing the structural basis of gender inequalities' (6), a strategy which has been consistent with the dominant approach to HIV prevention. Recent work has challenged the dichotomies of 'men's promiscuity vs women faithfulness; men's violence vs women's victimisation; or men's (ir)responsibility vs women's rights' in HIV, sexual health and development approaches (Edstrom, 2011: 74). But in the context of development, there has been, with a few exceptions, little acknowledgement of the way that racism has structured these constructions of masculinities.[4] Two aspects of this are particularly striking in the context of HIV interventions. First, since the era of slavery the notion of male hypersexuality has been central to colonial racialised tropes relating to African men, reinforcing the notion of black people as lacking rationality and self-control, and therefore not fully human, as well as black men in particular as 'dangerous' and needing to be violently controlled.

While dominant development discourses relating to HIV have moved away from the sensationalism of the early years of the epidemic when it was attributed to a range of wildly imaginary 'African' sexual practices, and the word 'promiscuity' is now less widely used, the notion of African men as the main drivers of the spread of HIV by engaging in exceptional and excessive sex is resurrected in the new emphasis on the effects of cultural expectations around masculinities (which frequently assumes that there is one 'culture' for the whole of Africa, betraying its underlying racialised assumptions). Thus, for example, an article written for a general readership in 2007 explains that

> traditional concepts of masculinity and 'normal' (accepted and expected) male sexual behaviour are a key factor in Africa's HIV epidemic. The 'custom' of having several concurrent sex partners – wives, girlfriends, prostitutes; the hospitable practice of 'wife-sharing' with visitors; men taking on their brother's widow as well as his property when he dies – all contribute to the spread of the disease. Men simply put it about. (Daniel, 2007)

The notion of male 'irresponsibility' as essentially African is also deeply racialised, invoking concepts of amorality and the absence of self-regulation which were central to eighteenth- and nineteenth-century constructions of the racialised other; it also indirectly references colonial constructions of 'lazy' African men, which, as Ann Whitehead has pointed out, 'have a long history in European discourses about rural sub-Saharan Africa, occurring whenever rural men resisted colonial labour regimes and coercive forms of rural development' (Whitehead, 2001: 42)

At the same time, this construction of specifically 'African' masculinity is both premised on and reinforces notions of white, Western masculinity as unproblematic. In a process that mirrors the oppressed Third World woman/liberated Western woman binary (Mohanty, 1986) and the 'death by culture' approach to gendered violence, in which domestic violence in the West is rendered invisible (Narayan, 1997), an essentialised normative white masculinity is reproduced within these discourses that is defined by its deviant other. While white/colonial hegemonic masculinity has always been produced in this way (Sinha, 1997; Grieg, 2011), dominant white masculinity as embodied by the development worker is now assumed to have transcended 'norms' of sexism and, increasingly, homophobia. Research, debate and policy recommendations relating to masculinity and development are predominantly conversations between white professionals, to an extent even more marked than in the wider field of gender and development. White men who have questioned their own earlier 'norms of masculinity' are constructed as well placed to teach (or rather train) African men to be 'better' men in the context of heterosexual partnerships. An adjunct to the ongoing colonial project of 'white men saving brown women from brown men' (Spivak, 1988) thus now appears to be 'white men saving brown men from themselves'.

Further, in contrast to HIV awareness campaigns in Europe and North America focusing on safe sex, approaches addressing masculinity that are based on behaviour change thus imply a much deeper level of intervention by NGOs and other development institutions in the African context, which is explicitly framed in terms of modifying and reforming what is defined as 'culture'. Once again, structural violence and the political economy of HIV and AIDS become largely invisible.

Relatedly, HIV/AIDS initiatives in Africa have been almost exclusively focused on 'heterosexual' relationships as 'geographic communities and – typically – heterosexual couples became the unit of analysis' (Edstrom, 2011: 72). This pattern emerged from the recognition from the 1990s onwards that the spread of HIV in sub-Saharan Africa affected entire populations and was not limited to people considered to belong to 'risk groups' identified in earlier epidemics. But the way this recognition has been reflected in behaviour-change interventions has been informed by heteronormative and racialised constructions of sexuality.

Much has been written about the transformative impact on understandings of sexuality of colonialism, which both linked sexuality irretrievably with nineteenth-century notions of morality and was premised on the racialised construction of the sexual deviance of the colonised, and involved direct intervention, surveillance and control of sexuality (Sangari and Vaid, 1989; Tharu and Lalita, 1993; Musisi, 2002; Tamale, 2006). Central to this process were the consolidation of European conceptions of homosexuality in the nineteenth century and its increasing criminalisation. The role of the colonial state in defining, stigmatising and criminalising sexual intimacy between men in particular and the subsequent continuation of this legislation and the ideas which underpin it by nationalist movements and post-independence regimes has been widely identified (Patton, 1990; Vanita, 2002; Phillips, 2004; Alexander, 2005; Hoad, 2007).[5] Further, it has been argued persuasively that the binary categories 'homosexual' and 'heterosexual' have themselves been imposed on much more fluid and varied understandings of sexual identity in many contexts (see, for example, Gosine, 2006; khanna, 2011).[6] Thus, notwithstanding the discourses of 'African authenticity' which a number of states currently engaged in homophobic campaigns and legislation deploy, such actions are deeply colonial in origin, as well as today being extensively funded and promoted by the US religious right (Kaoma, 2009).

Within development interventions relating to HIV and AIDS in sub-Saharan Africa, all of these processes have combined to marginalise people who do not conform to the 'model' of heterosexual partnerships, although they remain among those most affected (Edstrom, 2011). Further, as Andil Gosine argues, the adoption of the term 'men who have sex with men' (MSM), although designed to avoid the fixedness of 'homosexuality' as a category, in fact reveals 'a troubling adherence to traditional processes of racialisation that reduce non-white peoples to their bodies – and bodily functions – alone' (Gosine, 2006: 32). Examining its use by UNAIDS and other development organisations, he suggests that MSM have been primarily constructed as a 'threat' to their female sexual partners, as 'to blame' for HIV transmission, and as 'selfish and deceptive men who exercise little control over their primal urges' (32), reanimating once again the tropes of racialised masculinity.

This has taken place in a wider context in which homophobia is increasingly portrayed as inherent in 'African culture', and, more generally, the notion of 'tolerance' of homosexuality is appropriated within imperialist discourses (see, for example, Ekine, 2009; Haritaworn et al., 2008; and the analyses of the Abu Ghraib torture by

Puar, 2004; and by Butler, 2008 for discussions of this). Thus, while sexual intimacy between men, especially when it takes place outside the framework of gay identity, continues to be associated with the deviant hypersexuality of the racialised other (as it was in the 1950s when a report on population control in Bolivia referred to 'the ideal macho ... who flaunts his maleness, excelling in sexual activity, either heterosexual or homosexual'; Mass, 1976: 225), simultaneously homophobia is located as an essential characteristic of the African man and his problematic masculinity. This not only renders invisible the political economy and histories of current onslaughts on LGBTIQ people's rights, it also serves to obscure the heteronormativity of development interventions.

The response to HIV/AIDS: race, capital and ARVs

The second half of the 1990s saw significant changes in understandings of HIV and AIDS, with the development of antiretroviral (ARV) therapy,[7] which meant that if people with HIV were provided with lifelong treatment, it was now possible for them to live healthy lives. This clearly had enormous potential for combating the epidemic, since there were also symbiotic effects on prevention: access to treatment could reduce the stigma of HIV, which was no longer regarded as a 'death sentence', making it far more likely that people would be prepared to test for HIV before they became seriously ill, thus limiting transmission of the virus. Further, recent studies have shown that persons living with HIV who are on antiretroviral treatment are much less infectious and therefore much less likely to transmit HIV to others (World Bank/USAID, 2010). This process of change has indeed largely taken place in Europe and North America, where antiretroviral therapy is now routine for people who are HIV-positive.[8]

The fact that this process did not simultaneously occur in sub-Saharan Africa and elsewhere in the global South[9] and that, as of 2010, only 49 per cent of people in sub-Saharan Africa needing antiretroviral therapy were receiving it (WHO/UNAIDS/UNICEF, 2011) testifies to the 'necropolitics' of global capital and global financial institutions

(Sitze, 2004), and the obscene racialised dispensability of lives within the contemporary global order. Like famine, which from the late nineteenth century onwards came to be represented as part of the essence of the body of the colonised, at the same time as it became in material terms limited and specific to experiences of the global South of colonial integration in world markets, HIV/AIDS has come to be represented as synonymous with a dehumanised, essentially African poverty, inscribed within and on the bodies of African people.

By the end of the 1980s, it was abundantly clear that the previous decade of structural adjustment policies and economic liberalisation had had devastating effects: the 1980s came to be known as the 'lost decade' in Africa. As Adam Sitze explains,

> it is no accident that the states which implemented structural adjustment plans in the 1980s were the same ones which found themselves most unable to respond effectively to the spread of HIV/ AIDS in the 1990s. Forced to cut social spending and even urged to charge for health care facilities in IMF-designed plans to stabilize currencies and facilitate WB debt repayment, these states and their diminished healthcare systems were incapable of addressing the manifold medical needs of people living with HIV/AIDS. It was thus adding insult to injury when, after years of creating this capacity as a reality, the World Bank issued a 1996 study regretfully confirming the unaffordability of HIV/AIDS treatment in sub-Saharan Africa on the basis of a 'realistic estimate' of the region's low total health expenditure rates. (Sitze, 2004: 774)

Rather than question the rationale of neoliberalism, development institutions – led by the World Bank – responded by shifting the focus once again to the pathology of Africa. The failure of neoliberal policies was now attributed to the excessive greed of corrupt dictatorial rulers (the Western aid which kept them in power throughout the Cold War years conveniently forgotten) on the one hand, and on the other to the excessive desire of their people to survive, manifested in environmental degradation and 'unsustainable' population growth. A key text articulating this shift was the 1989 World Bank Report *Sub-Saharan Africa: From Crisis to Sustainable Growth* (World Bank, 1989).

The World Bank's focus on Africa as a target for population control only developed fully at the end of the 1980s in the context of the devastation wreaked by economic liberalisation. As we saw in the previous chapter, in the earlier period it was Asia and Latin America, not coincidentally the Cold War battlegrounds, which were the main targets for US-led population control policies. The 1990s saw the Malthusian 'nightmare' of 'overpopulation' being invoked with increasing frequency in Africa in the context of economies ravaged by the operation of global markets and by globalised conflict.

What this meant was that global responses to HIV and AIDS in Africa in the 1990s took place not only in the context of the continuing war of attrition waged by the IFIs on already decimated health services, but in a climate in which market-supremacist neoliberal policy prescriptions were combined with the racialised Malthusianism of population control to create a unique conjuncture in which the deliberate failure to prevent the deaths of millions of poor people could be legitimised.

Thus the World Bank argued that 'If the only effect of the AIDS epidemic were to reduce the population growth rate, it would increase the growth rate of *per capita* income in any plausible economic model' (1992 World Bank *Population and Human Resources Report*, cited in Gellman, 2000). This position was elaborated by those who argued, for example, that

> in the South African case, there is very strong evidence for the neo-Malthusian position ... there is a strong correlation between high population growth rates and the entrapment in poverty of the majority. To the extent that AIDS will bring about an overall reduction in population growth rates, there is thus a *prima facie* case that the effect on economic growth – and of course on *per capita* income, though this in itself is no very satisfactory indicator – will from one point of view be positive. (Cross, 1993, cited in Sitze, 2004: 801)

This implicitly racist logic in turn made it possible for the IMF to insist on low inflation targets for African states experiencing HIV/AIDS epidemics, which clamped down on health spending even further, preventing them from even beginning to address the crisis. These IMF stipulations led, for example, to the Ugandan government attempting to turn down a $52 million grant from the Global Fund to Fight AIDS, TB and Malaria in 2002 (ActionAid 2004).

The same logic is also reflected in some of the clinical trials which have been conducted in Africa. Wang notes that

> in 2000, Marcia Angell, the editor of the *New England Journal of Medicine*, wrote a lead editorial denouncing the unethical nature of HIV trials applied to 15,000 people in rural Uganda ... in September 2004, further ethical protests led to the suspension of an AIDS drug in Cameroon, a test organized by the Bill and Melinda Gates Foundation which involved 400 sex workers. Other findings estimate that recent clinical trials of anti-retroviral drugs in Africa, predominantly funded either by the US government or UNAIDS, have led to approximately 1,500 unnecessary infant deaths. (Wang, 2008: 11)

There are clear continuities with the infamous Tuskegee experiment on poor African-American men which took place from 1932 to 1972, and the less well-known US-government-led experiment in Guatemala in the 1940s.[10]

But it is possibly in the context of the attempts by transnational drug corporations to obstruct the manufacture of generic antiretroviral drugs which poor countries could afford that we can see most clearly the direct link between racialised Malthusianism and the related discursive constructions of pathological African sexuality, and the reproduction of material relations of power, exploitation and profit.

In the year when South Africa's apartheid regime ended, the power of transnational corporate capital was significantly consolidated when the Uruguay Round of the General Agreement on Tariffs and Trade (GATT) was concluded with the establishment of the World Trade Organization (WTO) and the codification of the highly contentious Trade-Related Aspects of Intellectual Property Rights (TRIPS) clauses, establishing a system of what Sitze (2004) calls 'global apartheid'. These clauses gave the transnational pharmaceuticals corporations powers to secure intellectual property patents, and therefore monopolies, on essential medicines. Backed by successive US administrations, 'Big Pharma' duly used the clauses to ruthlessly attack governments in the global South which initiated policies based on the local production of generic ARVs that could be made universally and freely available. When Brazil succeeded in halving AIDS-related deaths through the use of generic ARVs (which was actually fully consistent with TRIPS) 'Brazil's trade law was opposed first by the Clinton administration, which filed formal complaints against the law with the WTO on January 19, 2001, and then by the Bush administration, which refiled the same complaint two weeks later' (Sitze, 2004: 779).

Most notoriously, in 1999, thirty-nine of the richest pharmaceuticals companies filed a suit against the South African government in Pretoria's High Court to prevent the manufacture of affordable generic drugs (Wang, 2008: 11). In April 2001, the combined strategies of the Treatment Action Campaign, the South African government and global protests succeeded in forcing the pharmaceuticals companies to withdraw their case.

Despite this significant defeat, pharmaceuticals corporations and the US administration have continued to block access to treatment, refusing to lower prices and opposing generic manufacture. As a result, although generic drugs became increasingly available during the following decade, in 2006, 98 per cent of the market remained dominated by the leading ten corporations (Wang, 2008: 10). They have claimed, among other things, that generic manufacture may lead to failure to take the drugs correctly, and thus to the emergence of resistant strains. (In reality, of course, it is the prohibitively high costs of patented ARVs which can lead to people being compelled to take them irregularly.) The way racism has been used to legitimise this stance was made particularly explicit in a press interview by Andrew Natsios, administrator of USAID in the George W. Bush administration, in 2001, when (in the context of the lack of US support for ARV programmes) he expounded on the view that

[Africans] don't know what Western time is. You have to take these drugs a certain number of hours each day, or they don't work. Many people in Africa have never seen a clock or a watch their entire lives. And if you say, one o'clock in the afternoon, they do not know what you are talking about. They know morning, they know noon, they know evening, they know the darkness of the night. (*Boston Globe*, 7 June 2001)[11]

Since 2005, developing countries that are members of the WTO (which include manufacturers of generic ARVs such as India, Thailand and Brazil) have been required under TRIPS to issue patents. This has again made provision of treatment in the global South more difficult, since although patents have expired on a number of first-line AIDS drugs (making them available cheaply from generic makers), they still exist on most new and second-line medicines. The new antiretroviral drugs are generally less toxic, easier to take and more effective. They are often needed when a patient has to change his or her antiretroviral regime due to toxicity or resistance, which occurs in an estimated 10–15 per cent of people within five years. According to the AIDS charity Avert,

in 2009 the median cost of the most commonly used second-line regime was US$853 in low-income countries, US$1378 in lower-middle-income countries, and $US3638 in upper-middle-income countries. The vastly more expensive second-line drugs mean that, despite very few people taking them, they still account for a large proportion of the overall drug expenditure. In Brazil for example, the Ministry of Health currently spends 80% of its budget on imported patented drugs, even though they represent only a small proportion of drugs used. (www.avert.org)

TRIPS is thus once again being mobilised in the interests of the transnational pharmaceuticals corporations, by stifling the competition from generic manufacturers that drove the price of first-generation antiretrovirals down, shoring up 'global apartheid', this time through huge disparities in the price of first- and second-line ARVs.

A key episode in the struggle for treatment in the last decade has been the period during which Thabo Mbeki's AIDS 'denialism' prevented the provision of ARVs to the people of South Africa between 1999 and 2003.[12] As Joy Wang argues,

> understanding Mbeki's AIDS denialism within the context of apartheid and colonialism is crucial in enabling us to read the tragic mismanagement of the epidemic beyond the most frequently employed explanations of South African racial paranoia, pathological despotism and/or scientific illiteracy. (Wang, 2008: 1)

In an in-depth study of the various discourses supporting and opposing Mbeki's position, Wang analyses his denialism as a 'reactionary response' to both the racist representations of HIV/AIDS as resulting from African cultural practices and sexual deviance, as discussed above, and ongoing racialised imperialism, and specifically the exploitative practices of the global pharmaceuticals industry in Africa, which have been predicated on a racialised hierarchy in which some lives are systematically devalued (Wang, 2008). In this context, Adam Sitze suggests that the 'exceptionalist' approach to denialism in which Mbeki 'would appear purely and simply irrational [and] emerge as the embodiment of every postulate of Enlightenment racism' serves to 'obscure a more general economy of denialism, a denialism *writ large*' (Sitze, 2004: 771).

The current global financial crisis is making the practices of the 'economy of denialism' and the centrality of the racialised differentiation of the value of human lives to strategies of capital accumulation and contemporary imperialism even more evident. The recent failure by donor countries to fulfil their funding pledges to the Global Fund to Fight AIDS, Tuberculosis and Malaria, which led to the cancellation of Round 11 funding by the Global Fund, will mean that only the costs of drugs for people already on treatment will be covered, and in many countries the initiation of treatment for new patients may come to a standstill as a result, putting efforts to combat HIV in Africa under serious threat. This led Stephen Lewis, former UN special envoy for HIV/AIDS in Africa, to ask

> is it [the shortfall] because the women and children of Africa cannot be compared in the eyes of western governments to the women and

children of Europe and North America? ... Is it because a fighter jet is worth so much more than human lives? Is it because defense budgets are more worthy of protection in an economic crisis than millions of human beings? (SAfAIDS, 2011)

The relationships between corporate capital, neoliberal global institutions and constructions of 'race', and the ways in which they shape people's experiences of HIV and AIDS and their struggles for support and treatment, emerge starkly from the analysis of activists and researchers discussed in this chapter. These relationships also lead us to further questions about embodiment: how 'race' comes to be materially inscribed, often fatally, on the bodies that it discursively constructs and differentiates, and how this is resisted.

CHAPTER 5

New uses of 'race' in the 1990s: humanitarian intervention, good governance and democracy

Which will be the next victim of mass murder cloaked as humanitarian action?

Eduardo Galeano (2003)

Since the end of World War Two, every US President from Truman to Bush has had to have a Third World leader as a demon.

A.M. Babu (1993)

We came, we saw, he died.

US Secretary of State Hillary Clinton 'jokes with television news reporters' on hearing of the killing of Muammar Gaddafi (CBS News, 20 October 2011)

When I began to write this chapter in early April 2011, three separate news stories were unfolding simultaneously in the media. The events these stories represented, and the ways they can be connected, illustrate very clearly some of the changes explored here, processes which, as I argue, began in the 1990s at the end of the Cold War, but cannot be clearly understood without looking further back. Dominating the headlines was the bombing of Libya by British, French and American air forces, ostensibly to enforce a UN-sanctioned 'no-fly zone' and prevent air attacks by Gaddafi's government forces on anti-government fighters. We can perhaps begin to get a sense of the scale of these bombings from the fact that

> the coalition forces staged on 20–30 March well over 700 air-attacks, dropping over 600 precision-guided munitions from aircraft and firing nearly 200 Tomahawk cruise-missiles from offshore warships.

> Over the twenty-four hours to midday on 31 March, they carried out fifty-five air-strikes; the aircraft used include the A-10 Warthog (which can fire armour-piercing shells fitted with depleted-uranium tips) and the extremely powerful AC-130 gunships. (Rogers, 2011)

In the mainstream Western media, however, nothing was reported about civilian casualties of the bombings. Initially euphoric, reporters began to convey a sense of disappointment that the fighting had reached a 'stalemate' and experts held forth on whether or not the CIA should 'arm the rebels', an option which President Obama had recently announced as being under consideration, although it was well known that, having previously sold arms to the Gaddafi regime for at least a decade, the NATO governments had in reality already been supplying a variety of insurgent groups with weaponry and training for some time with 'British and French special forces ... operating alongside the rebels, and the United States deploying CIA operatives inside the country' (Rogers 2011). It was to be another six months before the objective of the NATO intervention was achieved with the capture of Gaddafi and his brutal lynching, which was televised and savoured in the Western media, underlining once again the dehumanising effects of the 'race' and racism at the centre of the contemporary imperial project.

Meanwhile, and accompanied by relatively little media coverage, French special forces with the UN backing, along with rebel soldiers, staged a military assault on the residence of the president of Côte d'Ivoire, Laurent Gbagbo, and placed him under arrest. Like Gaddafi, Gbagbo had challenged US and European economic and geostrategic interests and in particular control over oil. Specifically, he

> favoured non-European and non-US oil companies to explore in the newly discovered oilfields at the border with Ghana and off the coast of the Gulf of Guinea. He had encouraged involvement of Chinese, Indian and Russian companies. Additionally he refused to make a payment of US$2.3 billion on Côte d'Ivoire's dollar bonds to foreign investors, to pay the interest on the country's foreign debt. And he pursued nationalisation of foreign banks that had suspended their operations. (Bush et al., 2011: 363)

International investors expressed their confidence that the newly installed government of Alassane Ouattara, ex-deputy managing director of the International Monetary Fund, would be more oriented to the requirements of global capital (364) in a period when military and economic control over Africa and its resources has become a priority for the USA. But, as in Libya, the attacks on Côte d'Ivoire took place in the name of humanitarian intervention to protect the human rights of its citizens.

The third news story was of a slightly different kind, and although it related specifically to Britain's history it barely merited a headline in the British media. In a landmark case, four elderly Kenyan survivors of the mass detention camps set up by the British during the Mau Mau uprising from 1952 to 1961 had travelled to Britain to seek compensation for the atrocities they had experienced. They had been whipped, beaten, sexually abused and castrated as part of the systematic torture of detainees in the camps where hundreds of thousands of people were held, one of which was described as 'Kenya's Belsen' by a judge in Nairobi at the time (*Guardian*, 11 April 2011). Investigation of the claims had revealed 'boxes of previously undisclosed documents, stored by the Foreign Office' (*Guardian*, 7 April 2011) detailing the extent of the atrocities and the full awareness and approval of the British government. This evidence added to what had already been exposed about the appalling scale of British colonial violence in Kenya (see, in particular, Elkins, 2005; Anderson, 2005) and elsewhere in the 1950s and 1960s. In July 2011, the courts were to overrule attempts to block the claims by the Foreign Office, which argued that all responsibility had been transferred to the Kenyan state at independence. But this violence and the struggles of its survivors for justice were made invisible within a dominant discourse in which 'human rights violations' were committed by racialised others, and Northern governments' duty was to intervene to prevent them, and in which humanitarian intervention was linked to a renewed celebration of the history of colonialism and its 'values'.

Sherene Razack, in her analysis of the 1993 US-led UN intervention in Somalia, has argued that contemporary interventions are 'deeply racially inflected' (Razack, 2004: 17). I seek here to place 'race' at the centre of a discussion of the mobilisation of ideas of humanitarian intervention, good governance and democracy, and their relationship to imperialism. As elsewhere in the book, the presence of 'race' is addressed in two closely interrelated ways: first, in terms of the mobilisation of racialised and colonial tropes to legitimise various forms of intervention, and second in terms of the materiality of racialised global relations of power and accumulation.

The beginning of the 1990s has been characterised as a historical conjuncture in which a number of global changes coalesced to produce a series of shifts in development discourses and practices. Like most such defining moments, however, it was marked as much by continuities with the past, and the rediscovery and redeployment of the strategies of earlier periods, as by innovation. In fact, as we will see, like the official post-World War II 'birth' of development, the new discourse of rights, ethics and human development that emerged in the 1990s was part of a strategic realignment and consolidation of imperial power and global processes of accumulation which relied precisely on the technique of what April Biccum calls 'narrative rupture' (Biccum, 2009) for its effectiveness.

In the same vein, an examination of development discourses in the 1990s allows us to challenge another point of 'narrative rupture' which is much more strongly anchored in common-sense understandings – the events of 11 September 2001. We can see that many of the processes which became more highly visible with the declaration of a 'war on terror' after 9/11 (including, crucially, the racialised construction of 'Islam' as the most significant threat to Western civilisation) were already in place in the preceding decade.

In the following section, we look briefly at three interrelated processes which spanned that decade: the shift from 'needs-based' to 'rights-based' approaches in dominant conceptions of humanitarianism; the emergence of the governance agenda and subsequently the Post-Washington Consensus (Stiglitz, 1998); and the decisive reconfiguration of the discursive relationship between development and liberal democracy. I argue that all of these processes involved not only temporal but spatial ruptures, in which not only historical continuities but contemporary global interconnections were erased. The empty spaces left by these erasures, I suggest, have been filled through the strategic mobilisation of 'race'. Rather than declining in significance, as many studies of contemporary 'empire' suggest, race has been re-provisioned with new sets of meanings which both evoke and extend older ones.

Towards 'rights-based' humanitarianism

David Chandler has traced the trajectory of humanitarianism 'from the margins to the centre of the international policy agenda' (Chandler, 2006). Initially, he suggests, the dominant model of humanitarian aid was that of relief charities providing material assistance to those in need of it regardless of political affiliation, a model based on the principles of neutrality of the International Committee of the Red Cross (ICRC) and sharpened by the exigencies of the Cold War (Chandler, 2006). Chandler argues that, in a context where official aid was primarily bilateral between states and explicitly geopolitical in its motives, NGOs sought to occupy a space of 'neutrality', providing

> aid where the international geo-political divide meant that leading
> Western states were not willing to assist those in need. The
> Biafra crisis in 1968 was one of the first examples of humanitarian
> aid NGOs mobilizing in the face of British and international
> disapproval. In the 1970s, NGO relief intervention was repeated in
> Bangladesh, Ethiopia, the West African Sahel and Cambodia after
> the defeat of the Khmer Rouge government. (Chandler, 2006: 25)

But the intervention in Biafra in south-eastern Nigeria – in which international NGOs and church organisations became the main source of support for Igbo secessionist forces against the Nigerian federal government – can also be cited as an early example of the 'new humanitarian' rights-based intervention, in which human rights were explicitly pitted against notions of 'sovereignty'.[1] Biafra indicated a new way of operating, which came to be epitomised by Médecins Sans Frontières (MSF), whose founder, French doctor Bernard Kouchner,[2] had been a vocal critic of the ICRC's non-interventionist stand during the Biafra crisis. The campaign on Biafra was also marked by its extensive circulation of racialised images of severely malnourished children, which set a precedent for later NGO representational practices (Benthall, 1993; DeWaal, 1997).

With the rise of neoliberalism in the 1980s, this change in approach began to have a much more wide-ranging impact. NGOs increasingly took centre stage with the 'privatisation' of aid which accompanied neo-liberal reforms leading to the massive growth and proliferation of competing NGOs and an increasingly symbiotic relationship between NGOs and the media (Benthall, 1993; de Waal, 1997). 'International NGOs were increasingly relied upon to administer government and institutional relief funds in disaster situations in the 1980s. By the mid-1980s, 70 per cent of UK aid to Sudan and 50 per cent of British relief to Ethiopia was managed through NGOs' (Searls, 1995, cited in Chandler, 2006: 32). As the Cold War came to an end, 'the growing pressure from increasingly influential NGOs for cross-line interventions' led to a new patterns of collaboration between relief agencies and the UN, which negotiated access for NGOs to conflict zones in Sudan in 1989 and Ethiopia and Angola in 1990 (Duffield, 2001: 77).

A turning point was the establishment of the UN 'safe haven' for the Kurds in northern Iraq after the 1991 Gulf War. Such interventions had more to do with the increasingly central objective of containment – preventing people from crossing borders as refugees (and in particular preventing 'Third World' refugees from entering Europe and North America) than with saving lives within the designated areas (Chimni, 2000; Roberts, 1998).[3] At the same time, the failure to protect lives within these zones contributed to legitimising the idea of military intervention to facilitate humanitarian assistance. 1992–93 saw 'armed humanitarianism' in Cambodia, Croatia, Bosnia and Somalia. By the end of the decade and the 1999 NATO intervention over Kosovo there had been a further shift to intervention in the name of protecting human rights.

Underlying this were changing approaches to the political sovereignty of the 'non-West', culminating in the UN secretary general Boutros Boutros-Ghali's report, adopted by the General Assembly in 1992, in which he stated that 'the time of absolute and exclusive sovereignty … has passed'.[4] Many critical accounts of the overt interventionism which was to follow focus attention on this significant discursive shift away from the right of 'absolute and exclusive' sovereignty and towards the human rights of populations. In the process, however, these accounts risk reinscribing the 'narrative rupture' inherent in the interventionist rights discourse of the 1990s, which posits a 'misguided' period when postcolonial states were granted untrammelled sovereignty, followed by one in which the need for regulation and discipline of the 'natives' was once again recognised (for an example of this racialised discourse of trusteeship, see Helman and Ratner, 1992–93). In fact, as Siba Grovogui points out, 'there has never been a uniform international system of sovereignty across time and space' (2002: 316). The period shaped by the Cold War and by protracted, diverse and often bitterly resisted struggles for national independence from colonial rule was marked by continuous interventions in supposedly independent states. William Blum documents fifty-five major US military and CIA interventions between 1945 and 1991 (Blum, 2003). Many of these operations were of course covert, and their full extent only came to light through subsequent in-depth investigation (see, for example, Wilson, 1989 on CIA intervention in Zanzibar in 1963–64).

These interventions were not simply strategic in the narrow sense of installing or protecting Cold War allies; they aimed to protect and extend the interests of metropolitan capital in ways that involved actively obstructing the transformation of colonial economies which had been structured around the extraction of resources for metropolitan production. Third World Marxist thinkers theorised this neocolonialism and the operation of late-twentieth-century imperialism in a variety of ways. This was an era in which different meanings of 'development' struggled for dominance, with the 'developmental state' being mobilised for economic nationalist projects in some contexts (particularly in those countries that were part of the Non-Aligned Movement (Babu, 1991). This contestation over models of development would effectively be brought to an end by the imposition of neoliberal orthodoxy in the 1980s – although, as Owusu (2003) argues in the context of Africa, it was not until the 1990s that it became fully hegemonic among ruling elites, while popular resistance has continued to grow.

In the context of US foreign policy, William Robinson locates a change in the nature of intervention well before the end of the Cold War. He argues that turning points such as the defeat of the USA in Vietnam and the fall of pro-US regimes in Iran and Nicaragua triggered an apparent shift in the 1980s from reliance on covert destabilisation and 'dirty tricks', which were now seen as 'discredited', to more overt intervention in the name of 'democracy' (although covert interventions continued and still exist). This open intervention ranged from the funding of opposition parties and groups by organisations like the Washington-based, US Congress-funded 'National Endowment for Democracy' (NED), to the massive US military support to right-wing armed forces waging war on the state, as in Nicaragua, Afghanistan and Angola. Robinson directly links these new forms of intervention to the emergence of new strategies of accumulation based on the rapidly growing mobility of capital and neoliberal globalisation (Robinson, 1996).

By contrast, the narrative that posits an abrupt transition from Cold War sovereignty to post-Cold War intervention not only works to erase the history of Cold War interventions; more importantly, it often suggests that geostrategic objectives which influenced the foreign policy of Western governments only acted to reinforce sovereignty (this is usually described as Western governments 'tolerating' human rights abuses by 'friendly' dictatorships). The implication is that geostrategic concerns ceased to be significant in the post-Cold War, more 'ethical' 1990s. Even many critical observers accept this dichotomy: for example, in their characterisation of the post-9/11 aid regime as a 'new Cold War', with Western donor governments using international aid to bolster military allies like Pakistan at the

expense of some of the poorest countries, N
and Action Aid validated the construction of the
of 'genuine' attempts to use aid for poverty alleviaᴛ
2003; Black et al., 2004).

Approaches which foreground analysis of imperialism
this apparent rupture between periods of 'sovereignty' and   ᴄr-
vention', and are oriented more towards analysing the reconfiguration of strategies for sustaining dominance and how these changing
strategies are related to changing patterns of global capital accumulation as well as multiple forms of resistance. In particular, they
focus on the economic devastation wreaked by the liberalisation
policies imposed on the global South in the 1980s, and the ways
in which the causes of the crises these engendered were ascribed
to Third World states in the 1990s, in an attempt to sustain the
legitimacy of the neoliberal model (Gills et al., 1993; Abrahamsen,
2000).

These processes are explored in more detail below, but they also
help to contextualise the consolidation of 'rights-based humanitarianism' and the related notions of cosmopolitanism and 'transnational
governance' in response to the civil wars of the 1990s that took
place, predominantly, in sub-Saharan Africa and Eastern Europe.
This theorising emerged against the background of dominant media
representations of the conflicts in Africa as the 'story of a civilised
West faced with the disintegration of African states and their descent
into barbarism' (Razack, 2004: 47). The host of ever-present racialised
colonial tropes of 'irrationality', 'savagery' and figurative and literal
'cannibalism' were once again reanimated. Particularly influential
was American journalist Robert Kaplan's apocalyptic 'The Coming
Anarchy' (1994), which portrayed a future where 'scarcity, crime,
overpopulation, tribalism, and disease' spread from Africa to engulf
the planet.

The 'new wars' approach pioneered by Mary Kaldor, one of the
leading proponents of cosmopolitanism (Kaldor, 1999), rejected the
explicitly racialised imagery, but shared the obliteration of external
causes of conflict in Africa – both historically, in terms of the

dynamics of colonialism, its systemic violence and the divisions it generated and sustained (Mamdani, 1996, 2001; Prunier, 1997), and contemporarily, in terms of both the ongoing plunder of valuable resources by corporate capital and the economic devastation and social disintegration induced by liberalisation policies imposed by the World Bank and the IMF.

Further, the focus on the targeting of civilians for brutal killings and mass rapes, which was represented as an entirely 'new' form of warfare in a post-Cold War world (Kaldor, 1999), further dehistoricised the approach: by contrasting these atrocities with earlier 'Westphalian' conflicts where national armies engaged with each other according to predetermined rules, the 'new wars' theorists effectively collude with the racialised exclusion from full humanity of the colonised, to whom these rules of engagement never applied. From the massacres of entire villages by British forces in India in 1857, through the aerial bombing and gassing of civilians in what is now Iraqi Kurdistan in the 1920s, to the Mau Mau concentration camps in Kenya in the 1950s, whose full horrors are only emerging today, the history of brutal repression of diverse manifestations of anti-colonial resistance – termed 'mutinies', 'riots' 'rebellions' and later 'emergencies', but never recognised as wars, is once again denied in the 'new wars' paradigm.

In the post-World War II period, these colonial wars overlapped both temporally and in terms of their objectives with US-led Cold War interventions. Cold War atrocities were no less shocking than those of the civil wars of the 1990s – even Kaldor acknowledges that 'the new warfare borrows from counterinsurgency techniques of destabilisation aimed at sowing "fear and hatred"' (Kaldor, 1999: 8). But where the 'internecine' violence of the 1990s is constantly reinvoked as proof of unfathomable 'barbarism', the horrors engineered by the CIA were erased, or in some cases celebrated, in the Western media. As Tariq Ali reminds us, the massacres of half a million people as suspected communist sympathisers in Indonesia in 1965–66 were heralded in *Time* magazine as 'the West's best news for years in Asia' (Ali, 2003: 342).

It is from this starting point, at which a mountain of accumulated violent incursions have been set aside and rendered invisible or irrelevant, that the cosmopolitan approach puts forward the argument for a more interventionist, 'more political' humanitarianism that prioritises protecting human rights, rather than providing material relief. Commentators like Kaldor (1999), Archibugi and Held (1995), and de Waal (1997) problematised the principle of neutrality and argued that rights-based humanitarianism may need to 'take sides' in conflicts.

NGOs became polarised over this approach in the context of the aftermath of the 1994 Rwandan genocide of the Tutsi population, and the provision of aid to the 2 million Hutu refugees who had crossed the border and were in camps in Goma, Ngara and Bukava in Zaire. Proponents of rights-based humanitarianism like Alex de Waal of Africa Rights argued in favour of cutting off humanitarian aid to the camps, claiming that it was saving the lives of 'genocidaires' who would regroup and return to Rwanda to carry out further attacks, and criticising the 'irreducible residue of naivety' of relief agencies which 'felt they had no moral choice but to respond to massive human suffering, even though it meant supporting the extremists' strategy' (de Waal, 1997: 196). Accordingly, 'in an unprecedented move, humanitarian agencies, including MSF, withdrew humanitarian aid from these camps' (Chandler, 2006: 44). In a scathing critique of this construction of the 'undeserving disaster victim' and its effects, Nicholas Stockton, Oxfam's emergencies director, noted that

> this story line was and is used by many, including Africa Rights, the US and Rwandan governments, to justify the forced repatriation of most of the refugees (or 'fugitive Hutu extremists' as they have been labelled), and the 'disappearance' of the remainder. This argument has also suited many official aid agencies who found in it an excellent reason to suspend humanitarian aid and to be 'pragmatic', i.e. to do nothing, irrespective of any further distress experienced by this group of pariah refugees. (Stockton, 1998: 354)

The result was that during 1997 as many as 200,000 people may have died in Zaire – fleeing from troops clearly seeking revenge for the genocide of 1994. A large proportion of the refugees were clearly not responsible for the genocide. As Stockton notes, 'some 750,000 of those forcibly repatriated or "lost in Zaire" were children under five. Over 1.5 million were under 16 years of age' (354).

Stockton and others have argued that the 'new' (or 'rights-based') humanitarianism thus 'violated the principles of humanism' by creating 'deserving and undeserving victims', and in wielding power to decide who should live and who should die in the name of a 'greater good' (Stockton, 1998: 354). But I would suggest that what is visible here is not a new departure from long-established practices, but rather a new manifestation of processes which are in fact inherent in racialised imperialism. 'Race' and the dehumanisation associated with it made it possible for colonial powers to except colonised people from the 'rules' of nineteenth- and early-twentieth-century military engagement; 'race' made it possible to herald the Cold War massacres in Asia as 'good news'; similarly, 'race' in the 1990s made it possible for the deliberate refusal to save lives to be recast as 'humanitarianism' and for the foundations of the full-scale re-assertion of the colonial notion of trusteeship to be laid. By 2001, the liberal media in Britain could argue that even if the continued bombing of Afghanistan led to an additional 100,000 children dying, as UNICEF had warned, 'a greater good [would be] squandered' if the bombing ceased because the fall of the Taliban was 'the only truly humanitarian outcome for Afghanistan's starving' ('Fighting for a Better Future: This War Must Save Afghanistan', *Observer* editorial, 21 October 2001, cited in Chandler, 2006: 51).

While liberal cosmopolitans distanced themselves from the explicit racism of a world-view which saw 'ancient hatreds' inevitably and lethally resurfacing when the restraints of Cold War support for multi-ethnic states fell away (Huntington, 1993), their more nuanced and ostensibly radical arguments share the assumption that the causes of conflict are exclusively internal and the solutions external. And they lead to the same conclusion: what is required is 'trusteeship' of those racialised others – both those cast as 'victims' and those identified as 'perpetrators' – who have shown that they cannot govern themselves. In theory this trusteeship is to be invested in 'transnational civil society' comprising UN bodies and NGOs; in practice the cosmopolitans accept that it will be administered by 'coalitions of the willing' and the international financial institutions. As Chandler argues, their ideas have been instrumental in 'resurrecting a new imperial "duty of care" on the basis of the human rights discourse of victims, abusers and international saviours' (Chandler, 2006: 241), what Michael Ignatieff approvingly referred to as 'Empire Lite' or the building of a 'humanitarian empire' (Ignatieff, 2003).

By the time of the US-led invasion of Afghanistan, the discourse of human rights had become fully incorporated in what Sherene Razack describes as the racialised 'moral universe ... of white knights fighting for peace' against 'dark threats' (Razack, 2004: 12). It was also a central element in the open celebration of a 'new' imperialism. Robert Cooper, a key adviser to Tony Blair and subsequently director general for external and politico-military affairs at the General Secretariat of the Council of the European Union, made this explicit when he wrote in 2002: 'What is needed then is a new kind of imperialism, one acceptable to a world of human rights and cosmopolitan values. We can already discern its outline: an imperialism which, like all imperialism, aims to bring order and organisation but which rests today on the voluntary principle' (Cooper, 2002: 17–18). That this 'new' imperialism was, however, to be structured and sustained by the same racialised violence and racist tropes of 'civilisation' and 'savagery' as the 'old' one was evident:

> when dealing with more old-fashioned kinds of states outside the postmodern continent of Europe, we need to revert to the rougher methods of an earlier era – force, pre-emptive attack, deception, whatever is necessary to deal with those who still live in the 19th century world of 'every state for itself'. Among ourselves, we keep the law but when we are operating in the jungle, we must also use the laws of the jungle. (Cooper, 2002: 16)

Intertwined with this discourse has been a renewed triumphalist enthusiasm for the colonial past. This is articulated not only by historians like Andrew Roberts and Niall Ferguson (who is well known for advocating a formal US-run global empire on the lines of British colonialism) but notably by Gordon Brown, who in 2005 (as chancellor of the exchequer in the British government) chose a visit to Tanzania to tell the *Daily Mail* that

> the days of Britain having to apologise for its colonial history are over ... We should celebrate much of our past rather than apologise for it. And we should talk, and rightly so, about British values that are enduring, because they stand for some of the greatest ideas in history: tolerance, liberty, civic duty, that grew in Britain and influenced the rest of the world. Our strong traditions of fair play, of openness, of internationalism, these are great British values. (*Daily Mail*, 15 January 2005)

However, several simultaneous and related processes intersected to generate the rehabilitation of the notion of trusteeship, or what Helman and Ratner (1992–93) call 'conservatorship'. Equally significant was the emergence of 'good governance' as a central element within the prescriptions of powerful development institutions, which intersected both conceptually and historically with shifts in the discourse of humanitarianism. Once again, while the focus was the non-Western, and in this case specifically the 'Third World', postcolonial state, constructions of 'Africa' as uniquely dysfunctional pervaded its central legitimising narrative.

Good governance and the racialisation of corruption

In this section we will look at how development institutions promoting the good governance agenda have ignored the earlier critiques of the governance practices of 'neo-colonial' elites developed by activists and theorists of the left in Africa and articulated by political movements in a number of countries on the continent, and instead drawn upon and redeployed essentialised notions of 'Africa' as a source of corruption, chaos and conflict. They have structured the discourse around a series of racialised binary oppositions: corrupt, self-seeking African leaders on the one hand, incorruptible, accountable and compassionate Western institutions on the other; chaos and conflict on the one hand, order and stability on the other; despotism on the one hand, democracy on the other. This has allowed the elaboration of a neoliberal concept of corruption and poor governance that is both dehistoricised and decontextualised.

As with earlier moves to reinscribe notions of 'race' in understandings of development, this was simultaneously a response to resistance to capital and racialised imperialism – in the form of widespread popular opposition to the structural adjustment policies of the 1980s – and a strategy to extend and deepen processes of capital accumulation. The discourse of 'African exceptionalism' was central to this move, and, as in earlier periods, worked to obscure the paradigmatic nature of Africa's experiences of global capitalism. In the context of neoliberal globalisation, as Graham Harrison argues,

> many of the most damaging, recessive and ugly aspects … are (dis)placed onto Africa in order to represent them as manifestations of recidivism, anachronism and deviance. On the contrary – mass poverty, 'surplus' populations, state collapse and other features of Africa's development crisis are at the heart of globalisation. (Harrison, 2010: 6)

Systematic corruption and large-scale expropriation of resources by unelected rulers in states in Africa, as elsewhere in the global South, during the Cold War was inseparable from the extensive military assistance and aid provided by Western donor governments to those regimes seen as strategic allies and sources of key raw materials. It was African left and anti-imperialist thinkers and movements confronting these regimes that articulated cogent critiques of this corruption, which they placed in the context of a much wider Marxist analysis of the role of the dominant classes and their patterns of accumulation in supporting and furthering the interests of imperialism in the post-independence era. In these analyses, corruption was an inevitable by-product of the failure to transform structurally dependent, primary-export-based colonial economies (Babu, 1981, 2002a; Iyayi, 1986; Rodney, 1972).[5] A.M. Babu argues that

> the cheap labour in neocolonies helps to create a colossal return to the capital … invested. For instance, in developed capitalist

countries the average return to capital is about 5% while in our countries it ranges from 40% to 200% as in gold mining and petroleum. Thus, the huge transfer of wealth from the neocolonies to the metropolitan countries takes place through the exploitation of our workers and the looting of our peasants. Why we allow this to happen is another question. The politicians and bureaucrats in underdeveloped countries who supervise this exploitation and plunder are not themselves underdeveloped. They enjoy as high a standard of living as their counterparts in the developed capitalist countries; and through bribery and corruption, some enjoy even higher standards. They have therefore developed a vested interest in the system which they are reluctant to change, whatever they say to the contrary. There is also emerging a new group of local millionaires who benefit from this exploitation and plunder of their people by their foreign masters; they also take advantage of the economic chaos which the system has brought about. Both groups are developing material bases for reproducing themselves as a class whose vested interest is inextricably bound to neo-colonialism. (Babu, 2002a: 268)

The corruption of neocolonial elites was also frequently satirised – one example being Ousmane Sembene's classic 1975 film *Xala*, a scathing and hilarious critique of the post-Independence rulers in Senegal. In one memorable scene, the new national leaders have just seen off the French colonial administrators and taken office. They are shown sitting down to a meeting in the Chamber of Commerce in which each minister is modestly presented with a briefcase by the former rulers – which (as we see when each discreetly peeps into it and then sits back with a look of barely concealed pleasure) turns out to be stuffed with banknotes.

Development institutions and donor governments continued to support notoriously corrupt leaders like Kenya's Moi and Zaire's Mobutu during the 1980s. As Rita Abrahamsen notes, the notion of 'good governance' in fact makes its first appearance in the World Bank's highly influential 1989 report *Sub-Saharan Africa: From Crisis to Sustainable Growth* (Abrahamsen, 2000). Produced in the context of both the end of the Cold War and incontrovertible evidence of growing poverty, unemployment, worsening levels of child nutrition and overall economic crisis across the continent after a decade of IMF-dictated economic reforms and structural adjustment policies, as well as growing popular protests against neoliberal policies in many African countries,[6] the report was a strategic intervention which aimed to shift responsibility for the crisis to internal factors through a new dual focus on problems of governance and population growth, and in the process reiterated a commitment to the core principles of neoliberalism and globalised capital accumulation.

These ideas quickly became part of a donor consensus and gained a new prominence in the repertoire of racialised representations of 'Africa'. If the overarching tone of the good governance discourse was that of a facile populism, invoking 'bad policemen and greedy officials, abusing power to oppress the poor' (Craig and Porter, 2006: 8) it was shot through with deep-rooted colonial constructions of Africans and African rulers in particular as innately lazy, greedy, cruel and given to excess of all kinds, and African people as in need of the protection of benevolent and civilised external trusteeship. The resurgence of this trope reflected and reinforced the silencing of analysis of the specific class alignments and international affiliations of these regimes, in favour of racialised narratives of African exceptionalism.

Thus for Alison Rosenberg of USAID, Africa was 'a breeding ground for corruption' (1993: 173, cited in Szeftel, 1998: 226); for British ex-Tory MP Matthew Parris, writing in *The Times*, 'Corruption [had] become an African epidemic. It is impossible to overstate the poisoning of human relations and the paralysing of initiative that the corruption on the African scale brings' (*The Times*, 8 August 1997, cited in Szeftel, 1998: 226). James Thuo Gathii highlights the proliferation of epithets used to describe the essentialised 'African state' that emerged in this period: '"kleptocratic" state; "vassal" state; "vampire" state; "receiver" state, "prostrate" state, "fictitious" state, "collapsed" state, "predatory" state, "parasitic" state, "neo-patrimonial" state, "lame leviathan" and so on' (Gathii, 1999: 68).

This binarised discourse also served to obscure both the much larger 'scale' of corruption outside Africa and the evidence that corruption is not only intrinsic to capitalism but, under some conditions, may allow it to operate and develop more effectively. Earlier, this observation had been strategically mobilised to legitimise US support for corrupt dictatorships, but more recently it has become the preserve of more critical commentators on neoliberal globalisation (see, for example, Chang, 2007). The key question for domestic capitalist development, some have argued, is not the presence or absence of corruption, but rather whether the capital accumulated through corruption is reinvested in the national economy, or siphoned out to bank accounts in Europe (Chang, 2007: 164; Moore, 1999: 79; Grovogui, 2002), as was the case in US-backed dictatorships in several continents (including, notoriously, Marcos in the Philippines, Mobutu in Zaire, and the Duvaliers in Haiti), thus strengthening processes of imperialist capital accumulation.[7] This, then, returns us to the questions about the nature of postcolonial ruling classes and their insertion into global processes of imperialism which were addressed by African Marxist commentators much earlier.

If the World Bank's 1989 report, along with its study *Governance and Development* (1992), represent the 'locus classicus of the governance literature' of the 1990s (Abrahamsen, 2000: 48), the Bank further elaborated its agenda in its 1997 report *The State in a Changing World*. David Moore argues that whereas the era of economic policies of the 1980s and early 1990s represented 'attempts to "get the prices right" and to hack away indiscriminately at the state', the 1997 report heralded 'the age of "getting the state right" to implement the same goals as before' (Moore, 1999: 64). The role of the state was to provide the 'institutional framework for markets to flourish'; its priority must be to establish the 'pure public good' of property rights (World Bank, 1997). At the same time, the Third World state was once again identified as the biggest obstacle to development, as 'rent-seeking' by state personnel undermined 'free market' capitalism. As Moore summarises the report's message: 'It is now admitted that the third world state is necessary, but still it is not trusted. How can it be made to police itself?' (Moore, 1999: 68).

As Szeftel points out, in the discourse of the World Bank corruption is equated with 'rent-seeking', and

> the concept therefore neatly links state regulation to corruption. The rent-seeking behaviour of the state is deemed objectionable because it imposes economic and social costs – whether the rents are extracted legally or corruptly. For the Bank, corruption flourishes where 'institutions are weak and government policies generate economic rents'. (Szeftel, 1998: 225)

These policies can include virtually any form of regulation in which the state attempts to mediate the impact of global markets: for example, trade restrictions, subsidies, price controls, multiple exchange rates and foreign exchange allocation schemes. The vast opportunities for corruption which have been created by donor-driven deregulation and privatisation in Africa as elsewhere (Szeftel, 1998: 225; Hall, 1999) are, of course, excluded from the World Bank's governance narratives, as are the effects of New Public Management approaches, which seek to introduce the market into government itself, in increasing corruption (Chang, 2007: 168–70). More generally, the evidence that corruption often 'arises when capital and state intersect' (Szeftel, 1998: 237) is obliterated from these accounts.

The scale of corruption in Africa has been small in monetary terms when compared with the corporate financial scandals that have been exposed in Europe and North America and elsewhere in the world in recent decades (Szeftel, 1998: 222). But, not surprisingly, the neoliberal understanding of corruption promoted by the World Bank has continued to limit the location of corruption to the Third World state, excluding corporate interests as well as donor governments and international and local NGOs – not to mention the international financial institutions themselves – from its purview. As a result it has been central to the legitimation of new forms of imperialist intervention, including the configuration of 'civil society' as an arena for donor direction and control. Most recently, as the World Bank's publication *Africa Development Indicators 2010*, subtitled *Silent and Lethal: How Quiet Corruption Undermines Africa's Development Efforts*, indicates, the focus has shifted to the 'various types of malpractice of frontline providers (teachers, doctors, inspectors, and other government representatives) that do not involve monetary exchange' (World Bank, 2010: xi). The near collapse of the state brought about by neoliberal reforms – meaning that many such 'frontline providers' are rarely paid and are compelled to supplement their salaries in a variety of ways – is not considered central to the solution here. Instead, as Harrison and Mercer (2010) note, it is proposed that this 'quiet corruption' should be tackled by demands for better governance by 'civil society' in the form of NGOs – but the question of accountability of these organisations and their international funders, and of who decides who should be targeted, is once again marginalised.

The same processes of temporal and spatial rupture which operate in the new humanitarian discourses are at work in the context of good governance. If corruption is decontextualised from contemporary processes of class formation and global capital accumulation, and internalised to an essentialised and racialised 'African state', it is also dehistoricised.

Much has been written about the extent to which colonialism in sub-Saharan Africa has shaped contemporary political structures and practices (see, for example, Rodney, 1972; Mamdani, 1996; Mbembe, 2001; Grovogui, 2002). In particular, the role of Indirect Rule through Native Authorities in institutionalising what Mamdani (1996) has termed 'decentralised despotism' and in inscribing violence and coercion, ethnic essentialism and illicit accumulation within the post-independence polity has been extensively analysed. Under Indirect Rule, chiefs were expected to retain some part of the taxes extracted from the people on behalf of the colonial state, and to consume conspicuously the wealth they thus accumulated: both extortion and embezzlement were thus institutionalised. Further, it has been noted that at independence, colonial administrators deliberately concentrated power in the executive to ensure that the state passed into and remained in the hands of conservative interests. Elections were organised in such a way as to reinforce ethnic and regional patronage structures already developed through the bifurcated administrations of the colonial period (Allen, 1995; Szeftel 1998) and to intensify the divisions that colonialism had fostered and in some cases consolidated as a strategy for combating movements demanding independence (Mulinge and Lesetedi, 1998). This twin strategy of concentration of power and patronage-based politics further entrenched nepotism and other forms of corruption, in the context of dependent neocolonial economies.

But these historically contextualised accounts have been rejected within good governance discourses, which draw instead on racialised characterisations of 'African politics' as both internally undifferentiated and immutably 'different' from politics elsewhere. These representations and their academic elaborations either evoke an ahistorical notion of 'African' culture or, increasingly as the governance agenda has gained ground, go further in pathologising African politics as innately venal. As Grovogui observes,

> these scholarly works and chronopolitical narratives have helped to link African politics and the state of the state to the 'intrinsic nature' of endogenous 'cultures' and local institutions. Specifically, they have centred on particular but selectively chosen details of everyday politics that naturalize as culture all forms of politics, including the regional manifestations of global processes and local responses to such historical processes. (Grovogui, 2001: 442)

With the rise of the good governance agenda, 'African' corruption has become a key element in a discursive cocktail of dangerously contagious conditions of conflict and chaos. The flip side of this 'Africanisation' of corruption in development discourse is that 'developed' states (and IFIs) are free from any scrutiny of their governance practices, and are in fact assumed to be the model to which African governance must aspire.

This externalisation and racialisation of the financial practices defined as 'corrupt' has a long colonial history. Its genealogy can be traced to the early years of the East India Company. In 1787 the British House of Commons impeached Warren Hastings on charges of having engaged in corruption and bribery on a massive scale during his tenure as the governor general of Bengal from 1772 to 1785. Eight years later, in 1795, the House of Lords acquitted him of all charges. Hastings's defence centred upon the assumption that 'arbitrary power', corruption and despotism were part of the 'constitution of Asia', and therefore as governor general he had been obliged to conform to these forms of governance. Edmund Burke, who led the prosecution, condemned this as the rule of 'geographical morality' (Robins, 2006: 134), but it was Hastings's view of 'Asiatic' morality that informed subsequent moves undertaken by the new governor general, Lord Cornwallis, to curb corruption. In an early step towards the explicitly racialised hierarchies and racial segregation which were increasingly to characterise British colonial rule during the nineteenth century, these involved embarking on the 'Europeanization' of the civil services in India and purging the administration of Indians, who were considered incapable of honesty. Cornwallis notoriously remarked: 'every native of India, I verily believe, is corrupt' (Robins, 2006: 137).

As this suggests, the very practices that facilitated the plunder that laid the foundations of the European Industrial Revolution, and that have remained central to capitalist forms of accumulation, were externalised and projected onto the non-European other. This process was, of course, inseparable from the construction of what Said calls the 'idea of Europe', and in this case specifically the construction of notions of 'justice' and 'fair play' as uniquely British, which was consolidated during the course of the nineteenth century and is now, as we have seen, being invoked as part of the 'legacy' of empire. As Cowen and Shenton argue, in nineteenth-century discourses of development 'corruption' was closely associated with the stagnation that marked non-European societies, and this underpinned the necessity of 'trusteeship', which was to be exercised 'despotically by an incorruptible imperial cadre' (Cowen and Shenton, 1995: 41). Even more broadly, the racialisation of corruption coincided with the consolidation of the central trope of capitalism: that of capitalist markets as free, fair, impersonal and objective, and the accompanying assumption that injustice can only arise through interference in the operation of such markets.

As Padideh Ala'i points out, Hastings's principle of 'geographical morality' was re-invoked by ideologues of US capital throughout the Cold War period, who argued that different 'cultural practices' in relation to business justified kickbacks and other forms of bribery and extortion engaged in by Western corporations in their dealings with Third World governments (see Ala'i, 2000 for a discussion of this).[8] Today, however, its core assumptions of a racialised hierarchy of affinity with liberal morality have been incorporated into the good governance model – a new mode of intervention and control over these governments and their peoples.

This discourse has facilitated an unprecedented degree of involvement – by donor governments as well as international financial institutions, directly and via NGO networks – in the day-to-day decision-making of ostensibly sovereign states, leading to what Williams and Young (2009: 113) describe as an 'extraordinary range of forms of internal restructuring'. As Graham Harrison argues, 'rather than conceptualizing donor power as a strong external force on the state, it would be more useful to conceive of donors as *part of the state itself*' (Harrison, 2001: 669, emphasis in original). Harrison suggests that the governance architecture, which was underpinned by the World Bank's Highly Indebted Poor Countries (HIPC) scheme introduced in 1996, 'enabled the expansion of neoliberal social practice and facilitated increasingly ambitious discourses of social engineering – away from macroeconomic recalibrating "shocks" … and towards deeper social transitions' (Harrison, 2010: 42–3).

The imposition of conditionalities gave way to 'country ownership' as the preferred description of these relationships in the 2000s, reflecting the perceived success of earlier policies in consolidating leaders, ruling parties and administrators who fully shared a neoliberal consensus, and were now constructed as 'owning' the policies rather than being coerced into adopting them. But in practice this has meant more rather than less external control over policy. The 'ownership' approach, whose advent was heralded by the World Bank's 1998 'Comprehensive Development Framework' (CDF), did not in fact abandon conditionality; rather, it represented a shift from 'policy-change conditionality', in which countries were required to change policies as a condition for receiving loans, to 'selectivity', in which existing policies determine a country's eligibility for loans (Owusu, 2003; Harrison, 2010). At the same time direct control over policymaking has been extended. For example, the Poverty Reduction Strategy Papers which national governments have been required to formulate since 1999 have to be explicitly approved by the World Bank and the IMF (Cammack, 2003; Hulme and Scott, 2010).

It can be argued that the last decade, which has seen the emergence of the 'Post-Washington Consensus', incorporating strategies of managing poverty and 'social risk' into the neoliberal framework (largely by promoting 'participation', 'co-responsibility' and 'self-help' among the poor, as discussed in Chapter 2), has also witnessed a broadening of neoliberal hegemony among states and ruling classes. For example, Francis Owusu analyses the New Partnership for Africa's Development (NEPAD) programme adopted by the African Union in 2001, and initiated by Thabo Mbeki of South Africa, along with Nigerian president Olusegun Obasanjo and Senegalese president Abdoulaye Wade, as demonstrating an unprecedented convergence with the approach of the World Bank (Owusu, 2003). As Graham Harrison argues, 'it is through these reforms that neoliberalism has become increasingly "embedded" within African states, producing transnational communities of neoliberal practice within their broader ambit' even as the 'social base for neoliberalism' remains extremely narrow (Harrison, 2010: 59–60).

The World Bank's evident preoccupation with producing elites with a world-view and a transformative agenda compatible with the demands of globalised metropolitan capital – what the Bank's 1997 report described as 'competent and reputable technocrats', such as 'Chile's group of high-level advisers – the Chicago boys – and Indonesia's Berkeley mafia and Thailand's gang of four', who would be rewarded with large salaries, 'recognition, appreciation, prestige and awards' as they implement structural reform (World Bank, 1997) – reflects obvious continuities with modernisation models, as well as with the earlier colonial strategies from which they emerged. One is reminded irresistibly of Macaulay's view of the purpose of colonial education,

> to form a class who may be interpreters between us and the millions whom we govern, a class of persons Indian in blood and colour, but English in tastes, in opinions, in morals and in intellect. To that class we may leave it to refine the vernacular dialects of the country, to enrich those dialects with terms of science borrowed from the Western nomenclature, and to render them by degrees fit vehicles for conveying knowledge to the great mass of the population. (Macaulay, 1957: 729)

At the same time, and apparently contradictorily, by constructing the state and existing forms of social provision as an alien imposition, and capitalism as consonant with 'indigenous African values' (Abrahamsen, 2000: 49–51), the World Bank's governance discourse attempts to distance itself from the 'Westernising' project of developmentalism and claims to be reinstating and nurturing authentic 'African' traditions, a strategy which has a long colonial history. Where the European colonial powers selectively valorised the authoritarian and coercive aspects of social power within the multiplicity of social formations they encountered in Africa in order to consolidate indirect rule, the World Bank seized upon elements of 'indigenous' entrepreneurship and petty capitalism both to legitimise and to extend the contemporary imperialist project. This was made explicit in the 1989 World Bank report, which cited instances of 'Africa's market tradition' at some length (World Bank, 1989) and further elaborated in the 1997 report, which referred to 'traditions' of entrepreneurship and self-help as those characteristics of 'African' societies which a good governance approach would promote; not surprisingly, these are selectively chosen and reconstructed for their compatibility with neoliberal models. This strategy also illustrates how postcolonial critiques of 'Eurocentrism' have been selectively appropriated and incorporated into neoliberal discourses, a process I discuss further in Chapter 8.

Appropriating democracy

Coexisting with, and intimately related to, the governance agenda
was the decisive reconfiguration of the discursive relationship between
development and liberal democracy in the 1990s. The construction
of 'democracy' in many ways followed the same trajectory as that
of 'good governance' – shifting from a luxury which Third World
countries were not sufficiently 'civilised' to enjoy to a necessary
medicine for development which could only be correctly administered through the trusteeship of the West. In both these phases,
however, as in the case of good governance, the perceived presence
or absence of democracy was explained in ways which drew on the
notion of 'race' and racialised constructions of difference.

Within modernisation theory's narrative of linear progress for
developing nations, democracy had been seen as a long-term outcome
of development, one which would only come into effect at an
advanced stage of development. This approach, of course, was consistent with Cold War support for blatantly repressive regimes, covert
intervention to overthrow elected governments, and subsequently
sponsorship of anti-democratic armed insurgents in several continents. Walt Rostow, the founding father of modernisation theory,
and author of *The Stages of Economic Growth*, which was subtitled *A
Non-Communist Manifesto* (Rostow, 1960), was not only an economist
but directly involved in shaping US Cold War foreign policy in the
1960s as national security adviser to President Johnson, and is known
for his virulent anti-communism and his enthusiasm for escalating
the US war in Vietnam through bombing.

Abrahamsen points out that the intensification of Cold War
rivalries in the mid-1960s meant that there was a growing emphasis
on 'political order and stability' in dominant development discourses,
with democracy in Third World countries in the context of the rapid
changes associated with modernisation being increasingly constructed
as 'hazardous' (Abrahamsen, 2000: 27). In Chapter 3, we discussed
how this Cold War motif of poor countries in the global South as a
'breeding ground' for communism was informed by a longer history

of racialised fears of the dispossessed and their potential for changing the balance of power. In a widely cited example of this discourse, US social scientist Ithiel De Sola Pool wrote that

> in the Congo, in Vietnam, in the Dominican Republic, it is clear that order depends on somehow compelling newly mobilised strata to return to a measure of passivity and defeatism from which they have been aroused by the process of modernisation. At least temporarily, the maintenance of order requires a lowering of newly acquired expectations and levels of political activity. (Pool, 1967: 26)

With the advent of structural adjustment policies and neoliberal economic liberalisation in the 1980s, popular resistance to repressive regimes grew, and initially the ideologues of neoliberalism had no qualms about admitting that intensified repression and authoritarianism were inevitable if the reforms were to be implemented. World Bank economist Deepak Lal argued that a 'courageous, ruthless and perhaps undemocratic government is required to ride roughshod over newly created interest groups' (Lal, 1983, cited in Abrahamsen, 2000: 30).

In fact the pro-democracy movements which emerged in a number of African countries in the 1990s arose in opposition to the effects of economic reforms, as A.B. Zack-Williams emphasises:

> whilst external pressure grew after 1990 ... the decisive pressure for democratic change came from within Africa and this was very much precipitated by the economic crisis ... the collapsing infrastructure, the deteriorating economic situations, the falling standard of living and the absence of political space to express some of these concerns. (Zack-Williams, 2001: 217)

Partly in response to such movements, formal liberal democracy was increasingly incorporated into the neoliberal model of development as part of its recalibration in the 1990s, and donor governments introduced political as well as economic conditionalities. Electoral democracy was now specifically constructed within neoliberal discourses as inseparable from (and impossible without) economic liberalisation. The transition to electoral democracy was thus accompanied by an intensification of neoliberal restructuring, and not surprisingly in many countries the transition was also followed by popular unrest and resistance to these policies, and renewed state repression, as in Ghana (Osei, 2000), Zambia and Côte d'Ivoire (Abrahamsen, 2000).

As has been widely observed by activists and critical scholars, in the context of neoliberalism in Africa the democratic accountability of the government to the electorate is severely limited by external control over economic policies. The outcome of the transitions promoted by the representatives of global capital has thus been characterised as 'thin' democracy (Saul, 1997), with a key distinction being drawn between the 'liberal democracy' espoused by the IFIs and 'popular democracy' based on mass movements, which implies 'an ideology of resistance and struggle ... which articulates anti-imperialism and anti-compradore state positions' (Shivji, 1991: 255).

Crucially, the 'democracy' being promoted by Northern donors does not offer people the choice of challenging the terms of their insertion into a racialised global hierarchy; nor does it allow them to make claims on their state which might protect them from its fatal material and embodied effects. Thus, for example, while Amartya Sen identifies democracy as an important safeguard against famine (Sen, 1999), the existence of electoral democracy in Malawi failed to prevent the deaths that took place during the 2002 famine, which was caused largely by agricultural policies dictated by the IMF and donor agencies, in particular the dismantling of the system of grain reserves and the removal of food subsidies under the direction of the IMF (Devereux, 2002; Owusu and Ng'ambi, 2002). As Dzodzi Tsikata argues in the context of the current promotion of 'rights based approaches' (RBAs) by development institutions and NGOs,

> Much of the discussion about responsibility and accountability has been in terms of what governments of developing countries need to do differently. Given the dismantling and disabling of the state under structural adjustment, the proactive role being given to the state under the RBAs is unrealistic. Even more significant is the fact that not much is being directed towards the accountability

of the IFIs, transnational corporations, western governments and international NGOs. Thus it seems that it would not stick if citizens of certain African countries were to accuse the IMF and World Bank of human rights violations on account of SAPs resulting in increased levels of poverty. Or would it? (Tsikata, 2004)

The concepts of good governance and democracy, underpinned as we have seen by racialised notions of trusteeship, and operating to sustain and extend global structures of inequality, also intersect with the 'humanitarian imperialist' approaches discussed earlier in this chapter, and their preoccupation with the identification of 'failed', or, as they are now known in the ever-changing discourse of neoliberal imperialism, 'fragile' states. These in turn became targets for intervention, with the avowed goal, in the words of the US government's 2006 National Security Strategy, of 'bring[ing] ungoverned areas under the control of effective democracies' (Ploch, 2011: 14).

On the one hand, then, these concepts are a part of the architecture of development aid, which works to promote neoliberal economic and social transformations and to produce 'native' elites prepared to declare 'ownership' of them. On the other hand, equally importantly, surveillance of governance, democracy and rights can be used to demonstrate that states are failing, in order to legitimise even more direct military intervention.

Since the decade of the 1990s, which has been the focus of this chapter, this distinction itself has become increasingly blurred as the development/security approach becomes central to the framing of the imperialist project. So-called 'civil–military operations' are defined by the US military as 'the activities of a commander that establish, maintain, influence, or exploit relations between military forces, governmental and nongovernmental civilian organizations and authorities, and the civilian populace ... in order to facilitate military operations, to consolidate and achieve operational US objectives' (US Joint Chiefs of Staff, 2008). They aim to 'synchronize military and nonmilitary instruments of national power, particularly in support of stability, counterinsurgency and other operations dealing with asymmetric and irregular threats'. These 'threats' include 'ethnic and religious conflict, cultural and socioeconomic differences, terrorism and insurgencies, the proliferation of weapons of mass destruction, international organised crime, incidental and deliberate population migration, environmental degradation, infectious diseases, and sharpening competition/exploitation of dwindling natural resources'. Civil–military operations may involve US military forces taking over 'activities and functions normally the responsibility of the local, regional, or national government' (US Joint Chiefs of Staff, 2008: I–3). Such operations are becoming an increasingly central mode of development intervention, not only in occupied countries like Afghanistan but also in many parts of Africa, where control over resources and governments has become, as the establishment of AFRICOM highlights, a geostrategic and economic priority for the USA,[9] and are currently being visualised as the setting for intensified competition and even projected conflict between the USA and China (Holslag, 2009). The following chapter considers questions of 'race', imperialism and accumulation in the context of the development/security paradigm.

CHAPTER 6

Imperialism, accumulation
and racialised embodiment

I still think today as yesterday that the color line is a great problem
of this century. But today I see more clearly than yesterday that
back of the problem of race and color, lies a greater problem which
both obscures and implements it: and that is the fact that so many
civilized persons are willing to live in comfort even if the price
of this is poverty, ignorance and disease of the majority of their
fellowmen; that to maintain this privilege men have waged war
until today war tends to become universal and continuous, and the
excuse for this war continues largely to be color and race.

W.E.B. Du Bois, preface to the 1953 edition
of *The Souls of Black Folk* (Du Bois 1962)

The early twenty-first-century conjuncture of aggressive neoliberal
imperialism, in which development has been increasingly recast
and revalorised as metropolitan security, has been the context for
more focused theorising of the relationship between 'development'
and notions of empire, variously conceived. However, as we will
see, with some notable exceptions[1] 'race' remains curiously elided
from much of this work, which has taken place primarily within
an international relations framework. This chapter engages with
this approach and in particular its use of Foucauldian notions of
biopower. It argues that while there are important insights to be
gained from these analyses which focus on sustainable development
as a 'security technology' of containment, they fail to acknowledge
the extractive and accumulative aspects of global capitalist processes
taking place within the framework of 'development'. It suggests
that this neglect of the material processes underpinning imperial
intervention, and the related understanding of race as an exclusively

discursive concept, may help to explain why 'the racial ... aspects of colonialism' are assumed to have been superseded and to be 'now routinely rejected' (Duffield and Hewitt, 2009: 10) in these accounts. The chapter then goes on to discuss attempts to 'research racial formations beyond ideology, through materiality, embodiment and spatiality' (Chari, 2008: 1907), which have characterised some recent work in critical human geography. The third section focuses on the importance of addressing questions of racialised embodiment in the context of global processes of accumulation. It draws on feminist poststructuralist and postcolonial insight into the production of the embodied subject alongside Marxist theorising of the relationship between capital and embodiment, and historical materialist analyses of 'race' in the metropolis, to move towards an understanding of development, 'race' and racism which encompasses key questions of embodiment, labour, land, processes of accumulation and contemporary imperialism.

Development as biopower

Foucault's notion of biopower, in which populations are managed and regulated through technologies of surveillance and monitoring, has been a productive one for recent critical work on development.[2] This understanding of biopower is predicated on a shift in the nature of power associated with the emergence of capitalism. Pre-existing 'sovereign' power, defined as the power to 'let live or make die', is replaced by biopower, which conversely seeks to 'make live' within a framework of far more intensive – while less visible – processes of intervention, regulation, surveillance and discipline, which produce the 'docile bodies' and the subjectivities required for capitalist production. The Foucauldian approach has a number of aspects which have seemed to make it particularly appropriate for theorising development (and in particular its continuities with colonialism): its emphasis on the regulation of populations through enumeration, categorisation and measurement; its conceptual focus on the discursive production of consent through 'processes of subjectivisation' rather than the coercive aspects of power; and its theorisation of the co-constitutive relationship of power and knowledge. Foucault's ideas were incorporated extensively in the work of postcolonial theorists (most notably in Said's concept of Orientalism, 1978), but a number of writers have commented on the absence of any explicit engagement with colonialism in Foucault's own work; and on the apparent failure to recognise that the practices he describes were not merely adopted but originated and were perfected under conditions of colonial rule (Young, 1995; see Stoler, 1995 for a different reading of Foucault).

Mark Duffield (2005, 2006), who has deployed a biopower framework extensively in his work on contemporary development and the emergence of the development/security nexus, highlights, however, that Foucault drew a distinction between the biopolitics of 'mass society' in advanced capitalist/metropolitan social formations with various forms of state provision ensuring the reproduction of life, and that of populations in the global South which are 'non-insured' and expected to be self-reliant and self-reproducing (Duffield, 2005: 145–6). 'Self-reproduction', Duffield argues, 'has long been axiomatic for people understood through the register of tradition, simplicity, backwardness and race' (146). Maintaining this self-reliance in order both to contain migration to the global North and to counter 'extremism' and other 'threats to international security' becomes a key objective of contemporary biopolitics (Duffield, 2006). In this context, Duffield provides a powerful critique of discourses and practices of sustainable development which he sees as emerging from and structured by these objectives. He suggests that the rise of sustainable development as the dominant development paradigm marked a break with the 'aspirational goal' of modernisation theory, which claimed that living standards in the 'underdeveloped' world would eventually come to resemble those in the 'developed' countries (Duffield, 2005: 152). Instead, the strategy was now to promote self-reliance in the interests of containment. In a telling example, he cites an OECD Development Assistance Committee (DAC) report on 'terrorism prevention' which emphasises that 'education that spreads

faster than jobs is potentially destabilising since it heightens awareness of inequalities and hence breeds frustration' and that education
and training imparted to young people as part of donor-funded
programmes should be mindful of 'the feasibility of their aspirations'
(DAC, 2003, cited in Duffield, 2005: 155).

However, the biopower approach as adopted by Duffield and
other critical development theorists tends to marginalise processes
of extraction, exploitation and accumulation within imperialism.
Whereas for Foucauldian theorists, both colonial strategies and
contemporary development interventions have focused on managing populations and preventing or containing threats to security
through making these populations self-reliant, for Marxist theorists
of development, resources are continuously being extracted from
these populations through a variety of processes, and this (rather
than solely containment) continues to be the central *raison d'être* of
imperialism.

An analysis which excludes contemporary processes of extraction
of natural resources, exploitation of labour and expansion of markets
by global capital leaves much unexplained. In the context of the
discussion above, for example, it does not highlight that the shift
from modernising developmentalism to sustainable development as
the key development paradigm was driven by the rise to dominance
of neoliberalism as the strategy through which increasingly mobile
global capital would sustain and expand accumulation. This neglect
may be attributable to the adoption of Foucault's later conceptualisation of power as circulating and all-pervasive, which militates against
a focus on the class character or objectives of states or international
development institutions, or the concentration of power in specific
locations.[3] But it has significant implications. The recent trajectory of neoliberalism disrupts any clear-cut dichotomy between the
'insured' populations of the global North and the 'non-insured' and
self-reproducing populations of the global South, through both the
generalised dismantling of social provision in the countries of the
global North and the proliferation of excluded spaces and populations
within them. More importantly still, contemporary development

interventions do not always 'promote life' or self-reproduction: on the contrary, they frequently fatally disrupt these processes, as for example in the case of corporate displacement of poor communities in India for the purposes of extracting minerals or turning agricultural land into real estate, or, as we have seen, policies which allowed the withholding of treatment from people living with HIV in the global South in order to enhance the profits of pharmaceuticals corporations. Constructions of race which assign these lives less value make these deaths allowable.[4] Duffield mobilises Foucault's notion of the power to 'allow death' (or 'let die'), which complements the power to 'make live', in a discussion of the treatment of suspects in the War on Terror and other people considered 'threats to security' (Duffield, 2006), but in general there is little emphasis in the Foucauldian literature on the fact that the daily exercise of this power is integral to contemporary neoliberal development itself.

A recent collection of essays explicitly addresses the question of 'empire, development and colonialism', seeking to trace continuities and parallels between 'contemporary debates on socio-economic development, humanitarian intervention, and aid, and the historical artefacts and strategies of Empire' (Duffield and Hewitt, 2009: 1). Interestingly, with some notable exceptions (see, for example, the contributions by Patricia Noxolo, Paul Keleman and April Biccum), the contributors focus not on patterns of imperial accumulation, nor on constructions of race, but on liberal theory and practice as the locus of continuity between colonialism and development, primarily adopting a Foucauldian lens to theorise power. This produces some peculiar formulations and striking silences. For example, in a discussion of 'trusteeship and intervention' which aims to draw out parallels and continuities between colonial and contemporary forms of intervention for social transformation (with a focus on the World Bank), Williams and Young reduce the place of racism in the discourse of the civilising mission to an afterthought: a 'racial gloss' which makes it 'repulsive to modern liberal ears' but is merely a distraction from the 'very strong assertions of the universality of human nature' on which the authors wish us to focus our attention

(Williams and Young, 2009: 102). They go on to highlight the parallels between the nineteenth-century colonial civilising mission and elite interventions in the lives of the poor in England in the same period as evidence of this universalism. This ignores, first, the entire body of work which explains how evolving ideas about 'race' and racial superiority informed the pathologisation of the dispossessed poor in England (Magubane, 2004). In fact, ironically, this constant cross-referencing of racialised tropes is inadvertently underlined when the authors cite the construction of the Manchester masses as 'heathens' (Williams and Young, 2009: 103). Second, it bypasses extensive scholarship on the way constructions of 'race', and specifically of 'whiteness', evolved over this period in the nineteenth century, only gradually becoming inclusive of the metropolitan working class and, later still, the Irish. Williams and Young, in contrast, seem to regard racial categories as fixed and ahistorical, and apply contemporary definitions of whiteness anachronistically, writing for example that 'a kind of practical historicism was by no means limited to exotic "others" but informed thinking and practice about Ireland, Scotland and England itself' (103), in reference to a period when the Irish, in particular, were clearly 'othered' in ways which were unmistakably racialised.

Inextricable it seems from the disavowal of the centrality of race in colonial processes is the minimising of the processes of extraction and exploitation which shaped colonial interventions, in favour of an emphasis on the 'element of international tutelage' (Williams and Young, 2009: 103). Somewhat startlingly in the context of the critical approach of the volume and of earlier work by the authors themselves, the essay rehearses the well-worn discursive strategy of minimising the extraction underpinning colonial regimes in general by citing the deviant 'exception' which supposedly proves the rule: the Belgian Congo. 'The notoriously brutal and really extractive (private) regime of Leopold II in the Congo', we are reminded, 'was eventually terminated through pressure from the major powers' (103). Thus extraction and exploitation are characterised (along with brutality) as aberrations engaged in by the irresponsible lesser European powers, which had no place in the benevolent mainstream of colonial rule. The racialised colonial narrative of the civilising mission, then, is reconstituted, albeit in somewhat Foucauldian language.

Similarly, when Williams and Young turn to contemporary interventions, there is little consideration of the role of changing patterns of global capital accumulation in driving these interventions. The authors trace the increasing restriction of sovereignty in the post-Cold War period and examine the rise of various direct and indirect forms of intervention, particularly those led by the World Bank. But there is no clear distinction drawn in this approach between the (limited) form of economic nationalism tolerated by the Western powers in return for strategic geopolitical support in the era of developmentalism and the unflinching commitment to global capital and full 'ownership' of policies involving dismantling their national economies which leaders were required to demonstrate with the advent of neoliberalism. Strikingly, Williams and Young's critical account makes no reference to the extensive economic critiques of structural adjustment policies of the 1980s, seeming to take the World Bank's own explanation based on institutional failure (which became the justification for political conditionalities in the 1990s) at face value (Williams and Young, 2009: 109). This is consistent with their contention that conditionalities 'are not usefully understood as in the interest of more powerful states but are designed to effect policy changes within target states' (108).

The exclusive preoccupation with universalising tendencies within interventionist projects thus seeks to minimise their role in reproducing and intensifying both inequality and difference across space. In particular, as we saw above, it delegitimises the question of how these inequalities are structured by, and articulated through, race. Thus colonial interventions in practices deemed 'repugnant to civilisation' (such as *sati* in India, or polygamy), which have been the focus of an extensive postcolonial feminist critique, are here blandly cited as an inevitable consequence of 'a commitment to some notions of development which clearly tracked metropolitan norms (wage labour, housing, welfare and family structures, education)'

(Williams and Young, 2009: 104)[5] With race – as well as gender – apparently considered irrelevant even in the colonial context, it is hardly surprising that the racialised aspects of the contemporary 'liberal project in Africa' and its production of 'the right kind of individual' (113) are nowhere to be seen in this account.

I am by no means suggesting here that liberalism and universalist discourses should not be a central element in an analysis of imperialism – whether in its historical or contemporary manifestations. The shift in the approach of nineteenth-century liberal thought to the imperial project has been extensively analysed (see, for example, Mehta, 1999; Pitts, 2006). In a more general sense, as we have discussed, the key liberal concept of human progress has underpinned both colonial and development projects and is, as Duffield and Hewitt (2009: 2) suggest, an important basis for exploring comparisons and continuities between the two. Rather, I am concerned to highlight the silences and elisions that are produced when liberalism is considered in isolation from two other questions – those of race and capital. These three questions, I would argue, have been and remain mutually constitutive. The relationships between the development of Enlightenment liberal universalism, the consolidation of concepts of race, and the emergence of capitalism out of slavery and colonialism have been traced and theorised in depth elsewhere. I suggest that any project that seeks to explore the facets of contemporary development-as-imperialism must also consider these three questions in relation to each other.

The focus on liberal notions of social engineering as the main axis of comparison between colonialism and development also seems frequently to be associated with two assumptions: first, that coercion and violence have been overemphasised in earlier analyses of colonialism; and second, that coercion cannot be central to a characterisation of development. The starting point of Foucauldian theorists of contemporary development is clearly very different from that of the current crop of revisionist conservative historians of colonialism such as Niall Ferguson and Andrew Roberts: as Duffield and Hewitt stress, 'isolating a liberal colonialism should not be confused with attempts to rehabilitate the colonial project' (2009: 10). But, undeniably, they share with the latter a suspicion of analyses of colonial interventions (often by Third World Marxist scholars) in which exploitation and coercion are central.

Even more importantly for our current discussion, coercion is assumed to be marginal in contemporary development processes, to be, in fact, the grounds on which any comparison between colonialism and development must inevitably falter. Yet coercion and violence are inherent in development interventions. A broad conceptualisation of development such as the one used in this book encompasses the visceral corporate- and state-sponsored violence accompanying the contemporary extraction of resources – from the bauxite mountains of Odisha in India to the oilfields of the Niger Delta. But even if we accept a narrower understanding of development, one which is limited to the infrastructure of government aid departments, NGOs and international financial institutions, the structural violence of coercively imposed neoliberal economic policies seems difficult to ignore. The market fundamentalism and racialised disregard for human life of colonial administrations, which fuelled the El Niño famines of the nineteenth century, echo in the early twenty-first century's policy-driven famines and epidemics brought on by the dictates of the IMF.

It appears that many critical development and international relations theorists inspired by Foucault see capitalism as a set of relationships requiring constant management but as essentially static, in contrast to a Marxist understanding of capitalism as a mode of production with its own constantly expanding and changing dynamics, and multiple forms of articulation with other modes. The extent to which this reflects Foucault's own work is questionable. There is considerable scope for a different interpretation in, for example, Foucault's statement that 'bio-power was without question an indispensible element in the development of capitalism; the latter would not have been possible without the controlled insertion of bodies into the machinery of production and the adjustment of the phenomena of population to economic processes' (1980; cited in Chari, 2008: 1909). Relatedly, resistance tends to be underplayed in these accounts, although, again, Foucault's conceptualisation of resistance as always inherent within the operation of power is open to multiple interpretations.

My argument in this chapter is that neglect of the specificities of accumulation processes and the inequalities they build upon and reproduce, and of how these are experienced in ways which are material and embodied, actually makes it easier to marginalise questions of racism and racialised relations of power, and to view them as no longer relevant. Since race is understood solely as a discursive strategy of power in the critiques of the development/security paradigm, its apparent absence from development discourse[6] appears to render race unworthy of serious consideration in the context of development. As race is rarely explicitly cited as a justification for subordination, or for the treatment of certain groups of people as less than human, it is assumed to be marginal to the contemporary operations of power. This is the phenomenon David Theo Goldberg (2009: 1) refers to when he argues that 'being against race' does not constitute 'the end of racism', and that the disavowal of 'race' as a meaningful category or 'antiracialism' is not sufficient to bring down (and even helps to sustain) historically embedded racialised structures of inequality.

Some observers characterise this change as a shift from 'biological' to 'socio-cultural' racism: Étienne Balibar's 'racism without races' (Balibar, 1992). But it is important not to interpret this as implying a shift away from questions of embodiment in the operation of racism: rather, in this context 'culture' becomes inseparable from particular bodies; it comes to represent a series of essentialised and embodied characteristics in a way which is by no means completely distinct from biological definitions of 'race', a process which can be seen very clearly in the context of contemporary anti-Muslim racism and the 'War on Terror'.

In his recent book *The Threat of Race*, Goldberg argues that to understand these 'new modes of debilitation and degradation, humiliation and dehumanisation' (Goldberg, 2009: 361) we must think not only of 'racism without race' but of 'racisms without racism'. In explanation of this, he suggests that current processes in which certain groups come to be seen as less than human are increasingly detached from the particular histories of racialisation associated with biological racism: 'the modes, forms, sociologics, even their rationales more often than not mimic classic racisms. But they lack the sharpness of their identifying account or defining contours, torn as they are from the classic conditions of their articulation' (361). This view has become increasingly prevalent in critical understandings of the contemporary workings of race. Yet while it is crucial to recognise the mutability of racism and the changing forms of its articulation, it is surely also vital that we continue to historicise it, and perhaps inevitable that we do so when contemporary links and continuities with the forms of racialisation associated with Atlantic slavery and European colonialism are so glaring and so direct. Contemporary demonisations of Islam, for example, though nebulous and flexible, inescapably reflect, reproduce and extend their colonial precursors; on another, more specific, level, our understanding of the racialised dehumanisation which makes possible the official US use of the term 'bugsplat' to describe the killings of civilians (many of them children) in Pakistan in drone attacks deepens when we consider how 'classic' racism legitimated the bombing and gassing of unarmed Iraqi Kurdish civilians in the first ever aerial bombing in the 1920s. These connections, which relate to embodied experiences as much as to discursive constructions, suggest that it is still possible, and I would argue necessary, to consider 'race' as continuous, although changing, across time and space. I explore this further in the remainder of this chapter.

Space and race

In comparison to the fields of development and international relations, questions of race and racism have been addressed much more centrally in work that has taken place within the framework of critical human geography, which has addressed questions of 'spatial and racial control' and how 'racial geographies embed distributions of group-targeted fatalities viscerally and tangibly into bodies, landscapes, built environments and "second natures"' (Chari, 2008: 1911).

This strand of work roots race and racism strongly in the material: as Sharad Chari (2008) points out, it has drawn on influential Marxist thinkers in geography (notably Henri Lefebvre, David Harvey and Doreen Massey) who have theorised the production, structuring and destruction of space at multiple scales by capital. This work has also been informed by Foucauldian biopolitics, but significantly it has focused much more extensively on how biopolitics selectively excludes populations through racial differentiation and exercises the power to 'let die' in multiple contexts. This also reflects an engagement with Giorgio Agamben's influential conceptualisation of 'bare life' and 'spaces of exception' (1998). For Agamben, at the core of 'Western politics' or modern bourgeois democracy is the duality of bare life versus political existence, in which bare life is excluded from politics and devoid of rights – 'life exposed to death'. Agamben 'treats the concentration camp in general and Auschwitz in particular as the paradigmatic space of political modernity' (Gregory, 2006). In his analysis of the Nazi concentration camps, he argues that states and spaces of exception in which the suspension of the 'normal' becomes the rule and some human beings are constituted as bare life are 'the hidden foundation on which the entire political system rested' (Agamben, 1998: 9).

Agamben argues that the notions of bare life and states of exception are implicit in the relation between nation and citizenship in bourgeois democracy, and (like much critical race theory) focuses on exclusion as constitutive of political systems. Given this, it is particularly striking, and indicative of the extent of racialised silencing, that Atlantic plantation slavery as the primary paradigm for global capital accumulation, incarceration, bare life, and states and spaces of exception has not been addressed centrally in Agamben's analysis or in general in the work of those influenced by his ideas (a notable exception is Achille Mbembe's 'Necropolitics', 2003).

But Agamben's ideas of biopower, spaces of exception and bare life have been applied extensively in work relating to, in particular, the 'War on Terror' (including Agamben's own influential *State of Exception*, 2005), Palestine, HIV/AIDS, migrant domestic workers and immigration detainees. In many of these contexts, questions of how 'race' is embedded in and structures them are explored. This work also shares some key preoccupations with Fanon's analysis of colonised spaces in *The Wretched of the Earth* (Fanon, 1967b) and later scholarship on this theme by postcolonial theorists. As Gregory writes in the context of incarcerations in the War on Terror, 'I treat the global war prison as neither a paroxysmal nor a paradigmatic but a potential space of political modernity, which is given form and force through a profoundly colonial apparatus of power that the metropolitan preoccupations of Foucault and Agamben more or less erase' (Gregory, 2006).

However, the focus on control over spaces has meant that much of this work has been preoccupied with spaces of incarceration and/or military occupation, to the exclusion of wider processes which may be taking place beyond (as well as within) these delimited spaces in the name of development. These include both appropriation of land and resources and displacement of people, as well as direct exploitation of labour.[7]

Race, development and embodiment

In seeking to bring labour, capital and global circuits of accumulation within the same frame as the contemporary reproduction of race and the disciplinary technologies of development, questions of embodiment emerge as central.

As should be evident, the focus on the body here (and in the work of a number of writers whose ideas are discussed in what follows) reflects a complex engagement with the concept of 'race' itself. To recap, while rejecting biological explanations for the distinctions of race, and recognising race as a mutable and contingent social construction, I am simultaneously aware that this construction structures material relations of inequality in multiple ways. And while bodies do not bear race within them *a priori*, but are racialised through identifiable social processes, making possible specific forms of exploitation and expropriation, race is lived and felt through material and embodied experiences. In this sense, then, I echo Linda Martín Alcoff's reminder that 'race is real' (2001: 268).

In exploring the materiality of race in the context of global processes I highlight how social processes materially shape corporeality. Drawing upon Elizabeth Grosz's 'corporeal feminism', Alcoff writes that 'the body itself is a dynamic material domain, not just because it can be "seen" differently, but because the materiality of the body is … volatile.' Historical and social factors 'actively produce' the body (2006: 185). My approach is on one level consistent with Arun Saldanha's injunction to 'think and write about physical bodies' while recognising that 'corporeality is itself open to transformation and contestation' (Saldanha, 2006: 12–15). But whereas Saldanha focuses on corporeality as physical appearance, I am concerned broadly with the body as lived experience, and find that historical materialism is particularly useful in addressing these questions.

Producing racialised bodies

Sara Ahmed has explored how race is lived through the body in ways that are closely related to the racialisation of space. In *Strange Encounters* (2000) she examines how people are racialised by being recognised as strangers, as 'bodies out of place'. She describes 'how the recognition of strangers involves the demarcation, not only of social space, but also bodily space.… strange bodies are produced through tactile encounters with other bodies: differences are not marked *on* the stranger's body, but come to materialize in the relationship of touch between bodies' (2000: 15). As Ahmed suggests, this builds on and extends Fanon's idea of the gaze in which racialised subjectivities are generated through everyday encounters. Citing Fanon's *Black Skin, White Masks*, she writes: 'It is the seeing of the body which transforms it into both an object and other: "and already I am being dissected under white eyes, the only real eyes. I am fixed"' (Ahmed, 2002: 56). It is also closely linked to feminist theorising that questions the mind/body and sex/gender dualisms and investigates the social production of bodies. Rejecting the understanding of the body as a 'prima facie given' (Butler, 1990: 176), Judith Butler argues that the body is 'not a "being" but a variable boundary, a surface whose permeability is politically regulated' (189).[8] Further, the outcome of this regulation is not determined, as for Butler the constitution of the subject is a constantly repeated process, an iterable procedure open to resignification and subversion (189). Ahmed applies this to race in the sense that 'Racialisation involves the production of "the racial body" through knowledge, as well as the constitution of both social and bodily space in the everyday encounters we have with others"' (Ahmed, 2002: 47).

However, phenomenological feminist work has highlighted the limits to day-to-day mutability posed by material embodiment, while avoiding a return to essentialism through a central focus on 'the body as historical and social' (Alcoff, 2006: 163). This understanding becomes particularly important, I suggest below, in considering 'race' and racialisation in spatial contexts where 'the everyday encounters we have with others' are not *directly* structured by 'race'.

The racialised production of bodies

The discursively produced body within poststructuralist thought has often been contrasted with what is assumed to be a universal, natural, human body within Marxism. But historical materialism is distinct from other modern systems of thought in this respect. Bodies are understood as continuously produced by social relations, and Marx's and Engels's writing on the day-to-day experiences of workers in capitalist industrial production in England highlighted this corporeality inescapably. As Reecia Orzeck emphasises, 'Marx's ... basic argument is that *every* mode of production – that is, every *social* formation aimed at reproducing itself – produces bodies particular to it' (Orzeck, 2007: 500, emphasis in original). Further, the ways in which, through the division of labour, capital both incorporates and produces embodied difference are central to capitalism (Orzeck, 2007: 502; Harvey, 1998). This question of, as Stuart Hall has put it, 'how the regime of capital can function through differentiation and difference, rather than through similarity and identity' (Hall, 1996: 24) has been an important starting point for Marxist analysis of the body.

But diverging from poststructuralist approaches, Marxism regards bodies as produced not only through processes of signification, but materially through processes of production and reproduction. Social processes thus not only affect how the body is made visible and understood but also physically transform its materiality. Further, the historical materialist approach to the body, while it recognises the daily reproduction of social relations through repeated, although constantly reconfigured, practices within processes of production, circulation and consumption,[9] also places emphasis on historical processes of change. Arguably, then, there is more focus on the production of bodies as a historical process, or the embodiment of history through its accumulated effects, which may constrain the 'openness' and iterability of the production of the embodied subject. This is of particular relevance for an understanding of race and embodiment in the context of development, as we will see.

Within Marx's own writing – and Marxist work more generally – on embodiment, the focus has been on how capital produces particular bodies through the labour process. The corporeal experience of labour within nineteenth-century metropolitan capitalism and its long-term effects on labouring bodies is viscerally described in Marx (see, for example, *Capital*, Volume 1 on 'The Working Day') and in Engels's *The Condition of the Working Class in England* (see also Fracchia, 2008). As Orzeck elaborates in the context of contemporary capitalism,

> different types of labour transform the body in different ways. Workers lose limbs, digits, fingernails, eyes; they develop repetitive strain injuries, respiratory diseases, skin diseases, diseases from exposure to asbestos, pesticides, and other hazardous substances. Equally material are the transformations of the body that take place beyond the workplace which owe their existence not to a type of work but to a worker's location within the nexus of social relations which include uneven development and the division of labour as well as structural factors such as racism and patriarchy. Income, access to healthcare and education, environmental racism, etc. are all, like occupational injury and disease, factors that shape bodies, and frequently in ways that are both deleterious and indelible. (2007: 503)

The central place of race in the material production of labouring bodies by global capitalism is both epitomised by and still shaped by the rationalised racial terror[10] of Atlantic slavery, which underpinned and made possible the emergence of industrial capitalism in Europe. As we have noted in Chapter 1, a number of writers have explored the implications of a system in which not only labour but labourers themselves were considered to be commodities, arguing that the exclusion from 'personhood' of enslaved African people which this entailed is not an anomaly but rather is constitutive of capitalist universalism. Understood discursively, colonial racialisation, which was also inextricably gendered, was always inseparably linked to the global division of labour, legitimising the differential insertion of labouring bodies into the colonial economy.[11] But this process also differentially transformed bodies and lived corporeal experiences in ways that include, but are not limited to, the construction of racialised subjectivities.

If the effects of relations of production on labourers have understandably been the main focus of Marxist work on the body, in order to understand material embodiment in the context of imperialism and develop an approach to race that is useful beyond advanced capitalist contexts, we need to view the production of bodies through a wider lens, which encompasses but is not limited to the experiences of workers within direct capital–labour relations. Here we can make use of David Harvey's formulation, which seeks 'to broaden somewhat the conventional Marxian definition of "class" (or, more exactly, of "class relation") to mean *positionality in relation to capital circulation and accumulation*' (Harvey, 1998: 405, emphasis in original). This allows us to consider questions of the racialised production of bodies and the corporality of development more directly. It still allows us to look at the role of direct production relations (which itself encompasses, for example, women workers in global factories, but also women agricultural labourers employed by contract farmers supplying corporates, or women engaged in small-scale production for microcredit schemes financed by transnational banks). But it also means that we can consider other, closely related, processes associated with capital circulation and accumulation such as displacement and dispossession, population control interventions or denial of life-saving drugs, and their corporeal effects. Whether we look at the unequal and debilitating burdens of corporate environmental destruction, the impacts of imperialist war such as the use of depleted uranium, blockades and sanctions, the complex of forces which leads to 'foreshortened lives' among poor African Americans (Gilmore, 2007), or the invasive reach of population control technologies, those racialised bodies which are less valued and which it is considered legitimate to subject to these processes are also those which are shaped by the lived experience of them in multiple ways. These are, then, the bodies which become the racialised objects of development, essentialised as inherently 'less' healthy, nourished or productive.

How, then, do we avoid the trap of reinstating the idea of the body as a passive object, while taking into account the accumulated effects of these processes and the constraints they imply for the day-to-day reconstitution or contestation of corporeality? David Harvey has outlined some of the ways in which Marx's work may be used to address this question (Harvey, 1998), exploring how the concept of 'living labour', in combination with a Marxist understanding of the political, can be taken to imply both the production of the body by capital and the body as the 'locus of political action' (Harvey, 1998: 414). It seems evident that the many forms of collective resistance to the processes referred to above – for example, struggles for living wages, against food price rises triggered by neoliberal policies, against corporate takeover of land, or for access to ARVs – not only have bodily implications, but directly contest the racialised material production of bodies we have discussed. This perspective also opens up new possibilities for the theorisation of agency in the context of collective action (see Wilson, 2007, 2012) and, in particular, the implications for this when embodied experiences are shared.

While Foucauldian approaches to development have productively analysed the targeting and disciplining of the body by development interventions, they have not, in general, emphasised the materiality of these interventions and the resistance they generate, or their corporeal effects. The approach I suggest here may make it possible to link race more directly to accumulation processes, and may thus be applicable beyond specifically racialised social formations, helping us to locate race in the global political economy without universalising locally specific racialisations. To summarise, it may be useful to extend the focus from the (discursive) *production of racialised bodies*, to encompass the *racialised production of* (material) *bodies*.

As the preceding discussion suggests, this global racialised production of material bodies is by definition a process which operates differentially according to 'positionality in relation to capital circulation and accumulation'. While the discursive construction of racial categories is always contingent on other axes of inequality, particularly class and gender, it also acts to erase them, placing, for example, Ratan Tata, the billionaire chairman of the Indian transnational Tata Group, and the women, men and children his company has displaced from their land in India within a common racial category, thus making 'race' apparently irrelevant in a context where 'Indians are exploiting/oppressing other Indians'. If, on the other hand, we consider the racialised production of material bodies, as a historical and ongoing process inherent in global capital circulation and accumulation, then it is possible to look beyond this formulation and recognise the operation of 'race' in this scenario.

To elaborate, let us look briefly at an aspect of material embodiment, or what Orzeck calls 'corporeal differentiation' (Orzeck, 2007: 503), which relates very directly to successive eras of racialised global capital accumulation – the prevalence of malnutrition and the periodic generation of famine.[12] Ideologies of race legitimised the global plunder of colonialism, and the global operation of markets controlled by imperial interests in the nineteenth century was directly responsible for the 'making of the third world' in a material sense (Davis, 2001), so that by the end of the nineteenth century the biggest inequalities in standards of living were to be found no longer within but between different social formations. These huge inequalities have been perpetuated and intensified by subsequent phases of global capital accumulation (most recently neoliberalism in its various guises), which since the mid-twentieth century have been termed 'development' in dominant discourses. This is reflected in the contemporary global distribution of hunger. Hunger can be defined in many different ways. It has been measured by the Global Hunger Index in terms of three indicators: the proportion of the population who are 'undernourished' or have insufficient calorie intake; the proportion of children below the age of 5 who are underweight (low weight for age reflecting wasting, stunted growth or both), which is one indicator of child undernutrition; and the mortality rate of children below the age of 5, which partially reflects 'the fatal synergy of inadequate dietary intake and unhealthy environments' (IFPRI, 2011: 7). The 'industrialised' countries (Western Europe, North America, Japan and Australia) are not included in the Index because of the 'very low' prevalence of hunger thus defined.[13] According to the 2011 report of the Global Hunger Index, 'among the world's regions, South Asia and Sub-Saharan Africa continue to suffer from the highest levels of hunger.' The report warns that, despite reductions during the last two decades, food price spikes and volatility caused by the operation of world markets (including the financial crisis) risk reversing these gains, as the 2011 food crisis in the Horn of Africa indicated (IFPRI, 2011: 4). In India, the continuing pervasiveness of hunger has accompanied high growth rates and the 'success story' of neoliberal reforms, which have led to deepening inequalities. The report calculates, on the basis of surveys carried out between 2004 and 2009, that in India approximately 21 per cent of the population were undernourished, and nearly 44 per cent of children under 5 were underweight. In 2009, nearly 7 per cent of children died before reaching the age of 5 (IFPRI, 2011: 49).[14]

As we have seen, these inequalities have in turn been naturalised and racialised, so that the effects of poverty, malnutrition and destitution have come to be seen as essential embodied characteristics of particular racialised identities (and therefore ultimately acceptable), rather than the intolerable products of historical and ongoing economic and social processes which shape embodied lived experiences. The discursive production by development agencies of children, women and men experiencing hunger in the global South (obscuring the global forces generating these conditions) has been considered from the perspective of 'racialised regimes of representation' (Hall, 1994) by some critics. But the racialised differentiation of lived experience implied by global inequalities and relations of power which generate hunger in particular places and not others is yet to be addressed. An analysis of the latter also suggests a way that race and racism can be meaningfully considered globally (and thus in the same frame as development) and not only according to the specificities of those social formations which are internally structured by racialised relations, or 'racial formations' (Omi and Winant, 1986). Seen through this lens, race is inseparable from 'Euro-American' imperialism not only historically in terms of its conceptual origins, but also in terms of its contemporary material reproduction.

Similarly, the discursive association between 'disease' and racialised others has been deconstructed in detail by postcolonial theorists. But what does it mean for our understanding of race and development if we bring this critique together with analysis of how both historically and in ongoing imperial processes decimating viruses were exported; development interventions fatally undermined ecosystems (for example, colonial canal irrigation to increase the production of crops for export drastically increased the prevalence of malaria in parts of India [Whitcombe, 1995]); the destruction of livelihoods and people's insertion into superexploitative labour processes legitimised by ideologies of race left bodies vulnerable to ill health in new ways; and even as existing forms of bodily healing were undermined or outlawed, and new needs created, a massive gap in access to health care between North and South came to be consolidated.[15] It seems particularly important to foreground this analysis at the current juncture because it unequivocally reiterates the social basis of differences in epidemiological patterns at a time when we are witnessing attempts to 're-biologize' race in which the social concept of 'race' is once again 'imbued fallaciously with biological determinants.... through racial interpretations of human genomics findings' (Alcabes, 2006b: 413–25).

As we saw in Chapter 4, some researchers working on the HIV/ AIDS pandemic emphasise the link between the effects of malnutrition and vulnerability to HIV infection (patterned on the well-established relationship in the case of tuberculosis); many relate the spread of the virus to unequal power relations along lines of gender, class and age which have been intensified over several decades by neoliberalism – highlighting the 'positionality in relation to capital circulation and accumulation' of those who contract the virus. For many activists during the last decade, the most urgent task has been less to explain the spread of HIV than to resist attempts by pharmaceuticals corporations and the World Trade Organization to deny life-saving treatment to poor people in the global South living with it. But all of these approaches share the implication that certain bodies are rendered differentially vulnerable to the virus by global processes of accumulation in which race continues to be legitimating. Moreover, these processes are historical – corporeal experience being directly shaped by earlier colonial processes of articulation, incorporation and transformation which, for example, rendered agrarian livelihoods in much of sub-Saharan Africa acutely precarious, or reinforced and extended patriarchal relations – but also contemporary, with bodies destroyed by the imperialist plunder of the intellectual property rights regime and the neoliberal destruction of even the most skeletal of public provision; and these corporeal processes are repeatedly contested, derailed and reshaped by multiple forms of resistance.

I would like to reflect further on this in the context of rural Bihar, in Eastern India, where a movement of mainly Dalit agricultural labourers for land redistribution, a living wage and an end to gender and caste-based violence by landowners and the state, led by the Communist Party of India (Marxist–Leninist) is taking place, with women at the forefront of many of these struggles. While doing research on some aspects of agrarian transformation in the region, I had a number of conversations with groups of women who were involved with the movement. These women were mainly in their late thirties or older; most of them had grown-up children and were grandmothers. Several women on different occasions mentioned the fact that they regularly experienced pain, which they attributed to having had the 'operation' – that is, sterilisation. But as they talked further, it became clear that for them this was embedded in and could not be understood outside of a whole range of corporeal experiences shaped by multiple unequal relations. These included not only the policies that ensured that sterilisation would be the only effective means of contraception available to – and would be promoted among – poor rural women in India; or the absence in this region of even the most rudimentary health facilities for follow-up care. As they explained, the conditions of their lives as women landless wage labourers responsible for their households' survival was equally significant – although they had been advised to rest for a few days after the operation, this was impossible and they had returned immediately to the heavy work in the fields for which they were paid daily wages, as well as exhausting household work. These experiences of chronic overwork and ill health are shaped both by gender relations and by highly unequal land and labour relations, which are sustained and reproduced by the violence of the higher caste landed groups, a key focus of the movement (Wilson, 1999, 2008). Historically, the region's experience of colonial intervention, as we saw in Chapter 1, heralded chronic malnutrition among the rural poor as well as intensifying and consolidating unequal access to land, and reinforcing oppressive caste and gender relations. These processes are currently being extended in multiple and contradictory ways by neoliberal globalisation. But if it is all too evident that bodies are indelibly marked – or in fact materially produced – by the operation of capital on a global as well as a local scale, the testimonies of women agricultural labourers in Bihar also indicate how the resistance they are engaged in repeatedly challenges this process. Their practices in interlinked and sustained struggles for a living wage, for the redistribution of land, and against the gendered caste violence of the landowners and the state, and in challenging the gender division of labour within the household (Wilson, 2008), all have vital embodied implications.

I have outlined earlier in the chapter how this production of bodies when seen in a global context can usefully be understood as racialised. However, I should emphasise that race as a *system of categorisation* is clearly not significant in these struggles, or indeed in the day-to-day reproduction of subjectivities in rural Bihar, in contrast to the inescapable operation of class, caste and gender. For example, my own self-identification as someone of mixed South Asian and British heritage had very little meaning in the conversations referred to above, and factors which marked me as part of an urban educated class on the one hand, and as politically affiliated with the movement on the other, seemed much more salient. Further, the automatic association of visible difference with 'race' which is so ingrained in racial formations such as those of Europe and North America did not operate here. Ideas of 'whiteness' were often very indefinite, (particularly among women from rural poor households), if present at all. An Indian woman friend who spent many years as an activist and researcher in rural Eastern and Central India relates how, on entering a village for the first time, she was asked to her surprise if she was Norwegian. It turned out that a group of researchers from Norway had visited the village some weeks previously.

While it seems likely that processes of neoliberal globalisation are impacting on this in ways that are not fully predictable, these observations only serve to underline the socially constructed and historically and spatially contingent nature of 'race' as a system of categorisation. As other writers have argued, this may limit the contexts to which postcolonial theorisation of the racialisation of subjectivities can be productively applied, since in many places 'race' does not directly shape day-to-day encounters, notwithstanding the reconfiguration of identities such as those of 'caste' and 'tribe' by racialised colonial interventions. On the other hand, as I have suggested, racialised global processes of production of material bodies, while also mutable across time and space, remain centrally relevant to our understanding of these contexts.

In the next, and final, section of this chapter, I look at how mobilising this understanding of race in development, which is linked to embodied lived experience, labour, patterns of accumulation and struggles for transformation, also potentially delinks it from its association with a particular strand of elite nationalist projects. I would argue that it makes a consideration of race in the context of development consistent with more revolutionary and transformative forms of collective politics, in the process opening up new possibilities for anti-imperialist solidarity. In the following section, I elaborate on this in relation to questions of access to land, which, I would suggest, are intimately related to the shaping by race of lived material and embodied experiences and the 'racialised production of bodies', outlined above, as well as to the processes of perpetuation and contestation of a racialised global system of accumulation.

Embodiment, land and development

Said it was 96 degrees in the shade
Ten thousand soldiers on parade
Taking I and I to meet a big fat boy
Sent from overseas
The queen employ
Excellency before you I come
With my representation
You know where I'm coming from

You caught me on the loose
Fighting to be free
Now you show me a noose
On the cotton tree
Entertainment for you
Martyrdom for me...

Some may suffer and some may burn
But I know that one day my people will learn
As sure as the sun shines, way up in the sky
Today I stand here a victim, the truth is I'll never die

Third World, '1865'[15]

Changing people's relation to land, through myriad forms of forced cultivation, taxation, displacement and marginalisation, has been central to the processes of racialised global production of material bodies. And land and the terms under which people live on it and by it have been a central element in collective resistance to imperialism and systems of global capital accumulation among the exploited, oppressed and dispossessed. Many of these struggles organised 'from below' have directly challenged systems of power and production explicitly organised along racial lines – from the Haitian Revolution and its protracted aftermath (Shilliam, 2008; Trouillot, 1995; James, 1938; Bucks-Morss, 2000; Bogues, 2004; Sheller, 2000), Jamaica's 1865 Morant Bay rebellion (Sheller, 2000; Hall, 2002; Noxolo, 2009), the 1857 uprisings in India, and on to the Tebhaga movement,[17] the Mau Mau (Kenya Land and Freedom Army) uprising and many other anti-colonial struggles of the mid-twentieth century. The continuities with contemporary resistance to corporate appropriation of land under neoliberal development operate on multiple levels. They are present in the invocation of popular historical memory and knowledge, as when people resisting the acquisition of their land for a Special Economic Zone in Nandigram, West Bengal, resurrected the tactics of resisting state repression used in the Tebhaga peasant movement in the 1940s. They are evident in the operation of global capitalist markets in which power and resources continue to be massively concentrated in the North. But many of these struggles are confronting locally and nationally based ruling classes and groups, and increasingly Indian or East Asian transnational corporations – so is race still relevant?

In order to address this question, we need to consider two differ-ent strands of political thinking about race, and its relation to class, relations of production and, more broadly, capital accumulation. The first views race and class as competing ways of understanding power relations. Described schematically, political actions based on this perspective have started from the idea that in racialised states racism can, and should, be eliminated without disturbing capitalist production relations, and that the end of colonialism can allow a more just global capitalism to flourish. The second sees modern racism as intrinsic and essential to capitalism – and therefore sees struggles against racism as an integral, and non-negotiable, part of a transformative revolutionary project. This has been the approach of Marxist anti-racist thinkers who have theorised racism in the metropolis – thus Stuart Hall, in his early work, characterised 'race as the modality in which class is lived' (1978, 1980); for Sivanandan, 'capital requires racism, not for racism's sake but for the sake of capital. Racism changes in order that capital might survive' (2008: 89). It has also informed Third World Marxist anti-colonial thinkers, for whom (whether or not they spoke directly of race) struggles against racialised colonialism were always a part of – and necessary to – the project of overcoming global imperialism.

These two polarised positions are reflected within many anti-imperialist struggles – most notably perhaps within the Pan-Africanist movement. Reflecting on the history of the movement and his experience of it, A.M. Babu explains how at the 1945 Fifth Pan-African Conference held in Manchester

> the predominant theme ... was radical anti-imperialism in the context of nationalism. There were two distinct nationalist tendencies contending – political nationalism and racial nationalism. The former was led by people with strong socialist convictions ... as most of the delegates from Africa were labour leaders, the socialist tendency inevitably dominated the conference. (Babu 2002b: 100–101)

Babu goes on to describe the excitement and dynamism generated by the subsequent 1958 All-African People's Conference in Accra, held for the first time in an independent African state, which 'brought together for the first time all liberation movements in Africa' and 'sought to put into practice on the African continent that vision of liberation and socialism expressed in 1945' (101). However,

> throughout the post-colonial era, the two contending tendencies in Black politics which revealed themselves in 1945 – political versus racial nationalism – continued to dominate African politics with devastating consequences ... while the former continued the anti-imperialist struggle even after colonialism, the latter declared the struggle was over with the end of colonialism. This latter stance provided a fertile ground for the advent of neo-colonialism. (102)

In order to explore the implications of these different approaches for formulating an approach to race and racism in the context of contemporary development, and in particular in the context of struggles over land and its occupation, ownership and use, I propose to look in some detail at a recent article, 'What the Haitian Revolution Might Tell Us about Development, Security and the Politics of Race' (Shilliam, 2008), which seeks to bring at least some of these questions within the same frame. Robbie Shilliam is one of very few writers to address questions of race in the context of development, and his article shares some of the preoccupations of this chapter, though the outcome is somewhat different. A consideration of this article also in some ways brings us full circle to the discussion of the literature on development/security with which this chapter began.

Shilliam's argument revolves around the reinstatement of the 'co-constitutive relationship between First and Third Worlds' (Shilliam, 2008: 779) and, more explicitly, 'the threat to Third World development emanating from the First World' (787) into an 'account of the making of the modern world order' through a theorisation of the politics of race. Through this lens he investigates the Haitian Revolution, and specifically the institution of a coercive labour regime controlled by a centralised militarised state determined to maintain plantation production in the post-revolutionary period. Given what was at stake in the survival of the Republic (which went far beyond national independence and represented what was then the only existing refutation of racialised slavery, not simply asserting black people's right to citizenship but challenging their exclusion from personhood itself), Shilliam argues that we cannot understand the actions of Haiti's post-revolutionary black elite 'by reference to a singular logic of instrumental coercion derived from an intra-European model of geopolitical competition' (800), because 'to create a centralized sovereign integrity in Saint Domingue was at the same time to radically undermine the racial and hierarchical organization of the Atlantic world order itself' (791). By implication, this argument is extended to those states that are designated 'failed' – and therefore deemed subject to legitimate intervention – in the context of contemporary imperialism.[18]

For Shilliam, a Marxist historical materialist approach is by definition insufficient to assess the project of the black national elite (Shilliam, 2008: 782). This seems to imply a surprisingly Eurocentric

understanding of Marxism. As we have discussed, Third World na-
tionalisms have had a symbiotic relationship with Marxism throughout
the global South. From Mao onwards, Third World Marxist theorists
have repeatedly placed considerable emphasis on the potentially
progressive role of the anti-imperialist national bourgeoisie.

A perhaps more significant problem is that Shilliam repeatedly
invokes Fanon's injunction to adopt the perspective of 'exploited
men', but his argument actually sidesteps the key question of the
relationship between exploitation of labour and race in the events
he analyses, and focuses almost exclusively on the political projects
of elite groups. As Shilliam explains, the Haitian Revolution itself
was followed by an extended period marked by intense contestation
between black cultivators and the black elite over the relationship of
labour to land in the emergent republic, and between a militarised
plantation system, in which labourers were tied to the plantations
through annual contracts enforced through military supervision, and
the autonomous smallholder agriculture for which the ex-slaves had
fought (see Fick, 1990; Sheller, 2000 for a detailed exploration of this).
Shilliam argues that a historical materialist approach is inadequate
here because it can only understand this struggle through 'the dialectic
of capital and labour', which he distinguishes from 'the dialectic of
master and slave – the politics of race' (Shilliam, 2008: 782). The
latter perspective, he suggests, allows a clearer understanding of
the accumulation strategies of the Haitian rulers in the context of
'the logic of geopolitical contestation between colonial slaveholding
and anti-colonial anti-slaveholding powers'. However, a different
possible reading emerges from a shift in perspective which tries to
understand the political project of the ex-slave cultivators, and treats
race and class as inextricably related rather than alternative categories,
allowing slavery to be understood as a relation of 'capital and labour'
that is simultaneously one of 'race'. If, as we have argued, material
relations of production – in this case coerced plantation labour and
sustained alienation from land – were central to how race was lived
and experienced, then a decisive transformation of these relations
was central to the repudiation of race. The black cultivators' struggle

for land redistribution and the right to autonomous cultivation post-emancipation could be understood as an extension of their struggle against racialised slavery – and in this sense still (also) about race.

This becomes even clearer when we compare, as Mimi Sheller does (Sheller, 2000), the parallels between the Picquet Rebellion in Haiti in the 1840s (by which time the mulatto elite were entrenched) and the 1865 Morant Bay Rebellion in post-emancipation British-ruled Jamaica, and explore how those who took part rejected and resisted a transition from slavery to the economic coercion of racialised capitalist markets. A number of writers have highlighted the way ex-slaves and their descendants in the Caribbean extended the notion of freedom and democracy beyond that of liberal universalism, to encompass an explicit rejection of both racialised inequality and economic domination (Sheller, 2000; Bogues, 2004). What Sheller calls a 'subaltern political ideology' included 'an explicit critique of white racial domination and the unbridled market capitalism that built a world system of slavery. … this alternative path to a future free from domination provided not only a counter-narrative to modernity and an ethical critique of capitalism, but also an alternative vision of true grassroots democracy' (Sheller, 2000: 5). In this, I would suggest, they, along with many others in different parts of the world, were the predecessors of the strand of 'Third World' revolutionaries who would continue to struggle for social and economic transformation far beyond the end of formal colonialism.

In conclusion, then, although both national ruling groups and the transnational corporate elite are no longer racially exclusive, racialised patterns of global accumulation persist and are reproduced and extended. Making questions of labour and land central can further contribute to a historical materialist approach which considers race both discursively and in terms of its material, embodied effects, and locates it within historical and contemporary processes of global capital accumulation. In the next chapter, we look at some contemporary struggles over land through this lens and critically address ideas about race which are implicit in 'postdevelopment' approaches to these struggles.

CHAPTER 7

Worlds beyond the political?
Postdevelopment and race

This chapter looks at the critiques of development that have been brought together under the category 'postdevelopment', and their implications for understandings of race, racism and development. Like other theoretical trends, postdevelopment approaches have emerged from particular processes of struggle and contestation over development policies and practices. The discussion of postdevelopment is interwoven with reflection on various different aspects of the international campaign to prevent proposed bauxite mining in the Niyamgiri hills in the Indian state of Odisha[1] by a British-based, Indian-owned aluminium company, Vedanta Resources plc, with a focus on events that took place during the period 2009–11.

Vedanta is a London FTSE 100-listed mining corporation owned by Anil Agarwal (the seventeenth richest person in Britain according to 2010 figures) and his family through their Bahamas-based company Volcan Investments Ltd. The UK's Department for International Development and Department of Trade and Industry helped launch it on the London Stock Exchange. Vedanta's aluminium refinery at Lanjigarh in Odisha has been held responsible for polluting fertile agricultural land over a vast area in a region which has seen starvation deaths every year since 2007; contaminating drinking water sources by dumping fly ash and toxic red mud into rivers; and displacing thousands of people from their homes. For almost a decade, people who live in this region, mainly belonging to Kond *adivasi* (indigenous) communities, have been resisting Vedanta's plans for a 73 million tonne bauxite mine in the Niyamgiri hills and a sixfold increase in the Lanjigarh refinery's capacity, with massive blockades and protests. Their powerful people's movement has won some key victories, most notably in August 2010, when the Indian government prohibited Vedanta from mining bauxite in the Niyamgiri hills, but the struggle against the corporation, which is still pressing to be allowed to mine for bauxite and to expand its refinery, continues.

Post-development and race

Post-development has now become one of the 'development theories' routinely taught on development studies courses, along with modernisation theory, dependency theory and sustainable development. This is somewhat ironic given that its central project is the deconstruction of development, which is characterised as 'a pervasive cultural discourse with profound consequences for the production of social reality in the so-called Third World'. For post-development writers, this led to 'the possibility of imagining a post-development era, one in which the centrality of development as an organising principle of social life would no longer hold' (Escobar, 2000: 11). Post-development thus sought to transcend debates about the ways in which development could be best achieved and to question the very desirability of development as a goal, however it was conceived.

Unlike Foucault, postdevelopment thinkers located resistance as external to the circuits of power mapped by development: they celebrated 'local' and 'traditional' knowledges and practices, which were directly counterposed in a binary opposition with development and modernity. This romanticisation in postdevelopment writings of the non-West in a utopian era 'before' development has been highlighted by a number of critics, who point out that the 'communities' described in postdevelopment texts were thus constructed as 'timeless' and 'unchanging' until the moment of their encounter with development. Further, recognition of global economic inequality, let alone a desire to change it, was seen as an effect of development discourse. As Arturo Escobar summarises the postdevelopment position,

> Poverty on a global scale was a discovery of the post-World War
> II period ... If within market societies the poor were defined
> as lacking what the rich had in terms of money and material
> possessions, poor countries came to be similarly defined in relation
> to the standards of wealth of the more economically advantaged
> nations. (Escobar, 1995: 22–4)

As Escobar has himself warned, 'one must be careful not to naturalise "traditional" worlds, that is, valorize as innocent and 'natural' an order produced by history.... These orders can also be interpreted in terms of specific effects of power and meaning. The "local" moreover, is neither unconnected nor unconstructed, as is thought at times' (Escobar, 1995: 170). But this has rarely been heeded within postdevelopment work, as the following frequently cited passage from Majid Rahnema and Victoria Bawtree suggests:

> under the banner of development and progress, a tiny minority
> of local profiteers, supported by their foreign 'patrons', set out to
> devastate the very foundations of social life in these countries.
> A merciless war was fought against the age-old traditions of
> communal solidarity. The virtues of simplicity and conviviality, of
> noble forms of poverty, of the wisdom of relying on each other, and
> of the arts of suffering were derided as signs of 'underdevelopment'.
> (Rahnema and Bawtree, 1997: x)

This passage is in fact structured by many of the same binary oppositions that characterise colonial discourses: tradition vs modernity, simplicity vs sophistication, communality vs individuality, spirituality vs rationality. As Maria Baaz points out, 'while postdevelopment and the Eurocentric modernisation approach are on one level based on opposing strategies, the two discourses share a central discursive strategy – representations of *difference*' (Baaz, 2005: 160, emphasis in original). Similarly Kate Manzo argues that 'insisting that truth and meaning reside with 'the primitive' and not with 'the advanced' ... does not push beyond modern relations of domination but threatens to reinscribe them in their most violent form' (Manzo, 1995: 238). But although postdevelopment can be seen as simply reversing the hierarchy and revaluing the attributes that are ascribed to the 'derided' Other, it can also be understood as rearticulating and updating a strand that is in fact already pervasive within colonial discourse.

The notions of the 'noble savage' of the Americas tragically but inexorably doomed to extinction, of the 'dignity' of the 'Pathan warrior', or of the 'innocence and simplicity' of the Indian 'hill tribes' are examples of the many racialised representations that abound within colonial discourse which produced subjects who were simultaneously romanticised and infantilised. Signficantly, these characteristics – of nobility, dignity and simplicity – were continually contrasted not only with those of the European rational man with complex individual needs and desires, but also with those of other colonised subjects who were constructed as conspicuously lacking in these premodern virtues. Thus, for example, many of the *adivasi*/indigenous peoples of India were designated by British colonial administrators as 'primitive tribes'[2] at risk of exploitation by 'cunning' and 'avaricious' 'Hindus' from the plains and therefore requiring the protection of the colonial state. This obscured the role of colonialism in exploiting and dispossessing *adivasi* groups both directly and indirectly through local usurers, traders and landlords. It denied the underlying reasons for the series of *adivasi* anti-colonial uprisings against forced dispossession of land, oppressive taxation, forced and indentured labour and reservation of forests (Das, 1992: 69; Sundar, 1997), while it also legitimised strategies of surveillance and control over *adivasi* populations through special regulations which 'at best amounted to paternal despotism' (Das, 1992: 60). It also constructed the colonial state as protecting *adivasi* communities from exposure to the materially and morally destructive effects of modernity and progress in a discourse which strongly prefigures that of postdevelopment.

But it is important to remember that this discourse always coexisted with, rather than contradicted, the dominant strand within colonial discourse in which 'primitive', 'backward' groups were viewed as the objects of missions to civilise and develop, justifying brutal repression when they resisted. This is evident, for example, in colonial ethnologist W.W. Hunter's explanation of the uprising by the *adivasi* Santhal community in 1855: 'The inoffensive but only half tamed highlander had tasted blood, and in a moment his savage nature returned' (Hunter, 1875). As I argue later in this chapter, this coexistence also characterises contemporary development interventions, and has partially enabled the incorporation of postdevelopment critiques within dominant discourses of development.

The postdevelopment approach, with its emphasis on tradition and undifferentiated, unchanging communities, also, and relatedly, yet again raises the spectre of 'authenticity' and, like its colonial predecessors, arrogates to itself the power to identify the 'authentic' Third World. Postcolonial feminist writers, notably Rey Chow (1993) and Trinh T. Minh-Ha (1989: 88), have explored in depth the ways in which the construction of the 'authentic native', 'the unspoiled African, Asian or Native American who remains more preoccupied with his/her image of the real native – the truly different – than with the issues of hegemony, racism, feminism and social change' (Trinh 1989), sustains and reproduces contemporary racialised relations of power. The notion of 'inauthenticity' also becomes a weapon of dominant groups with an interest in maintaining the status quo, which, as in the Indian context, have mobilised conservative nationalism to discredit transformative politics such as those of Marxism and feminism as 'alien' (Narayan, 1996), and contributes to the peculiar convergence between the religious right and postmodernist thinkers (Nanda, 2003).

Protecting the authentic native in Niyamgiri

In 2010, the *Observer* newspaper published an article by the celebrity environmental activist Bianca Jagger entitled 'The Battle for Niyamgiri'. Jagger had visited the Indian state of Odisha on a trip organised by international NGO Action Aid to meet local people who are overwhelmingly opposed to the proposal by British-based aluminium company Vedanta to mine for bauxite in the Niyamgiri hills, and have been waging a sustained struggle against the company's incursions in the region. The people who live here are known as the Dongria Kond *adivasi* community; they depend on the hills and their complex ecology for their livelihoods, and consider the mountain targeted for mining as sacred. After explaining the situation with Vedanta, and the destructive impact of the aluminium refinery set up by Vedanta in neighbouring Lanjigarh, Jagger goes on to describe her 'sudden' meeting with 'a large gathering of more than 100 members of the Dongria Kondh':

> A group of smiling women surround me and put their arms around my waist, leading me to my assigned seat. They give me a bouquet of scented flowers and welcome everyone by putting the traditional 'tika' on our foreheads, made with the paste of turmeric and rice. The women and girls are wearing their traditional colourful clothes, beaded jewellery, hairpins, ear- and nose rings, and head necklaces. In contrast, the men wear plain dhotis. Many have long hair tied into a knot in the nape of their necks. Some are carrying axes on their shoulders and in their hands. One can already see the influence of 'development' in some of the young men wearing shirts and T-shirts. (*Observer*, 13 June 2010)

In this remarkable passage we can of course see in play many of the binary oppositions discussed above – the undifferentiated 'smiling women', the repeated use of the word 'traditional', which recurs throughout the article, and the detailed description of the 'colourful' clothes and 'beaded' jewellery worn by the women, combine to produce an image of the other both exotic and childlike. The reader is invited to share the experience and the anthropological gaze of the intrepid Western visitor, honoured and respected by these 'natives', who, we have been told earlier, are 'considered an endangered Primitive Tribal Group and are recognised as "a people requiring particular protection"'. Thus, while the article is framed as an appeal for support for the resistance of the Dongria Konds to the depredations of a British corporation, it does this in part by intertextual reference to a whole canon of narratives of white European exploration, 'discovery', conquest and benevolent trusteeship of 'primitive' peoples.

Consistent with these earlier accounts, there is an almost obsessive focus on racialised embodied difference: the clothing and ornaments of the 'beautiful young girls' are emphasised, but notably it is in Jagger's description of the Dongria Kond men that this is most evident. The description of the men's 'plain dhotis', 'long hair tied into a knot in the nape of their necks', 'axes on their shoulders and in their hands' and (in an earlier passage) 'hand-made drums' conjures up the full panoply of associations with the hyper-masculine 'noble savage' of colonial imagination, and the desire for the racialised other which this evokes. Echoing the postdevelopmentalists, Jagger plaintively decries the baneful influence of 'development' – not in the destruction of rivers and mountains and livelihoods that the Dongria Konds have organised to resist, but in the affective loss of embodied authenticity that she experiences when she sees 'some of the young men wearing shirts and T-shirts'!

Despite the representational violence that this implies, it could be argued that whatever tropes Jagger (probably unconsciously) mobilises, in this case it seems clear that she is using them to build opposition to Vedanta's destructive plans and support for the people who are resisting its incursion into their land. However, when we combine this with analysis of the material relations within which Action Aid (which organised Jagger's visit) and other development NGOs are positioned, and the implications for the struggle against Vedanta, we can see the symbiotic connections between the articulation of racialised postdevelopment discourses and the counter-strategies of neoliberal imperialism. Both the postdevelopment discourse and the groups articulating it can be seen as undergoing processes of appropriation and incorporation characteristic of the operation of neoliberalism.

The exponential growth and increasingly central role of the NGO sector in development from the 1980s onwards has been the subject of in-depth analysis and critique.[3] From the 1980s onwards we saw NGOs taking over the role of service provision in the wake of the dismantling of existing forms of social protection by the state, and mobilising people's – and particularly women's – unpaid labour to fill the gap. The period from the 1990s onwards, coinciding, as we have seen, with the rise of the 'good governance' agenda, has seen them simultaneously play a much wider role as the chosen representatives of 'civil society' as conceptualised in dominant neoliberal approaches. In some contexts, this takes the form of actively mobilising and expressing support for neoliberal economic policies or imperial intervention.[4] But they have also, and more subtly, played a key role *within* broad movements of people's resistance to the depradations of global capital, a role which has centred around delinking this resistance from political ideology and coherent visions of social transformation. This depoliticisation operates both at the level of the way this resistance is represented by NGOs, which by virtue of the scale of their funding have considerable control over the production and circulation of information, and at the level of direct intervention into and attempts to control people's movements. These multiple roles, and the big international NGOs' central positioning within the architecture of development (which also incorporates the donor governments that fund them as well as transnational corporations), makes their apparently contradictory actions easier to understand. These contradictions appear particularly marked in the case of Action Aid, which has been publicly critical of neoliberal policies and publicises its involvement in campaigns like that of Niyamgiri, but at the same time, particularly through its close links with (and funding from) the British government's international aid department DfID, is implicated in facilitating corporate exploitation. In the case of Vedanta, for example, it has been noted that

> Action Aid appeared to be campaigning vigorously against Vedanta only to apparently change course from time to time: on August 14th 2010, as part of its Corporate Social Responsibility project 'Partners in Change' it was part of a jury which awarded Vedanta the 'Best Community Development Programme Award' for its 'good work' around the Lanjigarh refinery at Niyamgiri hills, as advertised proudly on Vedanta's website ... Four days later Vedanta's Lanjigarh project was damned by the Indian government's Saxena Report for violations of tribal rights and illegal land grabbing. (South Asia Solidarity Group, 2011)

Samarendra Das and Felix Padel have traced in detail the ambiguous role of NGOs in the context of aluminium mining in Odisha.

They point out that while Action Aid 'has been one of the most pro-active' in the campaign against Vedanta in Niyamgiri, it also receives funds from DfID, which has actively promoted the company; and they trace the long-term relationship between the NGO's Indian organisation and corporate capital, which has developed in tandem with India's adoption of neoliberal economic policies since the early 1990s:

> as the New Economic Policy was coming into effect, Action Aid India formed a Corporate Partnership unit in 1993, which became 'Partners in Change' in 1995, with funding from the Ford Foundation, DFID and Novib, laying the ground for MoUs with Sterlite (part of the Vedanta Group), ICICI (one of its major investor banks) and other corporate houses: business partnerships that raise questions about AAI's involvement in the movement to save Niyamgiri. (Padel and Das, 2010: 524)

Against this background, the role of NGOs in movements such as that around Niyamgiri also raises questions about the reframing of practices of international solidarity, questions which, like Bianca Jagger's appeal discussed above, require an engagement with the ways in which 'race' and racism are implicated in this reframing.

NGOs and aliens in the London anti-Vedanta protests

The protests that took place outside Vedanta plc's 2010 AGM in Westminster in Central London brought together a range of groups and individuals with diverse political approaches. Having taken part in this protest (and similar ones in 2009 and 2011) I was struck by several aspects of it. In many ways the protest felt like a point at which two very different types of political action overlapped, without quite touching. The non-NGO protestors, mainly members of non-funded campaigning organisations and individuals, and many of South Asian origin, held huge hand-painted placards with photographs of Anil Agarwal, under the slogan 'Wanted – for Vedanta's Murders and Environmental Crimes'; they angrily yelled slogans like 'Anil Agarwal – blood on your hands' and 'Who killed Arsi

Majhi? [one of the leaders of the movement in Niyamgiri] Vedanta did!' Other placards targeted David Cameron for his collusion with Vedanta's crimes. On either side of this group of protestors stood two smaller groups, whose manner was quite different. On one side, members of Survival International stood quietly and slightly apart, all wearing yellow T-shirts printed with the Survival logo and holding matching printed placards with the slogan 'Vedanta's Profits – Dongria's Destruction' and the name of the organisation prominently displayed.[5] On the other side, again slightly apart, stood another group of half a dozen protestors, all in red T-shirts printed with the Action Aid logo. From time to time, this group launched into a group chant of their own, which ran: 'One, we are the people. Two, a little bit louder. Three, we've got to get Vedanta out of here!'

The protest is an interesting example of the way spatiality operates on a micro-level – first and most obviously in terms of the boundary between the shareholders' meeting, where decisions are taken inside a building guarded by the police (and which was on this occasion infiltrated by a number of activists who had bought shares in order to raise questions inside the meeting), and the street outside, where protestors raised the demands of the people whose lives were most directly affected by the decisions. But in terms of racialised space, it is also interesting to consider the unacknowledged boundaries within the space of the protest itself, and its reproduction of the wider positioning of NGOs in relation to people's movements.

However, in terms of the publicity the protests generated, a great deal of this focused on the presence of two actors who had been hired by Survival International to attend the protest in blue body paint to represent members of the Na'vi tribe – the inhabitants of the planet Pandora from the then recently released science-fiction film *Avatar* (2009). The two actors were photographed holding placards reading 'Save the Real Avatar Tribe'. This parallel had first been drawn by Survival International in February of that year, when they placed an advertisement in the entertainment magazine *Variety* invoking the idea that '*Avatar* is fantasy … and real' and appealing to James Cameron, *Avatar*'s director, to 'please help the Dongria'.[6] This notion of the 'real *Avatar* tribe' was taken up extensively in the media (including in Indian newspapers) and became a very popular theme of campaigning around Niyamgiri.

Mark Deuze highlights references to *Avatar* in the context of a discussion of how activists are engaging with media to make campaigns more effective (2010). Several groups made use of the *Avatar* theme. In Bil'in, a Palestinian village located in the central West Bank, where weekly protests have been taking place against the Israeli state's construction of a wall around its territory, five protestors wore Na'vi costumes in February 2010. A statement on Bil'in's website explained: '[l]ike Palestinians, the Avatars fight imperialism, although the colonizers have different origins. The Avatars' presence in Bil'in today symbolizes the united resistance to imperialism of all kinds' (Bil'in Popular Committee, 2010, cited in Deuze 2010: 6). But these two contexts in which the *Avatar* parallel was invoked have very different implications for questions of agency and representation. Significantly, in contrast to the Palestinian case, members of the Dongria Kond community have never dressed up as Na'vi themselves; whereas, as their statement clearly explains, the Palestinian protestors mobilised *Avatar* as a political metaphor, the Dongria Konds are represented by others as literally resembling the Na'vi.

I would like to ask how people in India who are organising to resist the plunder of their environment by corporate capital come to be represented in this way by their supporters in Britain and elsewhere. What does it imply for notions of solidarity? The aim of this questioning is not to undermine its impact in publicising the campaign, but to reflect on the particular discursive and material relationships which make this kind of representation possible, and which in turn are reproduced by its circulation.

Part of the effectiveness of the comparison with the film clearly stems from the parallels between the situation in Niyamgiri and the plot of *Avatar*, which revolves around a corporate/military mission from Earth to drive the 'native humanoid' Na'vi from their homes in order to mine for the valuable 'unobtainium ore'. But the parallel is taken much further: the focus in this campaign is not actually on the aggressors but on the irreducible 'otherness' of the Dongria Konds themselves – who have been represented as the embodiment of the 'real-life' Na'vi to the extent that several online photographic images used in campaigning fused the face of a young Dongria Kond girl with that of one of the blue-skinned Na'vi characters in a 'mirror' image. Further, the *Avatar* campaigning strategy 'worked', I would argue, precisely because the portrayal of the Na'vi in *Avatar* (unlike other science-fiction portrayals of 'aliens', sympathetic or otherwise) is clearly based on markers of difference more often constructed as racial. The Na'vi have exaggerated but essentially human features, with large, widely spaced eyes, flat noses and high cheekbones, and wear their hair in braids and beads. Their blue skin evokes the body painting practised by certain indigenous groups in the global South, while their lifestyle 'in harmony' with nature is also clearly intended to indicate their equivalence to these groups. Significantly, notwithstanding the use of make-up and CGI in creating the Na'vi on screen, none of the actors selected to play the main Na'vi characters is white. I would argue that the emphasis on racialised 'otherness' in the mobilisation of the *Avatar* parallel foregrounds understandings based on an ethos of morality, where people in the 'developed world' are made aware of an obligation to act to protect both the environment and those whose lives are lived in harmony with it and are apparently as yet untouched by 'development' – people who are assumed to live (like the Na'vi literally do) 'on another planet' from those campaigning on their behalf. Even more significantly, it forecloses certain kinds of political approach – those which recognise the collective political resistance by the people affected and take these as the starting point for actions based on an ethos of solidarity, linking it to struggles taking place in the global North.

This is linked to processes of depoliticisation on several levels. The construction of the members of the Dongria Kond community as pre-modern, innocent and uncorrupted authentic 'noble savages' of necessity precludes any consideration of their engagement in sustained political organising, which has made possible the series of protests, marches and blockades that prevented mining from 2002 onwards. It obliterates their historic and present relation to political structures, such as the various levels and arms of the Indian state and its colonial predecessor, and silences their articulation of any visions of the future which depart from a narrative of restoration of 'traditional' lifestyles and livelihoods. While the Dongria Konds are recognised to be overwhelmingly opposed to Vedanta's plans, the details of their campaign are kept vague. Whereas some observers in this and other contexts have characterised such tendencies as 'oversimplification', a side effect resulting from international NGOs' compulsion to attract public support in their home countries and compete with each other to raise funds, I would suggest that they can be understood as inseparable from racialised notions of people in the global South, and members of indigenous communities in particular, as irreducibly other and located in another world that is by definition outside the political. This racialised refusal to recognise the existence of conscious and collective political organising has also facilitated direct interventions by NGOs in these struggles. For example, NGOs selected the individuals who were brought to London as 'representatives' of the entire community as part of the international campaign.

By contrast, the possibility of collective action by an undifferentiated British public to bring about change is emphasised and valorised by the major NGOs involved in the Vedanta campaign. This public is expected to act on behalf of, rather than alongside, poor people in the global South, a transposition of agency epitomised by the British Action Aid volunteers' adoption of the 'we are the people' chant which originated in South Africa. This celebration of popular agency, however, is framed in terms of moral obligation towards 'other' worlds rather than a political project of transformation of one's own, as Survival International's slogan 'Their Future is in Your Hands' implies. Mutual solidarity, alliances between different but related struggles, or even the process of identifying shared interests in change (all of which require a much more extensive and committed engagement with actually existing struggles in the South) are precluded from this framework, which acknowledges North–South inequalities and the effects of overconsumption in the global North, but excludes a critique of global capitalism in which exploitation can be seen to characterise relationships in the global North as well.

A much larger-scale and more explicit version of this type of political practice was seen during the Make Poverty History campaign of 2005.[7] As Kate Nash suggests, Make Poverty History 'aimed to transform national citizens into global citizens by creating obligations towards people suffering outside the nation' (Nash, 2008: 168); in so doing, it sought 'to work with the structures of global governance rather than to destroy them' (169). While a detailed discussion of this campaign is beyond the scope of this chapter, it is worth noting that the campaign has been extensively analysed as an example of the way NGOs work to manage and appropriate resistance. In this case, popular support for the campaign's demands for radical change on issues of debt cancellation, aid and trade ultimately translated into Make Poverty History giving its stamp of approval to the neoliberal, pro-corporate agenda of the British government under Blair and Brown, as spelled out in the Commission for Africa, and the continuation and consolidation of neoliberal policies in Africa that emerged from the G8 Summit, both of which were represented as victories where, as Bob Geldof put it, 'the world spoke and the politicians listened' (Hodkinson, 2005). This was facilitated by what was argued to be the marked silencing of African critics of the campaign, and in fact the exclusion of any African commentators, recalling other more obviously imperial projects similarly informed by notions of cosmopolitanism citizenship, such as those discussed in Chapter 5. As Charles Abugre, then Christian Aid's head of policy, argued: 'what was the message? It was one of handouts and charity, not one of liberation defined by Africans themselves or the reality that we are actually resisting neo-colonialism and neoliberalism ourselves' (Hodkinson, 2005).

As in the campaign around Niyamgiri, within the discourse of Make Poverty History, according to Nash, 'compassion for distant suffering' was 'an important sub-theme', but overall 'the heroic rescue narrative was much more prominent' (Nash, 2008: 173). While she does not explore the racialised implications and colonial antecedents of this narrative, Nash interestingly highlights the repeated parallels drawn in the UK campaign's own material with the actions of British abolitionists (173).

Thus, even while development discourses bestow 'agency' upon people in the global South in the form of individual entrepre-neurialism and the moral imperative to help oneself (as we saw in Chapter 2), collective agency is located in and largely restricted to undifferentiated publics/civil society in the global north,[8] and here the imperative is again a moral one, to help – or rescue – less fortunate others. In this model, connections between campaigners in the North and those for whom they advocate can only be configured along two axes: that of the 'heroic rescue narrative', and that of obligation based on the benefits to the global North of unequal trade, resource extraction and environmental destruction in the South. The possibility of complicating and blurring this North/South dichotomy by acknowledging that the 'public' in the global North is itself riven by conflicting interests and a highly unequal distribution of these benefits along lines of class and 'race' in particular, and that there may be struggles taking place there which are confronting the same forces that are ravaging the global South, is not taken into account in this model. This strikes me as being particularly dangerous since it not only limits the scope and effectiveness of campaigning, but actively reinforces the 'development/security' model of relations between people in the global North and South promoted by British and US governments, in which people in (or entering from) the South are identified primarily as a racialised threat to those in the North, which can only be neutralised through neoliberal forms of development dictated by these governments. While campaigning INGOS articulate this differently, they arguably mobilise the same logic, which also contributes to the exclusive re-imagining of the 'British public' as a homogenous entity with shared national interests, in a manoeuvre characteristic of imperialism.[9]

Post-development policing

As portrayed in Britain, then, the struggle over Niyamgiri appears to epitomise the binary opposition that forms the core of the post-development approach – with Vedanta as the harbinger of development, on the one hand, and the Dongria Kond community representing tradition, simplicity and harmony with the natural world, on the other. This narrative is repeated in almost all the NGO-produced material on Niyamgiri on the web and in print and broadcast media. As in Survival's online film *Mine: Story of a Sacred Mountain* (narrated in the hushed tones usually reserved for wildlife films by the quintessentially upper-class English voice of actress Joanna Lumley), the emphasis is on the isolated existence of the 'remote tribe' and the idyllic environment in which they had been living until the advent of the mining company. However, other representations have also emerged from the people's struggle in Niyamgiri and the surrounding area which suggest that what people in Niyamgiri are actually saying is considerably more complex and does not fit neatly into the post-development paradigm. In what follows, I draw in particular on one of these, the film *Wira Pdika* (directed by Amarendra Das and Samarendra Das, 2005)[10] in which people from the Dongria Kond and Majhi Kond communities across a wider region which includes Niyamgiri speak about their lives and their struggles against 'the company'. As the film shows, a series of aluminium companies have been attempting to mine bauxite in the region since the early 1990s, and faced sustained resistance from the people living there. While I suggest that the variety of perspectives here and the virtual absence of voice-overs and narration make this film particularly important, it should be clear that this discussion does not seek to present some representations as 'more authentic' than others in the sense already discussed. The film does not make claims to present an 'unbiased' view of events; on the contrary, it is an example of politically committed film-making seeking to produce a film which can be widely used as a tool in the struggle. Rather, this discussion seeks to demonstrate how some ideas and perspectives come to be silenced in mainstream representations, how these representations have incorporated post-development approaches, and how this silencing relates to particular political projects and structures of power.

A number of points emerge from the film in this context. First, the Kond people's opposition to corporate mining has been sustained and organised and is informed by a history of struggles going back to the colonial period, with long and often bitter experience of interactions with politicians of major parties, the state in the form of the District and Block administrations and the police, and NGOs. For example, Kond activist Bhagaban Majhi, a spokesperson for Niyamgiri Surakshya Samiti (Save Niyamgiri Campaign), the movement against mining in the area, describes the prelude to the launch of the movement against corporate projects to mine bauxite in the area thirteen years earlier:[11]

> Anantaram Majhi, the Congress Party MLA, came to our meetings, he spoke against the company ... he said he will help us if we vote for him. We elected him but nothing changed, He didn't speak for us but took the company's side. That is how the movement started. (*Wira Pdika*)

What is clear is that, while marginalised and excluded on multiple levels, the Konds are in fact not isolated from the outside world as Survival's notion of a 'remote tribe' implies, but have been compelled to negotiate relations with other groups and with the state over several centuries. They are incorporated into the lowest levels of a social formation structured by class and caste, in which they are represented as other and inferior in ways which since the colonial period have involved ideas of 'race'. The people interviewed in *Wira Pdika* convey this powerfully in their frequent references to the discrimination and contemptuous attitudes towards *adivasis* that they face, and the way these attitudes are used to suppress dissent.

> We, the people of 12–13 villages wrote an application to the district administration saying 'We are not going to give up our water and forests, we won't part with our Niyamgiri.' Then [they said] – 'Who

has written this? A pig or a goat? Does he have a name or an address?' (Daisingh Majhi in *Wira Pdika*)

They ridicule us and say 'what are the Konds up to? What do they know?' (Bhima Majhi in *Wira Pdika*)

Second, while people express a sense of the sacredness of Niyamgiri, this is articulated in combination with an emphasis on their material dependence on the mountain, and also with an analysis of the possible ecological impacts of its destruction, in the context of already precarious livelihoods – concerns which in NGO representations are rarely attributed to the 'remote Dongria Konds' in their 'idyllic' surroundings. In the same interview cited above, Bhima Majhi explains: 'We are resisting for our motherland, for our mountain. The summer is very hot already. It will get hotter if [Vedanta] Sterlite comes. You won't get rain then. The summer is so hard for us already, so we want them to stop. So we oppose Sterlite, we oppose the government' (*Wira Pdika*).

This insistence that what is at stake is livelihoods, resources and sheer survival, as well as multiple forms of attachment to one's home, links the struggles in Niyamgiri to countless other movements against corporate displacement which do not mobilise notions of the sacred or cultural annihilation and have not attracted NGO support in the same way – notably the ongoing struggle against South Korean steel giant POSCO[12] which is taking place elsewhere in Odisha. Similarly, Bhagaban Majhi explains that

> we are tribal cultivators (*chasi adivasi*) ... earthworms (*matir poko*) ....
> we want permanent development (*sthayi unnati*). Provide us with
> irrigation for our land. Give us hospitals and medicines, give us
> schools and teachers. Give us our land and forests. We don't need the
> company. Get rid of the company. We have been saying this for 13
> years but the government is not listening. (*Wira Pdika*)

Third, as this makes clear, the Konds' struggle against Vedanta is not primarily conceived as a struggle against development and in favour of maintaining the status quo, or what Rahnema and Bawtree call 'noble forms of poverty'. In fact the notion of 'development' (*unnati*, which can also be translated as 'progress', anathema to post-development theorists) is one which is frequently mobilised to make concrete demands for change: for education, health care, irrigation, resources which the state has consistently failed to provide to their communities. The discourse that pervades *Wira Pdika*, then, is one in which people make claims not against development, but regarding the kinds of development they do and do not want. Further, this discourse consistently challenges the legitimacy of the corporates' claims to be bringing development to the region. They cite broken promises: local activist Sri Lasu Jani explains how NALCO had promised to provide facilities for a 10 kilometre radius around the aluminium refinery, including health centres; but this has not happened. Herabati Nayak of Amlabadi village describes how, despite NALCO promising jobs to graduates, although she graduated and is now studying for a postgraduate degree, 'I have not got any job … even though we have a quota for LDP [land displaced people] there are still no jobs for us' (*Wira Pdika*, 2005).

In this context, the post-development approach deployed by NGOs, which constructs all contact with the outside world as polluting the purity of the Konds' lifestyle, acts to silence these demands and construct them as inauthentic and illegitimate. As Maria Baaz writes,

> the problem of the post-development approach … is not only located in the risk of relegating questions of poverty and economic inequality to the margins by an infatuated interest in the authentic and the unspoiled. It is also about the ways in which demands for economic development and equality are delegitimized. (Baaz, 2005: 163)

Fourth, and relatedly, the people interviewed in the film make it clear that they conceptualise the activities of companies like Vedanta as representing not development but plunder. The opposition to 'the company' is articulated over and over again in terms of resisting the expropriation and seizure of resources – water, land, forests and mountains, and there is little reference, in either positive or negative terms, to any changes the companies will bring to the region, other than destruction and environmental degradation.

Postdevelopment and postcolonial critiques have highlighted the Eurocentrism of a monolithic developmentalism based on planning and characterised by 'the construction of roads, hydroelectric projects, schools, hospitals and factories' (White, 2006: 56). But this does little to address the decisive shift from the 'developmental state' to neoliberal globalisation, which by contrast has witnessed the destruction of such public services and infrastructure, and under which 'development' is more likely to entail the kind of unplanned and untrammelled incursions by footloose corporate capital seeking to extract and export resources that is being experienced in mineral-rich Odisha.

For the people resisting 'the company' in Odisha, however, this distinction is extremely important, and their movement incorporates a powerful critique of the hypocrisy of neoliberal imperialism as they are experiencing it. As Bhagaban Majhi explains:

> Where will the people go once the construction is over? Is this development? You say you are here for development – how many high schools, colleges, engineering colleges, health centres will you set up? When we ask these questions, they stay silent.... I had put a question to the SP [Superintendent of Police]. I asked him, 'Sir, what is development? What is development worth if it ends up in people being thrown off their land? The people for whom development is meant, if they don't benefit, what kind of development is that? Not only they, but all the generations who come after them should benefit. It should not be merely to cater to the greed of a few officers. Destroying age-old resources is not development.... Over the 23 years [that the bauxite will last] the government will get Rs 12–13 billion – but the company will grab Rs 2880 billion in 23 years. They will build red mud tanks and ash ponds – they will pollute our environment and export our resources abroad. How does our government benefit, the public benefit? Whereas the company benefits so much.' He had no answer. (*Wira Pdika*)

But fighting on this difficult terrain in which the notion of 'development' itself becomes a site of contestation also requires an awareness of how the people's demands for 'stable' (*sthayi*) development – for education, health care, irrigation and other forms of state provision – can also be appropriated and manipulated. Padel and Das explain how the entry of IFAD (the UN's International Fund for Agricultural Development) into the region in 1988, and the construction of roads, bridges and irrigation facilities that followed, prepared the ground for the arrival of the mining corporates in the 1990s (Padel and Das, 2010: 105–6). In *Wira Pdika* we hear how the companies used the familiar practices of Indian state developmentalism, with its preoccupation with enumeration and classification inherited from the colonial state, in order to gather information for their own purposes:

> Earlier when company people came, they would disguise themselves as veterinary doctors. They would get the information they required from us on the pretext of doing surveys about our cattle, sheep and chickens. They also came to us as ANM [auxiliary nurses and midwives] to ask about statistics of village population.... how many women, how many children ... After many such surveys, we became suspicious and would not let them carry out further surveys. (Bhagaban Majhi in *Wira Pdika*)

After this strategy failed, Bhagaban Majhi continues, the mining corporates set up their own NGOs:

> then they formed an organisation called URDS – Utkal Rural Development Society. They started free health check-up camps, free seed donation camps, free adult education in the area. We saw they were doing voluntary work (*seva*) but they were really company people. They aimed to win people's confidence and to divide people. So we protested against this organisation. Then they brought in BPD – Business Partners for Development[13] ... we also opposed them. After this there was repression, jail, false cases, *lathi* charges [police beating demonstrators]. (*Wira Pdika*)

Wira Pdika conveys the rich history of political organising and resistance among the *adivasi* people of the region, and their sustained struggles with corporate capital and the colonial and post-colonial Indian state. This is rendered invisible in racialised NGO representations, in which, as we have seen, the British public is called upon to prevent the primordial desecration of the 'unspoiled'. However, this elision is not only a question of representational violence. On a broader level, it is necessary in order to sustain the narrative of empowerment as a gift to be granted by development NGOs and their donors. But it also makes it possible for existing organizations and their demands to be marginalised and individuals to be hand-picked as representatives of communities, a strategy which has been seen as central to NGOs' role in diffusing and depoliticizing resistance to global capital.

Does the discussion of the struggle over Niyamgiri help us to conceptualise contemporary people's movements and their relation to 'development' in ways that differ from post-development theorists' understandings? On one level it is clear that 'people's movements' may not itself be a useful category – we need to look at who the people are who make up the movement, in terms of class, gender, race, caste and other social relations of inequality; and we need to look at the politics of the movement (not necessarily formally or explicitly expressed but still always present: what it is fighting for, and on what grounds). Not to do this would be to succumb to the tendency in post-development writing itself to essentialise 'the people' and to endow movements with a metaphysical quality.

But the emergence of post-development theory was in fact closely linked to the rise of a specific, though remarkably varied, strand of people's movements: those which developed in the 1980s and 1990s in opposition to displacement, environmental destruction, corporate takeover of resources and the effects of neoliberal globalisation and which have combined and mobilised a very wide range of discourses, including, as we saw in the case of Niyamgiri, those of alternative models of development.

Departing here from some of the earlier in-depth critiques of post-development theories, which have tended to minimise the significance and potential of such movements,[14] I have argued in this chapter that these movements have been subject to racialised representations within post-development discourses, and that this has made it possible for post-development approaches to be incorporated into the project of undermining and depoliticising the movements, in order to facilitate accumulation by global corporate capital, in which development institutions – and international NGOs in particular – are engaged.

Writing in the mid-1990s, Arturo Escobar explained the post-development understanding of 'New Social Movements', which, he suggested, represent 'the search not for grand structural transformations but rather for the construction of identities and greater autonomy through modifications in everyday practices and beliefs' (Escobar, 1995: 217). Nearly two decades on, not only have movements against neoliberal globalisation multiplied and intensified, but their articulation of collective visions of 'structural transformation', albeit often multiple ones, has become impossible to ignore. The practice of international political solidarity with these movements, I would argue, requires a sustained engagement with these visions, and a decisive break with the colonial relations that structure NGO campaigning.

CHAPTER 8

Reconfiguring 'Britishness':
diasporas, DfID and neoliberalism

Roll up Roll up for the Brown Sahib's burden.
Together, the diaspora and the developmentia industry can save
Pakistan. Presented to you this evening by a fully loaded barrel
of institutional (mi)stakeholders.

Post on *Developmentia* blog (14 November 2011)

This chapter examines the question of diaspora participation in development, in the context of shifting constructions of 'race' and 'belonging' in Britain, and their relationship with changing patterns of imperialism. It begins with a discussion of the existing literature that has directly addressed racism in development. A key argument that has emerged from this work, which has mainly been developed within a broadly postcolonial framework, is that critical approaches to racism that emerged in the countries of the global North (Britain and North America in particular) should inform development institutions. In particular, it is argued that the 'whiteness' of development can be challenged through greater engagement by these institutions with black and minority ethnic communities in the global North. In this context, the chapter reflects on the Department for International Development (DfID) policy of engaging with BME and Diaspora groups (Thornton and Hext, 2009). It goes on to examine the construction of diaspora participation in development in the context of racialised regimes of representation, through a discussion of several recent British television documentaries on 'development-related' themes.[1] In the second part of the chapter, we will explore these themes further through an examination of how initiatives which have taken place under the rubric of engaging with Indian diaspora organisations have been related to specific strategies of imperialist intervention and the consolidation and extension of neoliberalism.

Postcolonial critiques of racism in development

Within the vast sea of policy, advocacy and academic literature produced and reproduced under the auspices of development, the overwhelming silence on 'race' has remained, as Sarah White has argued, 'a determining silence, which both masks and marks its centrality to the development project' (White, 2002: 407). However, the last decade has seen the beginning of the breaking of this silence in a handful of contributions which have directly addressed questions of 'race' in development, notably those by Sarah White (2002), Paulette Goudge (2003), Uma Kothari (2006) and other contributors to the special issue of *Progress in Development Studies* devoted to 'race' and racism. These contributions form part of a wider and growing literature which brings postcolonial approaches to bear on development (see, for example, Sylvester, 1999; McEwan, 2001; Kapoor, 2002; Biccum, 2002; Baaz, 2005) and has significant implications for the theorisation of 'race' in development.

I argue in this chapter that while this work, written overwhelmingly from a postcolonial perspective, is particularly valuable in having broached the question, it needs to be considerably extended and deepened in the context of changes in development associated with neoliberalism, and in particular the processes by which neo-liberal development discourse has appropriated and incorporated critical concepts. Consistent with postcolonial approaches, these contributions focus on questions of representation, exploring the 'legacy' of colonial constructions and 'the articulations of "race" during the period of European, particularly British, colonial rule and how these were sustained and mediated following decolonisation to inform the west's current perceptions of the rest' (Kothari, 2006: 11). Kothari explains how racialised colonial binaries have been reproduced and reworked within discourses of modernising development, in which an emphasis on cultural difference replaces explicit invocations of 'race'.

> By sustaining, for example, the 'traditional' versus 'modern' dichotomy, mapped onto third and first worlds, respectively, development becomes a racialized project drawing upon a colonial imaginary when identifying who and what is 'progressive'/'backward'. Indeed within the discourse of modernization in development, progress is conceived as a shift from the traditional to the modern.... It is these racialized colonial dichotomies, such as 'modern'/'backward', 'order'/'chaos', 'reason'/'emotion', that ... provide rationales for the practice of some people intervening to develop others. Again, these distinctions are founded upon the racialized process of othering. (Kothari, 2006: 13)

Kothari argues that these processes have deepened as a result of the shift towards internalising the causes of conflict and 'under-development' which characterises dominant discourses of develop-ment: 'for instance, the whole of Africa comes to be identified with militarism, autocratic regimes and corruption, twisted by violence, war and famine. And, in contradistinction, the west is the epitome of morality, order, democracy and progress' (19). Similarly, White (2002) highlights the '"discursive *bricolage*" of development' in which older racialised discourses are modified and re-established in new forms (White, 2002: 415). She emphasises development's 'cultural constitu-tion as a "mode of knowing" or a set of regimes for the production of knowledge ... the structure of colonial thought turns on the central motif of self/other, subject/object. Development similarly rests fundamentally on notions of difference, between here and there, now and then, us and them, developed and developing' (413). Thus constructions of race continue to structure development discourses even as 'race' as a marker of inequality is rendered invisible within these discourses.

While White notes the importance of the 'materiality' of develop-ment (White, 2002: 412), these contributions do not in the main focus on exploring the racialised patterns of global accumulation which both underpin and are sustained by these discursive representations

– for example, the deepening neoliberal intervention and control and escalated processes of resource extraction, which, as we saw in Chapter 5, are legitimised by the 'racial imaginaries' of Africa as inherently corrupt, chaotic and violent. Their concern has been more to investigate the micro-level of practices in development organisations to illustrate and problematise the 'whiteness' of the development industry.

This builds upon a number of detailed ethnographies of development organisations and aid workers, which began to be published in the late 1990s – including notably Baaz's study of Scandinavian aid workers in Tanzania (2005), Crewe and Harrison's 'ethnography of aid' looking at fish-farming and stove development projects (1998), and Kothari's work on colonial administrators turned development professionals (2005). These studies have drawn on the theory of Orientalism (Said, 1978) and the postcolonial thinking that extended from it to explore how white Northern-based development professionals represent themselves, their 'partners' and 'users' and the enterprise of development itself, and how this both shapes and is shaped by the practices of development.[2] To different degrees, they also examine how the 'subjects of development' represent themselves within relationships with development workers in ways that both conform to these dominant constructions and also adapt, modify and subvert them (see, for example, Mosse, 2005).

Many of these studies have direct implications for understandings of racism in the context of development. This is taken further in discussions which focus on the 'whiteness of power' in development (Goudge, 2003). This is conceptualised in terms of the ways that 'authority, expertise and knowledge become racially symbolised' (Kothari, 2006: 9) and embodied in the white development practitioner. Thus Sarah White writes of her experiences in Bangladesh that, 'without my conscious intention, my whiteness opened me doors, jumped me queues, filled me plates, and invited me to speak' (White, 2002: 408), while Goudge (2003) explores this mapping of authority and expertise onto racialised bodies through interviews with white Northern development and aid workers in Nicaragua, emphasising the agency of the development workers themselves in reproducing these associations through their own expectations and assumptions.

Uma Kothari reflects on her own very different experiences as a Northern-based development consultant who is not white:

> 'local counterparts' have been visibly disappointed when they realized that their expatriate consultant was not white ... The appointment of a white consultant is seen to ascribe higher status to their own work whereas to be sent 'one of their own' devalues their organization.... These distinctions were also evident while working, again in Bangladesh, in a multidisciplinary team of white consultants where debriefing sessions were often awkward because the previously stable boundary between 'us' and 'them' had been breached by my presence. (Kothari, 2006: 16)

Constructions of the 'local' and the 'global' have themselves been structured by 'race'. As White notes in the context of gender and development 'expertise',

> while feminists of the South may speak on a global stage, their legitimacy is at least partially invested in their 'localized' status. Development, like globalization, lauds the local at the same time as it seeks to over-ride it. In one way the identification with 'the local' – even if it is as de-localized as the notion of 'the South' – enhances their voice. At the same time, however, it renders their voice marginal, with respect to the 'unmarked' voices of the North. (White, 2006: 63)

This perception of the North – and whiteness – as unmarked and therefore by definition pre-eminently universal or 'global' echoes Gayatri Spivak's observation (in relation to students at Columbia University, New York) that 'The student is encouraged to think that he or she is there to help the rest of the world. And he or she is also encouraged to think that to be from other parts of the world is not to be fully global' (Spivak, 2003: 622).

Racialised boundaries are constructed and maintained in multiple ways. Lisa Smirl (2008) has described the practices of international aid workers in humanitarian reconstruction initiatives and their construction of segregated spaces in ways that echo Fanon's description of the racialised spaces of the city in the settler colony (Fanon, 1967b: 30). The location of the 'expat aid worker' within these spaces often seems to legitimise behaviour and statements which are explicitly racist. White cites

> the British man who explained that his family had left for home because there were 'no children' in Bangladesh for his to play with; the expatriate club serving aid and embassy staff, which held a 'pyjama party' one week, and the next a 'Bengali party', in which the 'fancy dress' consisted of the clothes that Bangladeshis wear. (White, 2002: 409)

However, this is not primarily a question of geographical location. One has only to enter the offices of any of the major international NGOs or development bodies to find oneself in a space where mainly white staff work surrounded by glossy, larger-than-life photographs of smiling non-white children (and, more recently, adolescent girls) and be forcibly reminded of the racialised boundaries and relations of power between providers of development and their 'beneficiaries', 'users' and 'partners'.

The work discussed here has been instrumental in putting the question of racism in development on the agenda. But the postcolonial framework within which this work has taken place means that, although the discursive continuities between formal colonialism and contemporary development interventions are highlighted, there is relatively little emphasis on the material dynamics of resource extraction and accumulation of the colonial period, how these were racialised and the extents to which they have been both reproduced and changed in successive eras.

As we have seen, the discourse of developmentalism inaugurated by Truman's speech of 1945 and its racialised binaries of progress and backwardness, modernity and tradition, have been extensively analysed in both post-development and postcolonial work. Particular emphasis has been placed on the hierarchy implicit in modernisation theory's core concept of 'catching up': development as progress through a series of stages whose outcome would be the achievement of the 'advanced' US high mass consumption society. As Escobar has put it, 'people have first to be awakened to the new possibilities, they have to be taken by the hand into the new, exciting road ... It would be the task of the white fathers to introduce the good but backward Third World people into the temple of progress' (Escobar, 1995: 158). But little is written in this literature about the fact that developmentalism and its legitimising theory of modernisation were inseparable from imperialism and war. Development was conceived both as a Cold War antidote to communist revolution and as a means by which ex-colonies could be maintained as subordinate suppliers of resources and raw materials for Northern capital. As Walt Rostow, the 'father' of modernisation theory, wrote in a 1954 CIA position paper: 'In the short run communism must be contained militarily. In the long run we must rely on the development, in partnership with others, of an environment in which societies which directly or indirectly menace ours will not evolve. We believe the achievement of a degree of steady economic growth is an essential part of such an environment' (cited in Price, 2003). Further, as we saw in the context of population control, race was inextricably implicated in the Cold War fear of communism. Thus Cold War military strategist Thomas Schelling testified before the US House Foreign Affairs Committee, on 27 January 1966, while discussing the dangers if all Asia 'went Communist', that this would exclude 'the United States and what we call Western civilization from a large part of the world that is poor and coloured and potentially hostile' (cited in Chomsky, 2002: 329).

To comprehend the racialised violence of development in this era, then, we need to remember not only the mass displacement by hydroelectric projects and road building invoked by the post-developmentalists, but the racialised genocide and devastation of Vietnam, of which Rostow was a prinicipal architect.[3] We need to remember not only the erasure of 'traditional' knowledges about bodies, but the systematic racialised and gendered violence of population control as a weapon of the Cold War. We should perhaps think a little less of Escobar's 'problematisation' of poverty in this period and more of the long list of CIA assassinations of those who, like Patrice Lumumba in the Congo, were perceived as a threat to the global structures that perpetuated poverty, of the racialised dispensability of the millions of people killed in imperialist interventions, sponsored coups, wars and counter-insurgency operations.

To fully comprehend development and the way racism is imbricated within it, we need also to historicise it, a process which includes, but cannot be limited to, questioning the narrative fissure between colonialism and development. This historicisation, I would argue, is neglected in much postcolonial work. In highlighting the continuities in the 'meta-narratives' of development – the continuing centrality of discourses of progress, improvement and meeting goals – it obscures the successive substantial changes in global patterns of capital accumulation and, relatedly, in the dominant development approaches which have marked the period since 1945.

By retaining a critical focus on Cold War statist developmentalism and its discourse of modernisation and industrialisation, postcolonial critics of development are unable to engage meaningfully with the vast body of work, much of which has taken place in the global South, testifying to the destructive material impacts of neoliberal policies. These include the systematic dismantling of social provision and infrastructure, and the decisive move away from planning which has accompanied the increasing mobility of 'footloose' global capital and the integration of populations into global markets on highly unequal terms, with ever-deepening effects on peoples' daily lives and embodied experiences. This neglect of historical changes in development is particularly problematic because of the tremendous capacity of neoliberal discourses to flexibly incorporate critical ideas. Increasingly, the notions of 'difference' and multiple subjectivities, which poststructuralists have used to counter hegemonic constructions of knowledge, have, like the notion of agency, been appropriated, transformed and redeployed within neoliberal discourses of development. As we saw in Chapter 2, they reappear in the context of an emphasis on 'choice', individual 'empowerment' through the market, and users' co-management of (for which read responsibility for) social provision, legitimising policies of liberalisation, privatisation and outright corporate plunder, and marginalising questions of inequality, oppression and exploitation. Further, the notion of Eurocentrism itself has been mobilised to legitimise the neoliberal undermining of the state and the further opening up of economies to global capital. Thus, as discussed in Chapter 5, state structures and state responsibility for social provision have been constructed in World Bank discourse as an alien Western imposition bound to fail in Africa, while market forces are characterised as inherently and authentically 'African'. More broadly, as Duffield (2005) notes, development is no longer primarily constructed in the universalising terms of 'catching up with the West' critiqued by post-structuralists (Escobar, 1995); rather, with the shift to goals of 'sustainable development' prescribed for the global South, 'difference' is now celebrated in the form of permanent global inequality.

Chandra Mohanty has written that 'cultural relativist (postmodernist) models of scholarship and teaching are easily assimilated within the logic of late capitalism because this is fundamentally a logic of seeming decentralisation and accumulation of differences' (Mohanty, 2003: 524).[4] In line with this, the 'valorisation of ambivalence and hybridity' within postcolonial studies (Sylvester, 1999: 714) has increasingly been incorporated into dominant constructions of neoliberal globalisation. Within these celebratory discourses, hybridity is less a practice of resistance by the colonised and more a form of 'social capital' with which to negotiate globalisation successfully, and a potential resource for development interventions. I return to this point later in this chapter, in the context of the increasing emphasis on the role of diasporas in development.

Multiculturalism and development

As I have suggested, recent studies have tended to emphasise the contingency and mutability of day-to-day practices within and by development institutions at the expense of attention to their location within a racialised global political economy. Critics of the whiteness of development have attempted to combine postcolonial approaches with Gramscian-inflected sociological understandings of race – in particular, Omi and Winant's influential concepts of racial formation and racial projects, which they use to theorise racism in the United States (Omi and Winant, 1986). But the fact that these understandings implicitly construct the social formation as a bounded category for analysis and do not engage centrally with imperialism and global relations of power[5] constrains their critical potential in relation to development, and reinforces these studies' tendency towards a limited and limiting conceptualisation of development.

Thus (paradoxically, given the postcolonial critique of the very concept of development), when it comes to considering strategies for challenging the racism of development, these are usually conceived as operating at the level of practices within the frameworks of development institutions, defined as incorporating only those organisations – NGOs, government departments, international bodies – which are avowedly concerned with development and aid. These analyses convey a sense that development institutions based in the global North are temporally as well as spatially distinct from the societies in which they are located, that the racialised practices within them are a 'shocking' anachronism, and that they need to 'learn' from more progressive approaches to racism, which, it is implied, have become widely accepted in these societies. Vital to this process, it is argued, is the recognition of the 'links between black people in donor countries and those in aid-receiving countries' (Kothari, 2006: 21). The hope has been that 'debates around multiculturalism and anti-racism could inform a shift away from racialised representations and inequalities prevailing in development' (9).

In Britain in the 1980s multicultural policies were extensively critiqued by anti-racist activists and thinkers as a historically contingent state strategy for co-opting and undermining black radicalism and marginalising its analysis of racism as institutionalised and intrinsic and necessary to capitalism (Wilson, 1983; Sivanandan, 1985). The British state's adoption of multicultural policies which involved equal opportunities legislation, attempts to incorporate black and ethnic minority people into institutional structures, and the establishment of conservative elements within black and ethnic minority communities as spokespersons or community leaders, came in response to the culmination of a wide array of struggles against racist policing and immigration control, racist attacks on the streets and on people's homes, and racism in access to employment, education and health. In particular, multiculturalism was a strategy of fragmenting the black politics that had emerged out of these struggles, and that rejected biological conceptions of 'race' and redefined what it meant to be black as a political identity that brought together all those who experienced institutionalised racism. Multicultural policies actively sought to undermine this solidarity through initiatives (particularly related to the funding of community organisations) which encouraged people to come together on a much narrower basis of country of origin, language and, later, with the emergence in the 1990s of the notion of 'faith communities', religion (Alexander, 1998).

The emphasis on 'faith communities', however, also reflected the increasing centrality of global politics and the post-Cold War emphasis on Islam as the 'new enemy' of the West in shaping constructions of 'race' in Britain (Wilson, 1993). From the late 1990s onwards, the British state turned away from multiculturalism as a strategy in favour of a new assertion of 'Britishness' in the context of its domestic and global 'war on terror' (Kundnani, 2007; A. Wilson, 2007; Lentin and Titley 2011) and the emergence of 'new hierarchies of belonging' (Back and Sinha, 2011). While ethnic minorities continued to be represented as a part of the face of postcolonial Britain, this belonging now became conditional, as we will see, on identification with 'British values' and, more concretely, with the strategic economic and geopolitical objectives of the British state. Alongside and inextricable from these changes in state policy has been the reconfiguration of racism in Britain. While earlier racialised constructions and their material effects remain extremely powerful, anti-Muslim racism, which emerged as a key theme in the early 1990s, has now moved centre stage.

Not surprisingly perhaps, rather than a radical anti-racist critique, it is elements of the new approach of the British state, in which the earlier strategies of co-option have been adapted for a new era of imperialism, which are now informing initiatives to incorporate people from black and ethnic minority groups into Britain's development activities. In the following section, we will look at the implications for 'race' and racism in development of the Department for International Development's policy of engaging with BME and Diaspora groups.

The underlying preoccupation with changing the personnel of development – making the 'face' of development somehow less white – is of course one with a long history, and has repeatedly surfaced as a strategy for containing resistance and diffusing much more fundamental critiques of the development enterprise. Thus many colonial missionary groups and charitable organisations changed their personnel in the context of the rise of anti-colonial struggles and the pre-independence atmosphere of anti-imperialist nationalism in African countries (see Manji and O'Coill, 2002: 572, who refer to this process in Kenya in the 1950s; Christian Aid evolved out of a network of these organisations); while, as Julie Hearn describes, the proliferation of African NGOs in the 1990s 'characterized by external financial dependence and an external orientation' (Hearn, 2007: 1103) reflected a similar strategy: 'by the end of the 1980s it was clear to many that such a heavy white foreign presence, with its overtones of colonialism, was politically unsustainable. One of the most significant responses by NGOs and their sponsors was to indigenize the NGO-sector' (1101).

More broadly, the imperative of training and producing 'educated elites' who can be indigenous representatives of dominant Western ideas has been central to development discourse and practice at least since Macaulay's infamous Minute on Education of 1835. In the era of independence movements and the Cold War, the importance of creating modernising elites within 'backward' societies was a central tenet of modernisation theory, and was backed up by the CIA, the Ford Foundation (which produced Chile's Chicago Boys and

Indonesia's Berkeley Mafia, pioneers of neoliberal economics) and institutions like the notorious School of the Americas (now renamed the Western Hemisphere Institute for Security Cooperation). But, as we saw in Chapter 5, this imperative has returned in the 2000s with the notion of 'ownership', which emerged in response to the resistance generated by the economic and political conditionalities of the 1980s and 1990s and the critique of World Bank- and IMF-imposed neoliberal policies as a 'new colonialism'. With 'ownership', leaders are expected to be so steeped in neoliberal ideology that conditionalities are no longer necessary; in practice, this means that they will be consulting on a day-to-day basis with the representatives of the IMF and Northern government donors.

Diasporas in development, contemporary imperialism and reconfiguring racism: experiences from Britain[6]

The policy of the British government's Department for International Development of engaging with black and ethnic minority communities can be traced back to New Labour's 1997 White Paper on International Development, which emphasised 'building support for development in order to increase public understanding of our mutual dependence and the commitment to eliminate global poverty' (Thornton and Hext, 2009: 1), an approach that was consistent with the consolidation of the development/security paradigm under Tony Blair. This was elaborated in DfID's 'Building Support for Development Strategy' (BSDS), published in 1999. However, as noted by an evaluation of the policy ten years on, within this focus on 'public awareness', engagement with black and ethnic minority groups was 'not a particularly high priority'. But this was to change:

> The decade since 1997 has seen dramatic changes in the international development agenda ... Underlying these policy shifts were deeper factors – climate change, globalisation, the post 9/11 conflict agenda, wider issues of peace and security – which have changed public perceptions ... these changes were reflected in the approach to civil society. This is particularly evident in the engagement with BME

groups, the later focus on Diaspora networks and the changing role in relation to faith communities and faith based organisations. (Thornton and Hext, 2009: 14)

The evaluation observes that after the publication of the 2006 White Paper, there has been a further shift in DfID's approach to BME engagement: 'At this point the term "Diaspora" became more established in the development vernacular with BME groups valued more for the contribution they could make to economic and political development in their "countries of origin or heritage"' (14).

This is consistent with a wider rise in interest in the role of 'diasporas' in development. As Oliver Bakewell suggests in the context of African diasporas, 'the discovery of these developmentally-minded diasporas' by development institutions like DfID is quite recent (Bakewell, 2009: 1), with diasporas earlier being identified in development discourse with brain drain, remittances with increased inequality between households, and, in some contexts, diaspora political organisations with supporting and financing conflict.

With the advent of neoliberal policies, the shift to market-led development strategies, and the near collapse of state provision in many regions, migrants' remittances came to be increasingly viewed as an important safety net. More recently the emphasis on diasporas' role in development has gone beyond remittances to focus on their potential for investment and deployment of skills in countries of origin, and on diaspora organisations as a new channel for development initiatives. Again, this can be seen as linked to the rising emphasis on NGOs (particularly from the 1990s onwards) as the most suitable vehicle for both service provision and building a consensus around neoliberal ideas.

For donor governments and NGOs, working through diaspora groups is seen as a way of promoting 'ownership' of development interventions: 'through people who share the languages and culture' (Bakewell, 2009: 1). The dominant development discourse on diasporas has incorporated postcolonial notions of hybridity and transnationalism, which are seen as assets that can be instrumentally mobilised for the project of development. But this approach both assumes that diaspora communities are homogenous, failing to recognise the class and multiple other affiliations which shape their interaction with countries of origin, and ignores the fact that in the countries where they live, racism and 'hierarchies of belonging' structure their experiences in a variety of ways, and condition their ability to engage in 'homeland' development (Hammond et al., 2011). In fact the increased interest in diasporas in development has coincided with policies in the North which have led to escalating insecurity, precarity and exclusion for many people in these communities.

As we will see, the enthusiasm for diasporas in development has strong undertones of civilisational discourse, particularly in the context of the 'War on Terror'. For example, a recent report on 'The Pakistani Diaspora in Europe and its Impact on Democracy Building in Pakistan' argues that 'Diaspora members ... have a lot to contribute as they have seen how democracy and democratic institutions work' (Abbasi, 2010: 9). The diaspora involvement in Pakistan currently promoted by the British government is explicitly related to so-called 'deradicalisation' (Malik, 2011). Clearly, both Britain and the USA are increasingly seeking to incorporate diaspora organisations into the pursuit of broader strategic military, economic and political objectives.

Representing diasporas in development

The notion of the British diasporic subject as occupying a particularly appropriate location from which to intervene in development, which guides these policies, is also present in a number of recent popular representations of 'developing countries' in the British media in which we are invited to view them through the gaze of the young diasporic British citizen. The underlying assumption that diasporic communities can legitimise and give 'ownership' to existing development interventions by the global North is mirrored here, I suggest, in a sense that these 'second generation' diaspora commentators can effectively represent the perceived superiority of 'British' values over those ascribed to their country of origin while remaining by definition immune to accusations of racism. The emphasis here, however, is somewhat less on the unique potential supposedly stemming from hybridised cultural identities (though this theme remains), and more on the thoroughly 'British' outlook of the new generation of diasporic subjects, who, as we will see, are constituted in these representations almost as Trojan Horses being introduced into the alien cultural territory of their country of origin.

In order to explore this further, I briefly consider four documentaries, all of which were aired on BBC3 during 2010 and 2011. In *Women, Weddings, War and Me*, 21-year-old Nel Hedayat, who spent her early childhood in Afghanistan but has grown up in London, visits Afghanistan to find out about the position of women in the country. This was followed by two further documentaries using the same format: in *The World's Most Dangerous Place for Women*, 23-year-old Londoner Judith Wanga returns to the Democratic Republic of Congo and is reunited with her parents before visiting the conflict-affected region of Eastern Congo to speak to survivors of rape; while in *The World's Most Dangerous Place to Meet My Family* 21-year-old Dean Whitney from Sheffield, whose mother is from Yemen, visits his mother's family there, and reports on the human rights situation. Most recently, Nel Hedayet herself presented another documentary in a different though related format, *The Truth About Child Brides*, an investigation of child marriage in India and Bangladesh.

It should be made clear from the outset that the aim here is not to develop a comprehensive critique of these particular documentaries. *The World's Most Dangerous Place for Women*, in particular, largely deals sensitively with extremely complex and painful situations. Nor does this discussion seek to undermine attempts to make particular issues accessible in a popular idiom. Rather, the aim is to ask what representational work documentaries of this kind are doing in the context of wider racialised constructions of the diaspora's role in development. In order to explore this, we need to recognise that all forms of media production are processes of representation. The fact that we are discussing television documentaries should not obscure the fact that what is said and what takes place in them is not simply recorded but is constructed in specific ways in order to produce a particular set of narratives and particular 'understandings, subjectivities, and versions of the world'. The process of representing difference (such as that of 'race', gender or class) in media is thus also always a process of constructing it (Gill, 2007: 12). These representations also involve specific constructions of the projected viewer, while, as recent work by feminist media critics has emphasised, viewers actively engage with media representations in multiple, contingent and contradictory ways (Wearing, 2012).

All three of the documentaries portraying a 'return' to the country of origin open with scenes in which the protagonists demonstrate their 'Britishness', primarily through an affiliation to particular practices of femininity and masculinity. In the cases of Nel and Judith, this is portrayed in a strikingly similar way (despite the films having different directors): through demonstrating gendered and sexualised patterns of consumption and self-presentation which establish them as 'normal' young British women. Nel shows off the camisoles and 'short shorts' in her wardrobe, explaining 'I won't be able to wear any of this in Afghanistan', while Jude is first shown putting on mascara and, shortly afterwards, expressing alarm that she almost forgot to pack her hair-straighteners for the trip. Meanwhile Dean, the only male protagonist, explains that he finds it 'difficult to be a good Muslim in England because of the distractions. The Number One temptation? I would have to say sex, yeah (laughs).' Later, in Yemen, when he encounters young women at an amusement park wearing burkhas, he will reaffirm his British lad's masculinity with the comment 'I'm trying to think about what young boys talk about when they talk about girls.... You can't see their bum and you can't see their chest', while simultaneously rejecting what we are told are the markers of Yemeni masculinity ('He'd rather help his grandmother cook the sheep than kill it' according to the narrator).

While other commentators have noted that the discourse that constructs young diasporic subjects as 'caught between two cultures' or 'competing identities' is reiterated in *Women, Weddings, War and Me* (Ayaan, 2010), as where Nel states as one of the motives for her visit, 'I'm not fully British, and I can never be fully Afghan',

I would suggest that this is in fact less prominent here than a discourse of 'successful' assimilation. Both Nel and Jude are shown reacting strongly against day-to-day gendered practices that they encounter in their country of origin (arranged marriage in the case of Afghanistan, and in the Congo the insistence that young unmarried women should live with their families). But strikingly these reactions as they are portrayed in the film do not spring from long-term awareness of and resistance to the underlying ideas, but rather from the complete unfamiliarity, surprise and repugnance of the outsider: Nel is incredulous and 'cannot imagine' marrying someone she has not chosen, while Jude has 'never heard anything so ridiculous'. Their diasporic identities as constructed in the films seem to be predicated on a lack of prior knowledge which is not always credible, leading one to ask why it is clearly considered so important by the film-makers.

The later sections of both of these films explore issues of violence against women in the respective countries. Jude and Nel both meet women and children who have experienced horrifying gender-based violence. The focus here is on the traumatic effects of these encounters on the visitors, with the films building up to a climax where they are overwhelmed by what they see and hear about and break down. This focus is perhaps inevitable given the format of the films, but it raises once again long-standing questions raised by feminist postcolonial thinkers about representing others, who can speak, and whose voice can be heard (Spivak, 1988; Alcoff 1995). This is not to suggest that the women in the film are represented as 'passive victims': both Nel and Jude emphasise the courage and agency of women they encounter, several of whom are activists defending women's rights. But the voices of these Afghan and Congolese women (as well as those of the Yemeni men and women encountered in *The World's Most Dangerous Place to Meet My Family*) are filtered to the audience through reactions of the diasporic subject. Thus in place of the authoritative 'objective' voice of the white, middle-class reporter which still dominates representations of the global South in the media, what we encounter here is the privileging of the voice of the empathetic diasporic subject. The affective connection implied in being a member of a diasporic community is here expected to allay any concerns about representation, and at the same time facilitates an appropriation of affect and emotion, leading one to ask not only 'who can speak?', but also 'who can feel?' This echoes feminist anti-racist scholarship which highlights how the notion of empathy conceptualised as 'co-feeling' can in fact work to strengthen the voice and authority to speak of the already privileged empathising subject (Hemmings, 2011: 203; see also Ahmed, 2004; Pedwell, 2012).

So far we have discussed some common features of all three of the films in this format. But they also differ from each other in significant ways which relate to the reconfiguring of contemporary British racism. First, *The World's Most Dangerous Place for Women* differs from the other films in so far as it highlights the role of Western companies in fuelling the war and mass rape, through their demand for Congo's minerals (particularly emphasising the use of coltan in mobile phones, laptops and other electronic consumer goods). Although this is framed in terms of Jude coming to question her own consumption patterns (an established narrative of visits of young people from the 'developed' to the 'developing' world), rather than in terms of any more structural explanation, it contrasts with the marked elision of the role of the British state and British capital in generating the situations encountered in Afghanistan and Yemen.

Second, while, as we saw, all the films emphasise the 'cultural' Britishness of the diasporic subjects featured, the two films that feature young British Muslims seek to demonstrate their allegiance specifically to the British state and its imperial presence in their country of origin, in ways which, again, often appear contrived. Thus Dean, on entering the heavily fortified British embassy in Sana'a, describes it as 'a little piece of home'; Nel, while interviewing provincial prosecutor Maria Bashir, refers to 'our boys' who 'are here fighting presumably for your rights and your progress'.

In fact in both *Women, Weddings, War and Me* and *The World's Most Dangerous Place to Meet My Family* the visits are ultimately portrayed as redemptive journeys, where what Nel and Dean really discover is a deeper appreciation of the privilege of being British citizens. After visiting women imprisoned for so-called 'crimes of morality', Nel reflects: 'I've had so many opportunities … it humbles me to think, God, it could have been me.' The trip, we are told later, has made one thing clear: 'I can't be in Afghanistan.' This is even more explicit in the case of *The World's Most Dangerous Place to Meet My Family*, which concludes with Dean explaining: 'there are so many things which aren't there in Yemen – just even as simple as human rights. That is why I am proud to be British and I am honoured to live in this country. To be honest, I am really glad I live in England.'

Perhaps inevitably, given the current preoccupation with the figure of the young British Muslim man as the 'enemy within' on account of his perceived connections with the 'Muslim world', it is the film featuring Dean's visit to Yemen 'on the frontline of the War on Terror' which conveys this notion of a redemptive journey towards British values most directly. Prior to the trip, returning home from a football match, Dean reflects on the day-to-day racism he encounters: 'If I went to a pub now, I think I'd be beaten up.… I'm sure I'll die there [Yemen] to be honest. For people like me, who are trying to fit into, I don't want to be racist, but the white culture, the Western way, I don't think you do fit in.' These experiences are understood by Dean as shaping his identity without ultimately undermining his own sense of having a right to be in Britain, echoing anti-racist constructions of belonging: 'I would say I am a British Muslim, a steel-city Yemeni as we like to call ourselves.' But after encountering human rights violations in Yemen such as police firing on unarmed protesters and the disappearance of dissidents, Dean apparently learns to count his blessings: 'I didn't realise how comfortable we have it in England. Living where I live, police, they stop you in the street, you do get harassed, but it's nothing. Here if you say the wrong thing you'll disappear.' There is no indication here of the connections between the British government's engagement in the 'War on Terror' and these human rights violations, or indeed of the incarcerations without charge in Britain itself under anti-terror laws of people who have 'said the wrong thing' or, as in the cases of Babar Ahmed and

Talha Ahsan, allegedly looked at the wrong website,[7] often on the basis of evidence that is kept secret. Meeting a group of Yemeni men and women who talk about how the British government's actions in Iraq are generating sympathy for al-Qaeda, Dean has 'never felt so British', and, in case we haven't got the message, the narrator tells us that 'there is a kind of radical Islam getting a foothold here which Dean is beginning to realise he can never sympathise with'. Later, Dean meets survivors of a government missile attack on their village, Majala, in which US missiles were used, but unsurprisingly, perhaps, in this case his desire to tell people outside the country about such events is not followed up by the producers (unlike, for example, Judith's ongoing campaign to raise awareness of violence against women in the Congo). And things are soon back on track. By the time he returns to Sheffield, 'his journey of self-discovery cut short by Yemen's capacity for violence', Dean is shown to be no longer the confident, critical and potentially angry 'steel-city Yemeni', but affirms that he is now unproblematically 'proud to be British' and 'honoured to live in this country'.

The fourth documentary I will consider here, *The Truth About Child Brides*, is in many ways the most explicitly focused on issues perceived to be related to 'development', particularly in the context of gender relations, while it relies overwhelmingly on 'cultural' explanations for its analysis. While this film does not actually portray the return of the diasporic subject, it is similarly constructed around a central figure considered to be uniquely qualified to comment and empathise. Starting with the explanation that her grandmother and aunt 'were child brides', Nel Hedayat visits India and Bangladesh to investigate the practice of child marriage.[8]

In India, having attended a child marriage in rural Rajasthan, Nel meets a group of well-off teenage girls living in the state capital, Jaipur, to solicit their views on the practice. What is striking here is the construction of the girls as not only disapproving of, but completely ignorant of and bewildered by local forms of gender-based oppression in a way that mirrors Nel's own reactions. Even though one of the girls refers to a 'maid' employed by her family who arranged for her daughter to marry at an early age, the difference is explained in terms of a rural/urban rather than a class divide. Significantly, contemporary urban India, then, unlike any of the locations discussed earlier, is presented as a successfully developed, globalised space of unproblematic affluence and reassuring similarity rather than disturbing difference for the diasporic subject. This is clearly a growing (although by no means universal) theme in representations of India: in another recent programme, a BBC Radio 4 two-part series *Home from Home* (2011) about people of Indian origin who have moved from Britain to India, the emphasis is similarly on the increasing prevalence of shopping malls, spas and gated communities where 'everything' is available, which are portrayed as making such 'reverse journeys' possible.

In her quest for 'the truth' about child brides, however, Nel rapidly moves on to Bangladesh, where an auto-rickshaw ride through Dhaka's streets is enough to convince her that Bangladesh is 'much poorer' than India.[9] Here Nel meets several girls aged between 13 and 16 who are about to be or have recently been married. In this context the construction of the deviant Third World 'other' is explicit. The girls are portrayed as victims in a way which is literally dehumanising: one group of young women (who were in fact suffering from obstetric fistula and in hospital awaiting operations when interviewed) are described as not having 'had time to develop a personality'. Meanwhile the men are demonised: while questioning a 19-year-old man about his first impressions of his 13-year-old bride-to-be, Nel comments, 'men here clearly don't look at young girls the way we do in the West!' But while the latter remark might seem to invite awkward questions about objectification and sexualisation in the 'West', the fact is that, as in the films on Afghanistan and Yemen discussed above, oppressive gendered practices are being critiqued here less from a feminist perspective ('Western' or otherwise) and more in celebration of 'British' gender values. Nel repeatedly makes references to her own hypothetical wedding taking place in the future, as when, observing the anxious expression of a 13-year-old bride, she comments somewhat callously: 'I wouldn't want to look like that on my wedding day!' Later Nel meets Munni, an unmarried garment worker who supports her family financially, and, we are told, has worked forty hours a week since the age of 13, a neoliberal 'solution' which Nel assures us is 'the lesser of two evils'. But when Munni explains that she has no intention of getting married until she is 25, and is happy to remain unmarried if no husband is forthcoming then, Nel hastens to scotch this possibility, exclaiming 'No, no, you'll find *someone* in Bangladesh!' in a classic example of silencing and being unable to hear what is actually being said.

In terms of their approach to gender relations, these films are consistent with an aspect of contemporary British international intervention, and specifically its engagement in the 'War on Terror', which Vron Ware, in her study of the cultural activities of the British Council in the Middle East, describes as 'soft power' (Ware, 2011). This has centred around the active promotion, particularly among young people, of notions of emancipation conceived primarily in terms of gendered market-driven patterns of sexuality, sociality and consumption, which have been broadly characterised as 'postfeminist' (Gill, 2012) as part of a strategy to counter the rise of ideologies and movements considered hostile to the interests of British capital.

As the discussion above suggests, diasporic subjects are increasingly viewed as ideally positioned to further the imperialist project. Their involvement is located within a broader civilisational discourse and contributes to the production of particular representations of both contemporary Britain and those locations in the 'developing' world which become the target of intervention, for circulation within Britain and beyond. In this context, we need to further critically examine official initiatives for diaspora participation in development.

DfID, faith communities and the Hindu right

In this section we will look at DfID's engagement with black and ethnic minority communities, which as we have seen was first articulated by the Department as a desirable goal in the late 1990s (DfID, 1999). Clearly, in terms of concrete action this remained at best a very marginal concern for the department under New

Labour, while under the Coalition government that came to power in 2010 it appears to have been further sidelined, as indicated by the scrapping of the Diaspora Volunteering Programme in 2011. What is significant about this engagement, however, is the distinct framing of these limited initiatives, their contribution to constructing a specific version of 'ethnic minority communities' and their relationship with the 'developing world', and the ways in which certain kinds of relationships, and particular political forces, have been strengthened as a result. Exploring these processes in the context of India and the so-called 'Hindu diaspora', I suggest that these intiatives fit into both the neoliberal approach to development being promoted by DfID and the reformulation of domestic racism which has prefigured and accompanied Britain's engagement in the War on Terror.

In July 2006, DfID announced that it had awarded substantial grants from its Development Awareness Fund to 'three ethnic minority organisations' to 'teach schoolchildren, young people and community groups about the lives of people in Africa and Asia' (DfID, 2006). These organisations included Minorities of Europe, which was to 'train 150 14–24 year olds from black and ethnic minority communities .... as "champions" for international development', and the Muslim Council of Britain, which was to 'increase awareness of the role that can be played by faith communities in reducing global poverty.... produce teaching materials for Muslim schools and madresas [sic], a website focusing on work to reduce poverty and links between Muslim communities in the UK and in India, Bangladesh and Nigeria' (DfID, 2006). Most prominently featured in the announcement, however, was the slightly smaller grant of £137,532 to an organisation called Hindu Aid to 'work with the Hindu community in temples, schools and Asian businesses and at Hindu festivals to raise awareness of global development'. Ramesh Kallidai of Hindu Aid, the only beneficiary organisation to be quoted in DfID's press release, apparently saw the grant slightly differently, explaining that it would 'allow British Hindus, many of whom are already engaged in aid and poverty alleviation programmes, to organise their international development activities in a more structured manner' (DfID, 2006).

A number of questions arise from the DfID initiative. Most striking at first glance is the extent to which 'ethnic minority communities' have come by the middle of the decade to be reconfigured as 'faith communities'. What is more, it is along lines of 'faith' that these communities are posited as potentially engaging with – and furthering – Britain's securitised development objectives in the twenty-first century. The ascription of religion as the primary marker of identity for 'ethnic minority' subjects here seems particularly heavy-handed since clearly the rationale for such initiatives is in fact the existence of country of origin rather than faith-based links (hence the references to 'India, Bangladesh and Nigeria').[10] The inescapable implication of the insistence on 'faith' is that the British government is seeking to mitigate the effects of an apparently inevitable 'clash of civilisations'; it underlines the shift from a primarily technical discourse of progress through development interventions back to an earlier, avowedly civilisational one, which revolves around questions of faith and morality.

However, we also need to consider the significance of the particular emphasis placed on the 'Hindu community' in the DfID initiative.[11] The description of the role of the grant to the Muslim Council of Britain reproduces yet again the sense of the state's concern about, and imperative to intervene in, 'Muslim communities', with its reference to producing teaching materials for Muslim schools and 'madresas', an impression of anxiety which is only compounded by the admission that 'Final arrangements for this project are still to be agreed' (DfID, 2006). By contrast, the 'Hindu community' is presented as a robust and unproblematic partner, to be found in 'temples, schools and Asian businesses' (the latter presumably assumed to be all Hindu-owned) 'and at Hindu festivals' (DfID, 2006).

The fact that the self-styled representatives of the 'Hindu community' in Britain (including those who run Hindu Aid) are almost exclusively aligned with the far-right Hindu supremacist family of organisations in India, the Sangh Parivar, is not, as I argue in this section, in any way in contradiction with this assumption of shared developmental objectives. To understand this, we have to consider how support for the Hindu far right in Britain has been related to diasporic material and symbolic investment in particular forms of neoliberal corporate-led development taking place in India since the early 1990s. Further, we need to think about how the reconfiguration of constructions of 'race' in Britain and in globalised discourses associated with the War on Terror, in which the racialised and gendered figure of the Muslim 'other' has become central, have intersected with changing structures and discourses of power, exclusion and belonging within India.

The Sangh Parivar emerged as a major political force in India in the 1990s, the period coinciding with the introduction of economic liberalisation, following the launch of its campaign to build a Ram temple on the site of the Babri Masjid (mosque) at Ayodhya, which was accompanied by orchestrated communal violence. The main political party of Hindutva, the Bharatiya Janata Party (BJP), was in government at national level as the dominant party in the National Democratic Alliance (NDA) between 1998 and 2004 and continues to control several Indian state governments, including that of Gujarat. At the core of the Sangh Parivar, however, is an organisation formed in the mid-1920s, the Rashtriya Swayamsevak Sangh (RSS), an authoritarian, militarist, cadre-based organisation which shared many features with rising fascist parties in Italy and (in the 1930s), Germany, which were also a direct source of inspiration.[12] The RSS, which is organised through a system of *shakhas* (branches) in which young men and boys undergo physical training and the intensive inculcation of Hindu supremacist ideas, continues to provide the ideological direction – as well as being the source of most of the leaders – for the plethora of organisations which have been established around it. Known internationally as the Hindu Swayamsevak Sangh (HSS), it has branches in all parts of the UK with significant Indian Hindu (mainly Gujarati) populations. The Sangh Parivar actively targeted the Indian diaspora in the UK and North America from the 1980s onwards (Jaffrelot and Therwath, 2011: 48), and now draws upon it extensively for moral and, more importantly, material support for its project of establishing Indian as a Hindu *rashtra* or state, support which, as has been well documented, runs into millions of dollars. By setting up groups claiming to represent Hindu 'faith communities', the Sangh Parivar in Britain also has access to government funding for its activities. A number of local councils have directly funded the HSS, including Brent, Newham, Leeds, Bradford, Hillingdon and Coventry. In some areas local schools have provided free premises for *shakha* meetings (South Asia Solidarity Group, 2004). Pro-Hindutva groups in Britain also forged strong links with both the Labour Party and the Conservative Party. For example, in 2001, the Labour MP for Brent North, Barry Gardiner, representing the Labour Friends of India, visited Gujarat where he personally presented BJP chief minister Narendra Modi with a cheque for £1 million, collected in Britain by the charity Sewa International for earthquake relief (Awaaz South Asia Watch, 2004).

In the wake of the unprecedented violence of the meticulously planned, state-sponsored genocidal attacks on Muslims in the BJP-ruled state of Gujarat just the following year, in which an estimated 2,000 people were killed and more than 200,000 people displaced, the fundraising activities of Sangh Parivar organisations in Britain came under the spotlight, as progressive South Asian organisations stepped up their campaign to expose their links with Hindu supremacist violence against India's Muslim and Christian minorities. The biggest Indian charity in Britain, Sewa International, which had raised £2 million in Britain for Gujarat earthquake reconstruction and rehabilitation from 2001 onwards, was in fact the fundraising arm of the HSS, under whose name it was registered with the British Charity Commission. A Channel 4 television news report broadcast on 12 December 2002 revealed how one organisation funded by Sewa International, the Vanavasi Kalyan Ashram in Gujarat, was directly involved in the genocidal violence against Muslims in the state which took place in February and March of that year. Forensic evidence implicated a leading member, as 'leading a mob of 2,000 tribal people', in an attack on Muslims.[13]

The programme also reported that a Vanavasi Kalyan Ashram leader 'threatened the villagers saying that if they didn't join in provoking the Muslims and burning them, they would also be treated like Muslims and burnt', while another activist told the reporter: 'the Christians have made a church in our village. We have thought several times of destroying it. One day we will definitely break it down' (Channel 4 News, 12 December 2002).

A report by Awaaz South Asia Watch, *In Bad Faith? British Charity and Hindu Extremism*, published in February 2004, further detailed the role of Sewa International UK, the HSS and the Vishwa Hindu Parishad (UK) in financing communal terror in India, and in particular the diversion of funds raised for earthquake relief in Gujarat for this purpose (Awaaz South Asia Watch, 2004).

In September 2002, pressurised by South Asian organisations in Britain, the Charity Commissioners had agreed to undertake an investigation into the activities and goals of Sewa International and the HSS. However, the Commissioners admitted off the record that nothing would be done to stem the flow of funds without the go-ahead of the Foreign Office. In 2004, the investigation was dropped by the Charity Commission, which acknowledged, however, that they had not carried out any inquiries in India into the use of funds raised in Britain (South Asia Solidarity Group, 2004). Subsequently it emerged that the Indian government had denied the Commissioners visas to travel to India ('India Refuses Visas to Charity Investigators', *Guardian*, 27 February 2004).

However, as a result of this exposure of Sewa International, the Sangh Parivar increasingly began using other channels for fund-raising in Britain. One of these was Hindu Aid, the organisation which DfID, only four years after the Gujarat genocide, considered most suited to 'raise awareness of global development'. As was already widely known, Hindu Aid is an offshoot of the Hindu Forum of Britain, an organisation which has been vocal in espousing the Hindu supremacist ideology of *Hindutva*. As an investigation by Andrew Gilligan in the *Evening Standard* newspaper subsequently noted (Gilligan, 2007), while Hindu Aid describes itself as a British charity, it is in fact not a registered charity, but a limited company which has claimed exemption from the requirement to file detailed

234 | RACE, RACISM AND DEVELOPMENT

accounts. Ramesh Kallidai, who is quoted in the DfID press release, and is secretary general of the Hindu Forum and vice chair of Hindu Aid, works closely with the key Sangh Parivar groups in Britain, the Vishwa Hindu Parishad and the RSS/HSS, and has publicly celebrated the legacy of RSS leader M.S. Golwalkar (Gilligan, 2007), who notoriously viewed Hitler's treatment of the Jews as a model of 'race pride' which India should emulate (Golwalkar, 1944: 37).

However, perhaps even more startling than DfID's support for Hindu Aid was the fact that Kallidai had some months earlier been appointed to the government's Committee on Integration and Cohesion, a body set up by New Labour in the wake of the 7/7 bombings in London, and reflecting the ongoing shift in British state policy that involved publicly repenting the perceived errors of earlier multicultural policies and presenting integration and 'community cohesion' as a new salvation.

The inclusion of a figure like Kallidai in a committee whose brief was to 'produce a vision of society where people are committed to what we have in common rather than obsessing with those things that make us different' (Committee on Integration and Cohesion, 2007) may seem surprising, and for some commentators it represented another example of the state uncritically supporting conservative religious groups in the name of 'culture' (see, for example, Lord Desai, quoted in Gilligan, 2007). However, it can be argued that this does not take into account the specificities of the Hindu supremacist ideology. Within the discourses of *Hindutva*, Muslims, and Muslim men in particular, are identified as the primary threat to the nation, and made to represent symbolically a series of interlinked tropes including terrorism, fanaticism, allegiance to forces external and hostile to the nation, illegal immigration, rapid population growth and women's subordination. Indian 'national interests' within these hyper-nationalist discourses revolve around the perceived threat from Pakistan, and focus on Kashmir, and the bodies of Kashmiris, as the territory over which Indian 'integrity' must be violently reproduced. Clearly, this has multiple intersections with the post-Cold War shift which identified Islam as the new enemy of 'Western civilisation' (Huntington, 1993) and, post-9/11, the US-led War on Terror; the anti-Muslim racism which has become central following realignments in the dominant discourses of British racism; and the changes in the British state's approaches to 'race' which underpinned the emergence of the 'Community Cohesion' agenda.

This convergence was evident in February 2007 when Ramesh Kallidai and the Hindu Forum of Britain made allegations of 'forced conversion' of 'hundreds' of 'Hindu and Sikh girls' by 'Muslim extremists' at British universities. The allegation of forced conversion of young women is part of an arsenal of myths propagated by the Hindu right in India to incite violence against minority communities; inflammatory leaflets making these claims were in circulation immediately before the massacres of Muslims in Gujarat in 2002, and recently have resurfaced in the fabricated story of a so-called 'Love Jihad' in Kerala and Karnataka (Dube, 2010). In fact the notion of Hindu women needing protection from predatory Muslim men informs the core patriarchal-nationalist narrative of *Hindutva*, which appeals to Hindu men to reassert their masculinity through the performance of sexual and other forms of extreme violence against minority groups (Sarkar, 2002, 2011). In the British case, however, Metropolitan Police Commissioner Ian Blair, who was a guest at the HFB conference where the claims were made, seized the opportunity to commit his force to action, despite the absence of evidence that such conversions were in fact occurring. Blair's remarks were duly reported under headlines like 'Police Protect Girls Forced to Convert to Islam' (*Daily Mail*, 22 February 2007) and 'Hindu Girls Targeted by Extremists' (*Metro*, 23 February, 2007); readers were told that 'extremist Muslims who force vulnerable teenage girls to convert to Islam are being targeted by police' and that 'police are working with universities to clamp down on "aggressive conversions" during which girls are beaten up and forced to abandon university courses' (*Daily Mail*, 22 February 2007). The *Metro* reported that 'Scotland Yard is to set up a Hindu Safety Forum with "aggressive conversion" as its top priority' (*Metro*, 23 February 2007). Yet a few months later the police were apparently unable to cite a single such case (Gilligan, 2007).

Increasingly, in contrast to earlier constructions of 'Asians', 'British Hindus' are not only distinguished from 'Muslims' but represented as the acceptable, integrated face of 'difference', a process of redefinition with strong colonial antecedents which began in the 1990s and in which *Hindutva* groups actively collaborate. The summer of 2001, when Asian youth in the towns of Bradford, Burnley and Oldham in the north of England, mainly of Pakistani and Kashmiri origin, fought pitched battles with the police in riots caused by years of poverty, unemployment and racism, was one of a number of key moments in this process of differentiation. A vocal self-styled 'leader' of the 'Hindu community' in Bradford, Hasmukh Shah is also a leading member of the VHP in Britain. Shah attempted to project the disturbances as primarily Muslim violence against Hindus, telling BBC Radio 4's *Today* programme: 'This is a clear warning to the Home Secretary and the police that if they do not want the streets of Britain to be like the Taleban controlled Afghanistan, then they have to take immediate action (Choudhury, 2001).'[14] The government's response to the riots was to consolidate its 'community cohesion' agenda in which alleged Muslim 'separateness' and failure or refusal to integrate were identified as the primary obstacle and threat (Kundnani, 2007).

However, the symbiotic relationship between Hindu supremacist ideology in Britain and the dominant currents of British racism represents something more than simply a coincidental overlapping of demonisations or even a conjunctural convergence of different actors' political goals. To understand this, we need to look at processes of globalisation, development and imperialism, and how both twenty-first-century British racism and contemporary *Hindutva* are shaped by, and in turn impact upon, these processes.

Hindutva, development and neoliberalism

While the RSS has utilised the 'Swadeshi' rhetoric of economic nationalism, and continues to do so when convenient, Hindu supremacist forces played little part in the anti-colonial movement, focusing their attentions on Muslims rather than the British rulers as 'the enemy of the nation', and in fact actively collaborated with the British on a number of occasions. The more recent claims by the Sangh Parivar that their contemporary leaders like A.B. Vajpayee played a role in the independence struggle have been conclusively debunked (Chatterjee and Ramachandran, 1998; Krishnan, 2007). But what is perhaps more significant here is that the emergence of *Hindutva* forces as an effective political force in India from the beginning of the 1990s has been inextricably related to the restructuring of capital in the era of neoliberal globalisation and the Indian state's embrace of policies of economic liberalisation.

As many commentators have observed, the rise of the Sangh Parivar was in fact preceded by a marked shift towards explicit Hindu chauvinism in state policies in the preceding decade. Following the first IMF loan to India in 1982, the Congress Party government increasingly sought legitimacy for interlinked policies of economic restructuring and militarisation through mobilising *Hindutva*-inflected nationalist rhetoric. Further, the participation of national as well as local Congress leaders in communal violence marked a new phase in which Hindu chauvinism was explicitly visible in the material practices of the state. These trends were massively intensified after the second, larger, IMF loan of 1991, which was conditional on the extensive restructuring of India's economy, of which the now familiar features were removal of controls on foreign capital and import restrictions, cutting subsidies on basic consumer goods and public-sector spending, privatisation and the dismantling of labour protection legislation.

While the last two decades have seen all mainstream political parties adopt the neoliberal approach to development, the BJP has embraced it both ideologically and in policy. This was demonstrated during its rule at the centre between 1998 and 2004, notably through its establishment of a 'Ministry of Disinvestment', indicating 'both a firm retreat from public sector undertakings and a commitment to privatisation' (Sarkar, 2011: 76).

It was also under the BJP that the Indian government began targeting the diaspora for investment. As a DfID-commissioned scoping study on the diaspora role in poverty reduction noted approvingly, 'the government of India has moved ... [to] ... a multi-prong strategy, pursuing portfolio investment, direct investment, technology transfer and trade links through the Diaspora' (Newland, 2004: 5). The report goes on to explain that

> shortly after India's first nuclear tests in 1998, the Indian government launched a huge sale of 5-year bonds ... available only to non-resident Indians (NRIs). Named 'Resurgent India Bonds', the proceeds were in part intended to help offset the impact of the economic sanctions imposed after the nuclear tests.... the government understood it could not count on patriotism alone, and added significant benefits to make the bonds attractive: an interest 2 per cent higher in dollar terms than the US bond market, the option of redemption in US dollars or German marks, and exemption from Indian income and wealth taxes. (Newland, 2004: 5)

As this implies, the Resurgent India Bonds sale and the other initiatives for diaspora investment in India that followed (such as the setting up of L.M. Singhvi's High Level Committee on the Indian Diaspora and the first Pravasi Bharatiya Diwas [Overseas Indians' Day] conference, co-sponsored by the Indian government and the Federation of Indian Chambers of Commerce) were shaped both by a neoliberal framework of development and by explicitly Hindu supremacist notions of 'national pride'.

However, it is in Gujarat, which has been ruled by the BJP with Narendra Modi as chief minister since 2001, that the connections between Hindu fascism and corporate capital are perhaps most evident. The overwhelming evidence of Modi's personal involvement in the Gujarat genocide has not stood in the way of his self-projection as 'Vikas-Purush' (Man of Development). The development policies pursued, in which swathes of land and coastline have been converted into Special Economic Zones (and latterly 'Special Investment Regions') and handed over to corporates heavily subsidised by the state (Yadav, 2011), have meant that high levels of growth in relation to the rest of India have been accompanied by nutrition poverty levels higher than all-India levels (Dixit, 2011), and according to the recent *India Chronic Poverty Report* Gujarat is currently one of the states with the highest incidence of child malnutrition among the poor (Mehta et al., 2011). It has also seen severe curtailment of labour rights,[15] all under the shadow of the continuing activities of Hindu supremacist organisations, as a result of which many Muslim families driven from their homes in 2002 remain in camps unable to return safely.

As a result of this 'development' model, while the BJP is often still viewed as the party of small-scale domestic business and trade due to its core vote base, it is now the ruling party of choice for large sections of Indian and transnational corporate capital. With ongoing indictments against him for the 2002 genocide, Narendra Modi has been endorsed as the best person to be the next prime minister by India's leading corporate billionaires, including Ratan Tata, Mukesh Ambani and Sunil Mittal, the last claiming that 'CEO' Modi 'can also run the nation' (Bidwai, 2009). Tellingly, these statements were made at the Vibrant Gujarat Global Investor Summit, an annual event which targets the diaspora. Another guest was British MP Barry Gardiner, of the pro-Sangh Parivar Labour Friends of India, who went a step further to proclaim that 'Gujarat can lead the world' (Bhattacharya, 2009).

Gujarat has a particular salience in the context of the diaspora in Britain. This is partly because of personal connections with the state – most people of Indian origin who identify as Hindu in Britain are from families which originated in Gujarat and often still have relatives there, although many of these families migrated to Britain via East Africa, where Indians had been inserted into the colonial hierarchy at intermediate levels, as white-collar workers and as owners of small- and large-scale businesses. It is also because of the symbolic role the state has come to play within certain discourses as the epitome of a 'modern', developed and successful India, a construction which dominant sections of Gujarati communities are arguably particularly invested in. This is conceived in specifically neoliberal terms in which growing inequality is irrelevant, and persistent poverty invisible (see Dreze and Sen, 2011 for a commentary on how economic growth in India has perpetuated poverty).

The last decade has seen both the naturalisation of this approach to development, with mainstream political parties in India all adopting it, and the institutional entrenchment of *Hindutva*-inspired notions of citizenship, something which is much more tenacious than the fluctuating electoral fortunes of the BJP and its allies. Referring to the BJP-led coalition's slogan in national elections in 2004, 'India Shining', journalist Nadeem Asrar points out that

> India was 'shining' because it was 'growing' as well as becoming Hindu (at least in their perception). In fact, it is not an accident that the same terms that political Hindutva used – 'awakening', 'resurgence', 'new-found confidence' – are the terms that the champions of neo-liberal India use today to describe India post-1991. (Asrar, 2011)

These terms are also important in contemporary British media representations of India in which, as we saw earlier, urban India is portrayed as an affluent, entrepreneurial and therefore negotiable and 'safe' space for British diasporic subjects.

In fact, this construction of India is consistent with racialised notions of the good neoliberal diasporic subject her/himself. As Amrit Wilson notes, her/his 'difference' consists only of elements of 'culture' which are both essentialised and commoditised (Wilson, 2006), and does not imply any critical perspectives on global capital or imperialist intervention. As we have seen, this is a notion shared by the British state, for which this limited 'difference' is quite compatible with 'integration' and overarching 'British values', and by the organisations which claim to represent 'Hindus in Britain'.[16] The extent to which 'Hinduism' in the racialised discourse of British citizenship has come to be associated with an assumed allegiance to the ongoing British imperialist project was demonstrated in October 2011 when Prime Minister David Cameron spoke at a reception for 'prominent members of the Sikh and Hindu communities' hosted at 10 Downing Street to celebrate Diwali. In his first public comments on the lynching of Colonel Muammar Gaddafi by NATO-backed forces in Libya earlier that day, Cameron enthused that 'Diwali being the festival of a triumph of good over evil and also the death of a devil, perhaps there is a little resonance in what I am saying tonight' ('Confirmed Gaddafi Dead', *Mirror* online, 20 October 2011).

As I have argued in this chapter, DfID's partnership with Hindu supremacist groups in the context of initiatives to involve black and ethnic minority communities in development should not be regarded as an anomaly. It is consistent with the reconfiguration of the British state's approach to 'race' in the context of global changes in the 1990s and the 'War on Terror' from 2001 onwards. At the same time, it is premissed on a shared, neoliberal understanding of 'development' which involves facilitating the unlimited appropriation of land, resources and labour by capital. As we saw in the previous chapter, this approach to development has been vigorously promoted in India by DfID, whose programmes are primarily geared towards furthering the interests of British companies such as Vedanta. On the ground, paramilitaries and armed gangs, many though not all of whom are affiliated with the Sangh Parivar, work closely with transnational corporations to terrorise those who resist land seizure, displacement and environmental destruction. In Chhattisgarh, for example, both the BJP and the Congress were involved in setting up the Salwa Judum militia, which forced thousands of people from their homes and into camps. The Salwa Judum was later revealed to be sponsored by corporates Tata and Essar (Government of India, 2009).

Meanwhile the fact that Indian capital is playing an increasingly central role in the crisis-ridden British economy has only reinforced new representations of India as unproblematically affluent and 'civilised' and of its diaspora as loyal and deserving British citizens. However, these racialised representations overlap and co-exist with, rather than completely displacing, the representations of 'Asians' and India that existed earlier. They do not preclude the continuing reproduction, for example, of racist media representations of India and Indians as pathologically and comically 'unhygienic' or 'ignorant'.[17] Nor, of course, do they offer any protection against racist violence for people of Indian origin in Britain, like Indian student Anuj Bidve who was shot dead in a racist attack in Salford on Boxing

Day 2011. It is important to remember, too, that just as both the violence of the Hindu fascist organisations and the depredations of corporate capital have been continually resisted in multiple ways in India, in Britain also the activities of the Sangh Parivar described earlier in this chapter have faced sustained opposition and protest by people of South Asian origin organising across boundaries, and in the process repeatedly contesting the British state's constructions of 'identity', 'community' and 'race'.

In lieu of a conclusion ...

As I suggested in the introduction, this book should be read as a provocation to further engagement, exploration and elaboration in relation to its themes. The dominant framing of development research as culminating in the identification of a set of solutions to a set of predefined and limited problems (usually in the form of a list of recommendations) has given me a particular aversion to 'resolved' endings of this sort. But, more importantly, as should be evident, this book has not been about suggesting ways of 'doing' development better, of making it somehow less racist. As I have argued throughout, the ideas of race and development have been, and remain, inextricably intertwined with each other. Nor is this a matter of historical traces to be eradicated or legacies to be undone: rather, as I have sought to illustrate in different contexts, race is repeatedly reanimated and reconfigured through contemporary development interventions. Further, development, when understood in relation to global processes of capital accumulation and imperialism, is implicated in the production of material and embodied differences which are both legitimised by and come to be explained though ideas of racial hierarchy in multiple guises. My arguments in relation to development are distinct from those poststructuralist-influenced critiques which, I have suggested, have proved paradoxically amenable to incorporation within neoliberal discourses of development. In contrast to the tendency to suspect all 'progress narratives' within these critiques, I recognise that other possibilities for social transformation, ones which challenge the racialised perpetuation of global inequality, may be articulated in coherent (albeit often multiple) visions of change within collective political movements. One of the threads that run through this book is that of people's struggles to transform the unequal relationships which shape their daily lives, and for a more just world, struggles which disrupt the boundaries between 'global North' and 'global South', and range from nineteenth-century anti-colonial uprisings to movements for access to HIV/AIDS treatment; from movements resisting corporate takeover of land to campaigns against drone attacks, disappearances and incarcerations without end in the so-called War on Terror. As I have explained, all these struggles decisively challenge and potentially undo the effects of the relationship between race and capital on a global scale. As the crisis of capitalism deepens, it is to thinking about what an effective politics of transnational solidarity between these struggles might involve that I hope this book will in some way contribute.

Notes

INTRODUCTION

1. This understanding of race both as a social and discursive construct and as material and lived experience is reflected in my use of quotation marks to frame the word 'race' in some contexts but not in others.

CHAPTER 1

1. Kipling's oft-cited 1899 poem was actually an exhortation to the United States to take up the imperial mission in its newly acquired colony, the Philippines. Interesting comparisons have been drawn with historian Niall Ferguson's *Empire: How Britain Made the Modern World* (2003), which urges the USA to embrace explicitly the notion of 'empire' in the twenty-first century.

2. This extensive literature includes Williams, 1944; Palme Dutt, 1947; Rodney, 1972; Patnaik, 1972, 2006; Amin, 1977; Blackburn, 1997; Davis, 2001. Although it encompasses a range of theoretical positions and indeed debates, it has nearly all been elaborated within the broad framework of Marxist political economy.

3. Anthony Bogues suggests that the concept of a black republic was particularly significant. 'The Haitian revolution proclaimed, "the Haitians shall henceforward be known only by the generic appellation of Blacks."' Haitian citizenship was thus equated with blackness, and only citizens could own property. Within this understanding, not only the colonial hierarchies of 'race', but the meaning of 'race' itself was redefined – white people could be, and some were, 'naturalised by the government', but this citizenship was linked to 'a positive identification with blackness' (Bogues, 2004: 27–8).

4. This Act is currently being repealed, but its replacement, the Land Acquisition and Rehabilitation and Resettlement Bill, has been criticised for actually legalising and intensifying 'ongoing corporate land-grab' even while using terms such as 'informed consent' and 'partnership in development' (Liberation, 2011).

5. For example: '[Mirza Feroz Shah Shahzada]: To all Hindoos and Mahommedans of Hindoostan who are faithful to their religion, know that sovereignty is one of God's chief boons, one which a deceitful tyrant is never allowed to retain. For several years the English have been committing all kinds of excesses and tyrannies being desirous of converting all men to Christianity by force,

and subverting and doing away with the religion of Hindoos and Mahom-medans. When God saw this fact, He so altered the hearts of the inhabitants of Hindoostan that they have been doing their best to get rid of the English themselves' (cited in Ray, 2003: 385).

6. Ali points out that this narrative in which the uprisings were an almost exclusively Muslim affair has also been adopted by mainstream Pakistani historians (Ali, 2007a).

7. Polashi was named after the Polash ('Flame of the Forest') trees which grew there. The British anglicised it to 'Plassey'. The 100th anniversary of this battle is believed to have been one of the triggers for the uprisings of 1857.

8. This included contemporary Bangladesh, and, in India, West Bengal and parts of Assam, Odisha, Bihar and Jharkhand.

9. Irfan Habib notes that the sepoys 'asserted their "democratic" attitude by electing their officers (with, often enough, largely Hindu regiments electing Muslims, and vice versa)' (Habib, 2007).

10. Later versions of the legislation introduced for this purpose have been used in the twenty-first century for land acquisition by the state on behalf of corporates.

11. The liberal market orthodoxy and racist disregard for life which informed British famine policies enormously amplified the scale of this mortality. This is discussed in more detail in the context of 'race' and Malthusianism in Chapter 3.

12. In the context of growing inequality and polarisation of incomes, this represents an even greater decline for the direct producers.

13. Economist Utsa Patnaik has explained how the limited increase in productivity in British agriculture could not possibly have sustained the Industrial Revolution, whose demands were met from the output of far more productive tropical land, which Britain did not pay for: 'these imports created no external liability for the British economy since local producers were "paid" out of taxes they themselves contributed to the state. In India the colonial state guided and operated from Britain, extracted taxes from peasants and artisans, and used a portion of tax revenues to purchase their products including exported crops like wheat' (Patnaik, 2006).

14. Mamdani notes that the coercive violence implicit in the system of administrative chiefship established by the colonial powers was particularly significant because in Africa (unlike India) 'customary' law covered land. People could only access land as members of a community. Therefore, land was not directly subject to the pressures of the market. Thus the use of force was crucial to extract taxes, cash crops, and labour (Mamdani, 1996: 51–2).

15. See, for example, Ware, 1992; McClintock, 1995; Stoler, 2002; Magubane, 2004.

16. As Sumit Guha notes, 'the drive to understand social classification in terms of races of descent was a central element in mid-nineteenth-century science, predating the publication of *The Origin of Species* and the formulation of Social Darwinism.... As the development of geology and the sciences undermined the authority of the Church, and political and social change appeared to be destablizing western societies, the concept of race was invoked to support threatened hierarchies, both in colonies and metropoles' (Guha, 1998: 424).

CHAPTER 2

1. See, for example, Banerjee, 1989; Van Allen, 1972; Amadiume, 1997.
2. These issues have been raised, for example, by Dalit women in agricultural labour movements in Bihar in India (Wilson, 2007)
3. World Bank Gender Action Plan, 2007–2010; World Bank, 2011.
4. Magubane (2004), who also brings Marxist political economy to bear on constructions of 'race', has addressed this question in the context of South Africa.
5. For a discussion of this, see Manzo, 2008.
6. This is my own assumption: no information is provided about these women.
7. Interestingly Cafédirect apparently sees no contradiction between this and the fair trade approach outlined on the same page: http://brewing.cafedirect. co.uk/what-we-grow. Another example of the use of images to promote fair trade products is discussed later.
8. See, for example Hall, 1997; Dyer, 1986.
9. This introduction to the Nike Foundation draws extensively on a talk given by Caitlin Fisher, who worked closely on the Girl Effect campaign, at the LSE Gender Institute on 7 July 2010.
10. This is conceptualised in a way which is quite consistent with the neoliberal instrumentalisation of gender relations for household survival. For example, in a video clip on the Divine website entitled 'Women's empowerment' the national secretary of the Kuapa Kokoo cocoa farmers' co-operative is shown explaining how 'women are trained to embark on income generating activities ... women get money so that they can support their husbands, for the upkeep of their children like education and health'. www.divinechocolate. com/about/films3.aspx.

CHAPTER 3

1. In 1795 the Speenhamland Act had introduced a system where ratepayers effectively subsidised employers by providing relief to the working poor to bring starvation wages up to subsistence level. This did away with the Tudor system where the poor had to return to their parish of origin to claim relief, recognising the new requirements of the bourgeoisie for a mobile labour force. However, it led to a significant increase in the costs of the Poor Rate during the next four decades (Morton, 1938: 332).
2. The notion of a demographic transition refers to a situation where wide-ranging shifts in a large number of socio-economic variables, including urbanisation, industrialisation, rising standards of living, and improvements in public health, lead to a decline in death rates, followed, after a gap, by a decline in birth rates. This sequence of events cannot be assumed to always occur, but as Rao (1994: PE47) points out, what is significant is that the 'theory' of demographic transition involves 'a perspective that viewed population as a dependent variable; and socio-economic factors the determining independent variables': this view was overturned with the rise of the population control agenda.
3. The fundraising drives in Britain reflected contradictions in the colonial response to famine: these efforts were condemned by Malthusian free-market adherents.

Despite this, as Davis points out, the colonial famines have vanished in most modern historians' accounts of the nineteenth century (Davis, 2001).

4. This ambivalence towards birth control characterised eugenicists in this period, particularly as they observed that it was precisely those elite white women whom they wished to 'breed' who were most likely to gain access to contraception and had lower birth rates.

5. As early as 1951, an article in the US publication *Senior Scholastic* highlighted the idea that 'over-population creates a breeding ground for communism.... [because] Communist propaganda thrives on poverty and discontent' (cited in Ross, 1998: 86).

6. With its central concern with regulating populations and managing bodies and behaviour, as well its preoccupation with deviance, population control can be regarded as an almost paradigmatic example of the operation of biopower as defined by Foucault, and this approach has been elaborated by, for example, Briggs, 2002. For a brief discussion of the notion of biopower as it relates to 'race' and development, see Chapter 6.

7. It is striking that this 1950s' construction of *machismo* includes 'homosexuality' as part of its deviance. In Chapter 4, we discuss contemporary racialised accounts of 'deviant' hypermasculinity in the context of HIV/AIDS.

8. The experiences of Sarah Baartman, a member of the Khoikhoi community, who was taken from the Cape Colony in South Africa and taken to London in 1810 and 'publicly exhibited at the Piccadilly Circus because of the purported abnormality of her sexual organs' (Magubane, 2001: 817), were the focus of an influential article by Sander Gilman (1985) and have since been discussed in a number of key postcolonial texts addressing questions of 'race', gender and sexuality.

9. For example, Quinacrine, a form of chemical sterilisation, was promoted in a 'worldwide sterilization crusade' by two US doctors, supported by private foundations and anti-immigrant organisations in the USA. Despite opposition even from official population agencies due to the serious side effects and risks, they succeeded in distributing Quinacrine in the USA as well as in Bangladesh, Chile, China, Colombia, Costa Rica, Croatia, Egypt, India, Indonesia, Iran, Morocco, Pakistan, the Philippines, Venezuela, Vietnam, Malaysia and Romania, in a 'vast unethical experiment conducted on human subjects' permanently sterilising more than 104,000 women worldwide (Bhatia and Hendrixon, 1999; Committee on Women, Population and the Environment). The racist logic underlying this was made explicit by one of the proponents of Quinacrine, Stephen Mumford, who was quoted in the *Wall Street Journal* describing it as a means of reducing the potential number of immigrants to the USA from the global South. 'This explosion in human numbers, which after 2050 will come entirely from immigrants and the offspring of immigrants, will dominate our lives. There will be chaos and anarchy' (Freeman, 1998).

10. 'Developed in 1985 by geographer Gary Fuller during a stint as visiting scholar in the Central Intelligence Agency's (CIA's) Office of Global Issues, formal "youth bulge" theory originally aimed to provide ... a tool to predict unrest and uncover potential national security threats. It claims that a proportion of more than 20 per cent of young people in a population signals the possibility of political rebellion and unrest. It equates large percentages of young men with

an increased possibility of violence, particularly in the South, where, analysts argue, governments may not have the capacity to support them' (Hendrixon, 2004).

CHAPTER 4

1. Not surprisingly perhaps, given the behavioural preoccupations within existing research, more emphasis has been placed on the existence of untreated sexually transmitted infections as a risk factor in transmission. But the prevalence of untreated – or inadequately treated – infections of any kind cannot be fully understood except in the context of the global political economy of health care.

2. The assumption that it is men who overwhelmingly infect their partners with the virus in long-term heterosexual relationships has been challenged (Edstrom, 2011).

3. At the same time, conflict may open up possibilities for the reconfiguring of gender relations, with women taking on work previously monopolised by men (Jacobs et al., 2000).

4. See, for example, Gosine, 2006 for an exception to this.

5. According to a report published by Human Rights Watch shortly before a Delhi High Court ruling decriminalised 'homosexual conduct' in 2009, 'more than half of the world's remaining "sodomy" laws – criminalizing consensual homosexual conduct – are relics of British colonial rule ... laws in over three dozen countries, from India to Uganda and from Nigeria to Papua New Guinea, derive from a single law on homosexual conduct that British colonial rulers imposed on India in 1860' (Human Rights Watch, 2008).

6. The term 'men who sleep with men' (MSM), which ostensibly addresses this issue in the context of HIV/AIDS programming, has, as akshay khanna argues, in fact emerged as another category, overriding the complexities of people's multiple self-identifications, a category to which it has become necessary to conform in order to access resources (khanna, 2011).

7. In the USA, FDA approval for Zidovudine was granted in 1987, making it the first antiretroviral therapy to be used as a treatment for AIDS. However, it required considerable campaigning from activist groups for the government to promote further research and make drugs affordable. By the mid-1990s, 'the introduction of the protease inhibitors represented one of the biggest breakthroughs in AIDS treatment. Highly active antiretroviral therapy, a combination of protease inhibitors and two or three other AIDS drugs, helped transform AIDS into a manageable and chronic disease for many patients. In the USA, where the drugs were readily available, the death rate from AIDS dropped by 47 per cent in 1997, only 2 years after the introduction of protease inhibitors' (Nelson, 2006).

8. Access to treatment continues to be shaped by inequality and racism in these countries, however: see, for example, Appel, 2007.

9. For example, the UN special envoy for HIV/AIDS to the continent reported in 2005 that while the use of triple-dose therapy in the West had cut the numbers of children with HIV practically to zero, in Africa only 10 per cent of pregnant, infected women have access to the means of preventing mother-to-child transmission (Lewis, 2005).

10. The Tuskegee syphilis experiment was conducted in Tuskegee, Alabama by the US Public Health Service to study the natural progression of untreated syphilis. Investigators enrolled in the study a total of 600 impoverished African-American sharecroppers from Macon County, Alabama, of whom 399 had previously contracted syphilis. For participating in the study, the men were given free medical care, meals and free burial insurance. They were never told they had syphilis; nor were they ever treated for it. Instead they were told they were being treated for 'bad blood', a local term used to describe several illnesses, including syphilis, anaemia and fatigue. Researchers knowingly failed to treat patients even after the validation in the 1940s of penicillin as an effective cure for the disease they were studying, and prevented participants from accessing syphilis treatment programmes available in the area. The study was only terminated in 1972 after a whistle-blower exposed it in the press. In October 2010, research by historian Susan Reverby revealed that in Guatemala between 1946 and 1948 US Public Health Service researchers deliberately infected prisoners, soldiers and patients in a mental hospital with syphilis with permission from the authorities but not from those infected. A total of 696 men and women were exposed to syphilis without their informed consent ('US Says Sorry for "outrageous and abhorrent" Guatemalan Syphilis Tests', *Guardian*, 1 October 2010). When they contracted the disease they were given penicillin, although it is unclear if all were cured (Reverby, 2011).

11. Natsios repeated this theory to justify the lack of US support for ARV programmes in a hearing before the US Committee of International Relations: 'People do not know what watches and clocks are. They do not use western means for telling time. They use the sun. These drugs have to be administered during a certain sequence of time during the day and when you say take it at 10:00, people will say what do you mean by 10:00? They do not use those terms in the villages to describe time. They describe the morning and the afternoon and the evening. So that is a problem' (Committee for International Relations, 2001: 67).

12. Although no longer official policy, AIDS denialism has ongoing effects on access to treatment (Treatment Action Campaign, www.tac.org.za).

CHAPTER 5

1. The Joint Church Airlift not only supplied humanitarian aid, but attempted to establish a Biafran air force, leading to a federal ban on outside aid flights (Chandler, 2006: 30).

2. Kouchner later served as a minister in several French governments, including most recently foreign minister under Nicholas Sarkozy's right-wing administration from 2007 to 2010.

3. Refugee flows were identified as a major consideration in the decisions of the Security Council in six major crises in the 1990s: northern Iraq, Bosnia, Somalia, Rwanda, Haiti, and Kosovo (Roberts, 1998).

4. This position was to be further developed in the norm of the 'Responsibility to Protect', a United Nations initiative established in 2005, according to which if a state is seen as failing in its responsibility to protect its population from mass atrocities, the international community has a responsibility to intervene.

5. Corruption was also theorised as a form of 'primitive accumulation' in the context of the absence of structural transformation of the economy (see for example Iyayi, 1986 on Nigeria). A similar analysis of accumulation in Bihar, India was developed by Das (1992).

6. Manji and O'Coill (2002: 10) note that 'Between 1976 and 1992 there were 146 protests against IMF supported austerity measures in 39 countries around the world. These took the form of political demonstrations, strikes and riots. They took place almost exclusively in cities and they reached a peak in the mid 1980s. In many cases, the immediate response of governments was brute force. Demonstrations were violently suppressed, strikes declared illegal, universities were closed, and trade unions, student organisations, popular organisations, and political parties also became the target of repressive legislation or actions.'

7. Capital flight, 'in conservative reckonings', was estimated to account for about 37 per cent of African public and private wealth (Moore, 1999: 79).

8. This principle continues to be invoked when convenient, as in the remarks of Lord Young, a minister in the Thatcher government and former chair of Cable and Wireless: 'when you're talking about kickbacks, you're talking about something that's illegal in this country [the UK] ... But there are parts of the world I've been to where we all know it happens and, if you want to be in business, you have to do it' (cited in Hall, 1999: 540). This evokes the construction of colonial 'knowledge' of specific countries and cultures; see, for example, Uma Kothari's work about colonial administrators turned development professionals (Kothari, 2005).

9. The 2006 US National Security Strategy identified Africa as 'a high priority' and stated that 'our security depends upon partnering with Africans to strengthen fragile and failing states and bring ungoverned areas under the control of effective democracies'. The Obama administration's first National Security Strategy, issued in 2010, stresses the need to 'embrace effective partnerships' on the continent, highlighting as first priority 'access to open markets', along with 'conflict prevention, global peacekeeping, counterterrorism, and the protection of vital carbon sinks' (cited in Ploch, 2011: 14).

CHAPTER 6

1. See, in particular, Grovogui, 2001, 2002; Razack, 2004; Shilliam, 2008.

2. This approach to development has been particularly influential in anthropology. This considerable body of work includes Rankin, 2001; Ferguson and Gupta, 2002; Li, 2007; Karim, 2011.

3. A similar point is made by Bracking and Harrison (2010: 7), who point out that 'the increasing attention paid to networks (generated by theories of governance and their Foucauldian variants) opens a path to insightful research on global capitalism, but it also runs the peril of downplaying what is obvious to all observers: the *persistent, and historically structured concentration of power emanating from the West*' (emphasis in original).

4. This is a process which takes place in the global North as well. The experiences of refugees in the UK with 'no recourse to public funds' and legally forbidden from earning income, or of poor African American US citizens during and after Hurricane Katrina, for example, testify to this.

252 | RACE, RACISM AND DEVELOPMENT

5. Postcolonial feminist theorists, notably Stoler (1995, 2002), have used Foucault differently, emphasising how he viewed the production of difference as inherent in processes of regulation.

6. In fact race does structure the discourse in more subtle ways – this is the focus of some postcolonial critiques of development such as Kothari, 2006; and White, 2002, 2006, which are discussed in Chapter 8.

7. Both of these are at work in policies of 'sustainable development' – for example, microcredit involves both promoting strategies for survival in the context of denial of access to resources, and increasingly and inevitably direct exploitation by corporates.

8. See also Puar, 2004; Butler, 2008 on the construction of racialised subjectivities in the context of the Abu Ghraib torture.

9. Nicholas Thoburn in a discussion of the relationship of Deleuze's work to Marxism highlights the 'kind of permanent reconfiguration and intensification of relations in a process of setting, and overcoming, limits' as characteristic of capitalism, citing Marx and Engels's famous description in *The Communist Manifesto* of capital as a state of being where 'All that is solid melts into air' and where relations 'become antiquated before they can ossify' (Thoburn, 2003).

10. Gilroy, 1993: 220.

11. In a particularly striking example of this process, Alcoff describes the construction of the Panama Canal by the United States-owned and -run Panama Canal Commission, in which 'workers were divided and identified.... as "gold" (whites) and "silver" (West Indian blacks), denoting the form of currency in which they were paid. Gold and silver workers were given separate and differently constructed living quarters, different currency for wages, and different commissaries; they were assigned different tasks and also attributed different characteristics.... Here race explicitly determined economic and social status, but it was also understood by the dominant white authorities to be the determinate constitutive factor of subjectivity – involving personal character traits and internal constitution (blacks were thought to be more resistant to yellow fever)' (Alcoff, 2000: 144).

12. Amartya Sen (1981, 1999) defines famine as an eruption of severe deprivation, distinguished from endemic hunger and poverty. Also, Alex de Waal notes that 'famine is a broad economic, social and political phenomenon, with undernutrition as only one component among many' (de Waal, 1997: 55).

13. Aggregate figures for the indicators in these countries conceal inequalities within them which are themselves shaped by 'race' and racism: for example, Australia has an under-5 mortality rate of approximately seven per thousand children. But for Australia's indigenous (Aboriginal) population, available evidence suggests that, at current rates, as many as one in fifty children will die before reaching age 1, while an additional eight per thousand will have no chance of reaching their fifth birthday (Kinfu and Taylor, 2005). Within the United States, race, class and gender structure patterns of food insecurity and inadequate access to food, whose effects can include obesity (Firth, 2012).

14. Clearly, such representations of hunger in statistical form, mediated by states and international organizations, can be understood as simultaneously revealing and concealing lived and embodied experiences. While in themselves they do little to convey either the visceral effects of hunger and the pain inflicted by the

suffering and loss of loved ones, or the structural violence and unequal relations of power which produce them, neither is it useful to consider such statistics solely as the product of a regulatory technology or (as in the postdevelopment thinking discussed in the next chapter) as tools in a discursive process of 'inventing' poverty. Rather, we might also ask what is and what potentially can be done with them – and whether they are being used to promote, or to preclude challenges to the status quo (see, for example, Gupta, 2012).

15. For an interesting example of the embodied implications of this, see Boddy's discussion of experiences of childbirth in Sudan and Canada (2007).

16. A 1977 song by the reggae band Third World which tells the story of Paul Bogle, a leader of the 1865 Morant Bay Rebellion in Jamaica.

17. The Tebhaga movement in Bengal, India, was a militant and now iconic anti-colonial peasant struggle initiated by the Communist Party of India in 1946, in which sharecroppers who were compelled to pay two-thirds of their crop in rent to the landlords demanded that this share be reduced to one-third. The poor peasant sharecroppers, women in particular, put up sustained resistance to violent repression by the British colonial state.

18. This parallel is perhaps more appropriately drawn with those deemed 'rogue' states, such as Iraq, Iran and Libya. Early-nineteenth-century Haiti has little in common with the coercive states (later labelled 'failed' post-Cold War) in postcolonial Africa, for example, which were, by contrast, bolstered by the West in the interests of maintaining a racialised global capitalist order, as well as institutionally rooted in colonialism.

CHAPTER 7

1. In November 2009 the Indian state of Orissa was officially renamed Odisha.

2. As described in Chapter 1, these differences were defined as racial by colonial anthropologists in India.

3. See, for example, Petras, 1999; Manji and O'Coill, 2002; Hearn, 2007.

4. See, for example, Malik, 2011 on how NGOs have claimed that there is popular support for drone attacks in Pakistan.

5. This is not intended to reproduce ideas about authentic or inauthentic protestors (or placards!).

6. Cameron did not respond to Survival's appeal. He did go to the Amazon rainforest with another group, US-based Amazon Watch, to meet the Kayapo people, threatened by a dam planned by the Brazilian government.

7. Make Poverty History was a coalition of development NGOs, alongside religious groups, trade unions, campaigning groups and celebrities initiated by Oxfam in 2005 around issues of debt, aid and trade justice. It was formed to coincide with the G8 summit to be held in Edinburgh that year, the first five-year evaluation of progress on the UN Millennium Development Goals (MDGs) agreed in 2000, the 6th WTO Ministerial Meeting in Hong Kong, and the 20th anniversary of Live Aid.

8. Since the Arab Spring of 2011, representations of these protests are sometimes referenced in these contexts of mobilising of publics in the global North by NGOs, without, however, recognising them as having any specific politics or structure.

9. As I discuss in the following chapter, this is accompanied by the exclusion

from 'Britishness' of those who are constructed as not sharing these 'national' interests.

10. The film is titled *Wira Pdika* in the Kui language spoken by the Konds. In Odia it is called *Matir Poko, Company Loko*, which translates as 'Earthworm, Company Man', the film's English title.

11. The first of these was Utkal Alumina International Ltd (UAIL), which sought to mine bauxite deposits covering 10 or more square kilometres on top of the Bapla Mali mountain. UAIL was formed by Indal and Tata in a joint venture with Norway's Norsk Hydro (Padel and Das, 2010: 109).

12. POSCO is in fact largely controlled by a range of US, European and Japanese banks and corporations. The largest investors in POSCO include the Bank of New York Mellon, which controlled 18.44 per cent by September 2010, Japan's Nippon Steel Corporation and US investment company BlackRock Inc. (Samarendra Das, pers. comm., 3 September 2011).

13. The URDS was set up by Utkal Alumina International Ltd. According to Padel and Das, the World Bank 'listed it as a model project in its Business Partners for Development scheme (BPD), a worldwide scheme promoting "tri-sectoral partnerships" between government, companies and civil society. The UK was the only government that became officially involved, through ... DfID' (Padel and Das, 2010: 115). The BPD later withdrew from the project. It has also changed its name to Building Partnerships for Development.

14. See, for example, Kiely, 1999.

CHAPTER 8

1. The term 'diaspora' is currently used extensively within development initiatives but it is a highly contested concept (see for example Kalra et al, 2005, for a discussion).

2. These questions are also increasingly visible in popular discourse around development and aid workers. See, for example, the self-reflexive humour of the Stuff Expat Aid Workers Like blog (although, strikingly, in more than 100 entries there is no mention of racism to date).

3. Walt Rostow was national security adviser to President Johnson during the Vietnam War, when he was the principal advocate of escalating the conflict through US bombing of Vietnam. An obituary in the *Guardian* newspaper after his death in 2003 notes that 'Rostow developed an almost ghoulish enthusiasm for flip-charts detailing the "body count" on which his policies relied, an attitude wildly at variance with his gentler virtues. Ferocity towards theoretical Asian communists contrasted strangely with his kindness to actual human beings' (Hodgson, 2003). The author apparently completely misses the role of racism, and the tenacious exclusion of certain groups from the category of 'actual human beings', in making such 'strange' contrasts possible.

4. Mohanty argues that her earlier highly influential article 'Under Western Eyes' (1986) has been subject to 'postmodern appropriation' and 'misread' as arguing for 'difference' at the expense of all systemic connections, when in fact she had argued for the 'need for a materialist analysis that linked everyday life and local gendered contexts and ideologies to the larger transnational political and economic structures of capitalism' (Mohanty, 2003: 504).

5. This contrasts with the work of earlier influential theorists of racism in the USA, notably the later work of W.E.B. Du Bois.

6. I use the term 'diaspora' here in reference to the DfID initiatives that use it, bearing in mind that its use to indicate all migrants and their descendants has been heavily criticised. However, the term has become widespread in Britain, particularly in the context of African and South Asian communities.

7. Talha Ahsan is a British citizen born in London in 1979. A poet who suffers from Asperger's Syndrome, he is currently fighting extradition to the United States. He was arrested at his home on 19 July 2006 in response to a request from the USA under the Extradition Act 2003, which does not require the presentation of any prima facie evidence. He is accused in the USA of terrorism-related offences arising out of an alleged involvement over the period 1997–2004 with the Azzam series of websites, one of which happened to be located on a server in America. He has never been questioned by British police. Talha is currently in the final stage of proceedings at the European Court of Human Rights (ECHR). He has now served the equivalent of a ten-year sentence in high-security prisons without trial. If convicted in the USA he will spend seventy years in 'supermax' solitary confinement in ADX Florence.

Babar Ahmad, born in London, has been held in custody in the UK since August 2004. He has never been charged, but is also fighting extradition to the United States on allegations of involvement in websites. In March 2009, he was awarded £60,000 compensation at the High Court in London after an admission by UK anti-terrorist police that they subjected him to 'grave abuse, tantamount to torture' during his first arrest in December 2003.

8. The film does not make a very clear distinction between marriages arranged and performed (though not consummated) between young children and the marriages of girls in early adolescence.

9. A recent article by Jean Drèze and Amartya Sen shows how India's neoliberal model of growth has meant that it is actually falling behind other countries in South Asia, including Bangladesh, in terms of poverty-related indicators. They point out that 'during the last 20 years or so, India has grown much richer than Bangladesh: per capita income was estimated to be 60 per cent higher in India than in Bangladesh in 1990, and 98 per cent higher (about double) in 2010. But during the same period, Bangladesh has *overtaken* India in terms of a wide range of basic social indicators: life expectancy, child survival, fertility rates, immunisation rates, and even some (not all) schooling indicators such as estimated "mean years of schooling". For instance, life expectancy was estimated to be four years longer in India than in Bangladesh in 1990, but it had become three years *shorter* by 2008. Similarly, the child mortality rate was estimated to be about 24 per cent higher in Bangladesh than in India in 1990, but it was 24 per cent *lower* in Bangladesh in 2009. Most social indicators now look better in Bangladesh than in India, despite Bangladesh having barely half of India's per capita income' (Drèze and Sen, 2011).

10. Pakistan is notable by its absence here – presumably there was a decision not to highlight the connections between the diaspora and Pakistan, which have been tirelessly (mis)represented by the British state and the media as a nexus of 'terrorism', in this context.

11. In numerical terms, the grant to Hindu Aid represented almost 60 per cent

of the grant to the Muslim Council of Britain, although according to the 2001 Census just over half a million people in Britain identified as 'Hindu' as compared to 1.5 million identified as 'Muslim' (Mercia Group, 2006). The choice of particular markers of identity to generate 'knowledge' about populations is, of course, itself shaped by changing strategies of power.

12. See, for example, Casolari, 2000; Basu et al., 1993. Bhatt (2001: 125–6) briefly discusses some of the debates among the left in India regarding the fascism of the Sangh Parivar. A key point in these debates is the recognition that fascism may take different forms in metropolitan and colonial/neocolonial contexts (see, for example, Sarkar, 1993; Balagopal, 1993).

13. As Bhatt notes, the Vanavasi Kalyan Ashram was formed in 1952 with RSS support and 'by 1980 had become a nationwide organisation working among "tribal" communities in order to "integrate them into the Hindu mainstream", launch "reconversion" campaigns and combat the influence of "foreign" Christian missions. The name of the organisation is significant: *vanavasi* means forest dweller and substitutes for the accepted term *adivasi*, meaning the original (aboriginal) inhabitants of India; *ashram* denotes a Hindu religious instruction centre' (Bhatt, 2001: 114). Attempts to mobilise the most subordinated and marginalised groups for communal violence and divide the poorest communities have characterised recent Sangh Parivar campaigns – for example, the 2008 violence in Kandhamal in Odisha in which *adivasi* Konds were mobilised to attack Pano Dalit Christians (see *Kandhamal 2008*, dir. Samarendra Das, 2011).

14. In fact Shah's position led the BNP, whose racist violence had been one of the triggers for the riots, to suggest an alliance with the VHP (Choudhury, 2002). The discourse of far-right groups like the BNP and the English Defence League has also shifted in recent years to primarily targeting 'Muslims'.

15. According to a recent report by Anumeha Yadav, 'the shrill rhetoric has gone from "investment drive" to "inclusive growth", but the numbers reveal where the gains end up. The Survey of Industries data shows workers' share as wages in Gujarat has fallen from 23 to 8 percent.... Planning Commission data shows that between 1993 and 2005, Gujarat slipped from sixth to eighth spot among 20 major states in the percentage of poor living below the poverty line. Despite high growth, its rate of reducing poverty was among the lowest, worse than West Bengal, Uttar Pradesh, Andhra Pradesh and Bihar' (Yadav, 2011).

16. The promotion of this form of 'Indian-ness' has also been observed in analyses of Bollywood films and their relation to the diaspora. As Amrit Wilson observes, these films 'present a sanitised picture of India, with none of the poverty which might embarrass Asians living in the West and none of the 'strangeness' which might make them or their children feel uncomfortable in white society ... [they] focus on the consumption of commodities ... constantly redefining and strengthening ... a modern investor-friendly Hindu identity which appeals especially to the diaspora' (Wilson, 2006: 134–6). It is also consistent with the *Hindutva* project of homogenising Hinduism (prioritising upper-caste and patriarchal understandings and practices and excluding others) in a way which makes it intelligible within the framework of the global market.

17. A recent example of this was a *Top Gear* Christmas special shot in India, aired by the BBC on 28 December 2011, just two days after the murder of Indian student Anuj Bidve.

References

Abbasi, N.M. (2010) *The Pakistani Diaspora in Europe and Its Impact on Democracy Building in Pakistan*, International Institute for Democracy and Electoral Assistance, Stockholm.

Abrahamsen, R. (2000) *Disciplining Democracy: Development Discourse and Good Governance in Africa*, Zed Books, London.

Abu-Lughod, L. (2002) 'Do Muslim Women Really Need Saving? Anthropological Reflections on Cultural Relativism and Its Others', *American Anthropologist* 104(3): 783–90.

ActionAid (2004) *Blocking Progress: How the Fight against HIV/AIDS is Being Undermined by the World Bank and International Monetary Fund*, ActionAid International USA, www.actionaidusa.org/blockingprogress.pdf.

Agamben, G. (1998) *Homo Sacer: Sovereign Power and Bare Life*, Stanford University Press, Stanford CA.

Agamben, G. (2005) *State of Exception*, University of Chicago Press, Chicago.

Agarwal, B. (1994) *A Field of One's Own: Gender and Land Rights in South Asia*, Cambridge University Press, Cambridge.

Ahikire, J. (2008) 'Vulnerabilities of Feminist Engagement and the Challenge of Developmentalism in the South: What Alternatives?' *IDS Bulletin* 39(6): 28–33.

Ahmad, A. (1995) 'The Politics of Literary Postcoloniality', *Race and Class* 36(3): 1–20.

Ahmed, S. (2000) *Strange Encounters: Embodied Others in Post-coloniality*, Routledge, London.

Ahmed, S. (2002) 'Racialised Bodies', in M. Evans and E. Lee (eds), *Real Bodies: A Sociological Introduction*, Macmillan, London.

Ahmed, S. (2004) *The Cultural Politics of Emotion*, Routledge, London.

Akhter, F. (1992) *Depopulating Bangladesh: Essays on the Politics of Fertility*, Narigrantha Prabartana, Dhaka.

Ala'i, P. (2000) 'The Legacy of Geographical Morality and Colonialism: A Historical Assessment of the Current Crusade Against Corruption', *Vanderbilt Journal of Transnational Law* 33(4): 877–906.

Alcabes, P. (2006a) 'Heart of Darkness: AIDS, Africa, and Race', *Virginia Quarterly Review* 82(1): 5–9.

Alcabes, P. (2006b) 'The Risky Gene: Epidemiology and the Evolution of Race', *Patterns of Prejudice* 40(4–5): 413–25.

Alcoff, L.M. (1995) 'The Problem of Speaking For Others', in J. Roof and R. Wiegman (eds), *Who Can Speak? Authority and Critical Identity*, University of Illinois Press, Urbana.

Alcoff, L.M. (2000 [1995]) 'Mestizo Identity', in R. Bernasconi and T. Lott (eds), *The Idea of Race*, Hackett, Indianapolis.

Alcoff, L.M. (2001) 'Toward a Phenomenology of Racial Embodiment', in R. Bernasconi (ed.), *Race*, Blackwell, Malden MA.

Alcoff, L.M. (2006) *Visible Identities: Race, Gender and the Self*, Oxford University Press, New York.

Alexander, C. (1998) 'Re-imagining the Muslim Community', *Innovation* 11(4): 439–50.

Alexander, M.J. (2005) *Pedagogies of Crossing: Meditations on Feminism, Sexual Politics, Memory and the Sacred*, Durham, New York.

Ali, M (2007a) '1857: Shared History, Shared Struggle', unpublished MS.

Ali, M. (2007b) '1857 – Reconstruction of History', unpublished MS.

Ali, T. (2003) *The Clash of Fundamentalisms: Crusades, Jihads and Modernity*, Verso, London.

Allen, C. (1995) 'Understanding African Politics', *Review of African Political Economy* 22(65): 301–20.

Amadiume, I. (1997) *Re-inventing Africa: Matriarchy, Religion, and Culture,* Zed Books, London.

Amin, S. (1977) *Imperialism and Unequal Development*, Harvester, Brighton.

Anderson, D. (2005) *Histories of the Hanged: The Dirty War in Kenya and the End of Empire*, Weidenfeld & Nicolson, London.

Appel, A. (2007) 'HIV/AIDS: Racism, Gov't Apathy Fuel US Epidemic', 30 November, www.commondreams.org/archive/2007/11/30/5532.

Archibugi, D., and D. Held (1995) *Cosmopolitan Democracy: An Agenda for a New World Order*, Polity Press, Cambridge.

Arnold, D. (1988) *Famine: Social Crisis and Historical Change*, Basil Blackwell, Oxford.

Asrar, N. (2011) 'Why Globalisation is No Antithesis of Hindutva', *India Global*, 12 October, http://ibnlive.in.com/news/why-globalisation-is-no-antithesis-of-hindutva/172115–61.html.

Awaaz South Asia Watch (2004) *In Bad Faith? British Charity and Hindu Extremism*, www.stopfundinghate.org/resources/news.

Ayaan (2010) 'Homeland Insecurities: Nel Hedayat and Afghanistan', *Muslimah Media Watch*, www.patheos.com/blogs/mmw/2010/04/homeland-insecurities-nel-hedayat-and-afghanistan; accessed 7 November 2011.

Baaz, M.E. (2005) *The Paternalism of Partnership: A Postcolonial Reading of Identity in Development Aid*, Zed Books, London.

Babu, A.M. (1981) *African Socialism or Socialist Africa*, Zed Books, London.

Babu, A.M. (1991) 'Non-Alignment in the Post-Gulf War Era', *Inqilab*, Summer, http://ambabu.gn.apc.org/articles.htm#2article.

Babu, A.M. (1993) 'Third World Concern About "Humanitarian" Interventions', *Pacific News Service*, 11 January, http://ambabu.gn.apc.org/articles.htm.

Babu, A.M. (2002a [1982]) 'Introduction to *Dar es Salaam Debates on Class, State and Imperialism*', in S. Babu and A. Wilson (eds), *The Future that Works: Selected Writings of A.M. Babu*, Africa World Press, Trenton NJ.

Babu, A.M. (2002b [1995]) 'Visions of Africa', in S. Babu and A. Wilson (eds), *The Future that Works: Selected Writings of A.M. Babu*, Africa World Press, Trenton NJ.

Babu, S., and A. Wilson (eds) (2002) *The Future that Works: Selected Writings of A.M. Babu*, Africa World Press, Trenton NJ.

Back, L., and S. Sinha with Charlynne Bryan (2012) 'New Hierarchies of Belonging', *European Journal of Cultural Studies* 15(2): 139–54.

Bakewell, O. (2009) 'Which Diaspora for Whose Development? Some Critical Questions about the Roles of African Diaspora Organizations as Development Actors', *DIIS Briefing*, Danish Institute for International Studies, Copenhagen.

Balagopal, K. (1993) 'Why Did December 6, 1992 Happen?', *Economic and Political Weekly*, 24 April.

Balibar, É. (1991) 'Is there a Neo-racism?', in É. Balibar and I. Wallerstein, *Race, Nation, Class: Ambiguous Identities*, Verso, London.

Banerjee, N. (1989) 'Working Women in Colonial Bengal: Modernization and Marginalization', in K. Sangari and S. Vaid (eds), *Recasting Women: Essays in Colonial History*, Kali for Women, Delhi.

Basu, S. (2003) 'AIDS, Empire and Public Health Behaviouralism', *Zmag*, August, www.zmag.org/content/print_article.cfm?itemID=3985%20&%20sectionID=2.

Basu, T., P. Datta, S. Sarkar, T. Sarkar and S. Sen, (1993) *Khaki Shorts Saffron Flags*, Orient Longman Tracts for the Times, Delhi.

Bates, C. (1995) 'Race, Caste and Tribe in Central India: The Early Origins of Indian Anthropometry', in Peter Robb (ed.), *The Concept of Race in South Asia*, Oxford University Press, Delhi.

Bayly, S. (1995) 'Caste and "Race" in the Colonial Ethnography of India', in P. Robb (ed.), *The Concept of Race in South Asia*, Oxford University Press, Delhi.

Benthall, J. (1993) *Disasters, Relief and the Media*, I.B. Tauris, London.

Bhabha, H.K. (1994) *The Location of Culture*, Routledge, London.

Bhatia, R., and A. Hendrixon (1999) 'The Quinacrine Controversy', *Women's Health Activist Newsletter*, May/June, http://nwhn.org/quinacrine-controversy.

Bhatt, C. (2001) *Hindu Nationalism: Origins, Ideologies and Modern Myths*, Berg, Oxford.

Bhattacharya, D. (2009) 'Combating the Corporate Idolisation of Modi',

Liberation, February, www.cpiml.org/liberation/year_2009/feb_09/commentary_1.html.

Biccum, A.R. (2002) 'Interrupting the Discourse of Development: On a Collision Course with Postcolonial Theory', *Culture, Theory & Critique* 43(1): 33–50.

Biccum, A.R. (2009) 'Theorising Continuities between Empire and Development: Toward a New Theory of History', in M. Duffield and V. Hewitt (eds), *Empire, Development & Colonialism: The Past in the Present*, James Currey, Oxford.

Bilgin, P., and A.D. Morton (2002) 'Historicising Representations of "Failed States": Beyond the Cold-War Annexation of the Social Sciences?', *Third World Quarterly* 23:(1): 55–80.

Bil'in Popular Committee (2010) 'Bil'in Weekly Demonstration Reenacts the Avatar Film', 12 February, www.bilinvillage.avatar-film.org/english/articles/testimonies/Bilin-weekly-demonstration-reenacts-the-avatar-film.

Black, D., J. Davison, S. Halford, J. Melby and D. Nutt (2004) *The Politics of Poverty: Aid in the New Cold War*, Christian Aid, London.

Blackburn, R. (1998) *The Making of New World Slavery: From the Baroque to the Modern, 1492–1800*, Verso, London.

Blum, W. (2003) *Killing Hope: US Military and CIA Interventions since World War II*, Zed Books, London.

Boddy, J. (2007) 'Remembering Amal: On Birth and the British in Northern Sudan', in M. Lock and J. Farquhar (eds), *Beyond the Body Proper*, Duke University Press, Durham NC.

Bogues, A. (2004) 'The Haitian Revolution and the Making of Freedom in Modernity', www.polisci.upenn.edu/programs/theory/bogues.pdf.

Bracking, C., and G. Harrison (2010) 'Demanding Development', *Review of African Political Economy* 37(124): 119–22.

Bracking, S., and G. Harrison (2003) 'Africa, Imperialism and New Forms of Accumulation', *Review of African Political Economy* 30:(95): 5–10.

Briggs, L. (2002) *Reproducing Empire: Race, Sex, Science, and U.S. Imperialism in Puerto Rico*, University of California Press, Berkeley.

Buck-Morss, S. (2000) 'Hegel and Haiti', *Critical Inquiry* 26(4): 821–65.

Bush, R., G. Martiniello and C. Mercer (2011) 'Humanitarian Imperialism', *Review of African Political Economy* 38(129): 357–65.

Butler, J. (1993) *Bodies that Matter: On the Discursive Limits of 'Sex'*, Routledge, New York.

Butler, J. (2006 [1990]) *Gender Trouble: Feminism and the Subversion of Identity*, Routledge, New York.

Butler, J. (2008) 'Sexual Politics, Torture, and Secular Time', *British Journal of Sociology* 59(1): 1–23.

Cammack, P. (2003) 'What the World Bank Means by Poverty Reduction', *Chronic Poverty Research Centre*, www.chronicpoverty.org/publications/details/what-the-world-bank-means-by-poverty-reduction.

Campbell, C. (2004) 'Migrancy, Masculine Identities, and AIDS: The Psycho-social Context of HIV Transmission on the South African Gold Mines', in E. Kalipeni, S. Craddock, J.R.Oppong and J.Ghosh (eds), *HIV and AIDS in Africa: Beyond Epidemiology*, Blackwell, Malden MA.

Carby, H.V. (1982) 'White Woman Listen! Black Feminism and the Boundaries of Sisterhood', in Centre for Contemporary Cultural Studies, *The Empire Strikes Back: Race and Racism in 70s Britain*, Hutchinson, London.

Casolari, M. (2000) 'Hindutva's Foreign Tie-up in the 1930s – Archival Evidence', *Economic and Political Weekly*, 22 January.

Chandler, D. (2006) *From Kosovo to Kabul and Beyond: Human Rights and International Intervention*, Pluto Press, London.

Chang, H.-J. (2007) *Bad Samaritans: The Guilty Secrets of Rich Nations and the Threat to Global Prosperity*, Random House, London.

Chant, S.H. (2006) 'Re-thinking the "Feminization of Poverty" in Relation to Aggregate Gender Indices', *Journal of Human Development* 7(2): 201–20.

Chari, S. (2008) 'Critical Geographies of Racial and Spatial Control', *Geography Compass* 2(6): 1907–21.

Chatterjee, M., and V.K. Ramachandran (1998) 'Vajpayee and the Quit India Movement: Findings of a *Frontline* Investigation', *Frontline* 15(3), February: 7–20.

Cherniavsky, E. (2006) *Incorporations: Race, Nation and the Body Politics of Capital*, University of Minnesota Press, Minneapolis.

Chimni, B.S. (2000) 'Globalization, Humanitarianism and the Erosion of Refugee Protection', *Journal of Refugee Studies* 13(3), September: 243–64.

Chomsky, N. (2002 [1967]) *American Power and the New Mandarins*, New Press, New York.

Choudhury, B. (2001) 'Race Tension in Bradford', BBC Radio 4 Today Reports Archive, www.bbc.co.uk/radio4/today/reports/archive/politics/bradfordrace.shtml.

Choudhury, B. (2002), 'BNP Attempts to Forge Ethnic Minority Links', BBC Radio 4 Today Reports Archive, www.bbc.co.uk/radio4/today/reports/archive/politics/bnp.shtml.

Chow, R. (1993) *Writing Diaspora: Tactics of Intervention in Contemporary Cultural Studies*, Indiana University Press, Bloomington.

Comaroff, J. (2007) 'Beyond Bare Life: AIDS, (Bio)Politics, and the Neoliberal Order', *Public Culture* 19(1): 197–219.

Commission on Integration and Cohesion (2007) *Our Shared Future*, Final Report of the Commission on Integration and Cohesion, www.integrationandcohesion.org.uk.

Committee for International Relations (2001) *The United States' War on AIDS*, Hearing before the Committee on International Relations, House of Representatives, 107th Congress, 1st sess., 7 June, http://commdocs.house.gov/committees/intlrel/hfa72978.000/hfa72978_of.htm.

Committee on Women, Population, and the Environment 'Stop Quinacrine! Stop sterilization abuse', www.cwpe.org/taskforces/dctf/quinacrine.

Connelly, M. (2008) *Fatal Misconception: The Struggle to Control World Population*, Harvard University Press, Harvard MA.

Cooper, F., and A.L. Stoler (1997) 'Between Metropole and Colony: Rethinking a Research Agenda', in F. Cooper and A.L. Stoler (eds), *Tensions of Empire: Colonial Cultures in a Bourgeois World*, University of California Press, Berkeley.

Cooper, R. (2002) 'The Post-Modern State', in *Reordering the World: The Long Term Implications of September 11th*, Foreign Policy Centre, London.

Cornia, G., R. Jolly and F. Stewart (eds) (1987) *Adjustment with a Human Face: Protecting the Vulnerable and Promoting Growth*, Clarendon Press, Oxford.

Cornwall, A., and S. Jolly (2006) 'Introduction: Sexuality Matters', *IDS Bulletin* 37(5): 1–11.

Cornwall, A., J. Edstrom and A. Greig (eds) (2011) *Men and Development: Politicizing Masculinities*, Zed Books, London.

Cosgrave, J. (2003) *The Impact of the War on Terror on Aid Flows*, Action Aid International, South Africa.

Coulter, P. (1989) 'Pretty as a Picture', *New Internationalist* 194.

Cowen, M., and R. Shenton (1995) 'The Invention of Development', in J. Crush (ed.), *Power of Development*, Routledge, London.

Cowen, M., and R. Shenton (1996) *Doctrines of Development*, Routledge, London.

Craig, D., and D. Porter (2006) *Development Beyond Neoliberalism? Governance, Poverty Reduction and Political Economy*, Routledge, London.

Crewe, E., and E. Harrison (1998) *Whose Development? An Ethnography of Aid*, Zed Books, London.

Cross, S. (1993) 'A Socio-Economic Analysis of the Long-Run Effects of AIDS in South Africa,' in S. Cross and A. Whiteside, *Facing Up to AIDS: The Socio-Economic Impact in Southern Africa*, Macmillan, London.

Crush, J. (ed.) (2010) *Migration-Induced HIV and AIDS in Rural Mozambique and Swaziland*, Idasa, Cape Town.

DAC (2003) *A Development Co-operation Lens on Terrorism Prevention: Key Entry Points for Action*, OECD Development Assistance Committee, Paris.

Dalrymple, W. (2006) *The Last Mughal: The Fall of a Dynasty, Delhi, 1857*, Bloomsbury, London.

Dalrymple, W. (2007) 'Delhi, 1857: A Bloody Warning to Today's Imperial Occupiers', *Guardian*, 10 May.

Daniel, P. (2007) 'Africa and HIV/Aids: Men at Work', *Open Democracy*, 9 April, www.opendemocracy.net/globalization-fifty/aids_men_4509.jsp.

Das, A.N. (1992) *The Republic of Bihar*, Penguin, Delhi.

David, S. (2003) *The Indian Mutiny 1857*, Penguin Books, London.

Davis, A. (1982) *Women, Race and Class*, Women's Press, London.

Davis, M. (2001) *Late Victorian Holocausts: El Niño Famines and the Making of the Third World*, Verso, London.

de Waal, A. (1997) *Famine Crimes: Politics and the Disaster Relief Industry in Africa*, James Currey, Oxford.

Deuze, M. (2010) 'Survival of the Mediated', *Journal of Cultural Science* 3:(2): 1–11.

Devereux, S. (2002) 'The Malawi Famine of 2002', *IDS Bulletin* 33(4): 70–78.

DfID (1999) 'Building Support for Development Strategy Paper: Raising Public Awareness and Understanding of International Development Issues', DfID Strategy Paper, UK Department for International Development, London.

DfID (2006) 'Ethnic Minority Groups Share in £5 Million Fund to Raise Awareness of Poverty in the Developing World', press release, 25 July, UK Department for International Development, London.

Dirks, N. (2001) *Castes of Mind: Colonialism and the Making of Modern India*, Princeton University Press, Princeton NJ.

Dixit, A. (2011) 'Poverty and Food Security in Gujarat, India', *European Journal of Development Research* 23(1): 129–50.

Dogra, N. (2007) 'Reading NGOs Visually – Implications of Visual Images for NGO Management', *Journal of International Development* 19: 161–71.

Dreze, J., and A. Sen (2011) 'Putting Growth in Its Place', *Outlook Magazine*, 14 November.

Dube, M. (2010) '"Love Jihad" Was No Farce', *Countercurrents*, 9 February.

Du Bois, W.E.B (1962 [1903]) *The Souls of Black Folk*, Fawcett Publications, New York.

Dubois, J.A. (1906) *Hindu Manners, Customs and Ceremonies*, trans. H.K. Beauchamp, Clarendon Press, Oxford.

Duffield, M. (2001) *Global Governance and the New Wars: The Merging of Development and Security*, Zed Books, London.

Duffield, M. (2005) 'Getting Savages to Fight Barbarians: Development, Security and the Colonial Present', *Conflict, Security & Development* 5(2): 141–59.

Duffield, M. (2006) 'Racism, Migration and Development: The Foundations of Planetary Order', *Progress in Development Studies* 6:(1): 68–79.

Duffield, M., and V. Hewitt (eds) (2009) *Empire, Development & Colonialism: The Past in the Present*, James Currey, Oxford.

Dyer, R. (1986) *Heavenly Bodies*, Macmillan, London.

Edstrom, J. (2011) 'Masculinity and HIV: Di-visions of Bodies, Sex and Structural Context', in A. Cornwall, J. Edstrom and A. Greig (eds), *Men and Development: Politicizing Masculinities*, Zed Books, London.

Ehrlich, P.R. (1968) *The Population Bomb*, Buccaneer Books, Cutchogue NY.

Ekine, S. (2009) 'Don't Throw Anti-homophobic Stones in Glass Houses!', *New Internationalist* blog, www.newint.org/blog/majority/2009/11/30/homophobia.

El-Bushra, J. (2000) 'Transforming Conflict: Some Thoughts on a Gendered

Understanding of Conflict Processes', in S. Jacobs, R. Jacobson and J. Marchbank (eds), *States of Conflict: Gender, Violence and Resistance*, Zed Books, London.

Elkins, C. (2005) *Britain's Gulag: The Brutal End of Empire in Kenya*, Jonathan Cape, London.

Elson, D. (1991) 'Male Bias in Macro-economics: The Case of Structural Adjustment', in D. Elson (ed.), *Male Bias in the Development Process*, Manchester University Press, Manchester.

Engels, F. (2009 [1845]) *The Condition of the Working Class in England*, Penguin, London.

Epstein, H. (2007) *The Invisible Cure: Africa, the West, and the Fight against AIDS*, Farrar, Strauss & Giroux, New York.

Escobar, A. (1995) *Encountering Development: The Making and Unmaking of the Third World*, Princeton University Press, Princeton NJ.

Escobar, A. (2000) 'Beyond the Search for a Paradigm? Post-Development and Beyond', *Development* 43(4): 11–14.

Eze, E.C. (1997) *Race and the Enlightenment: A Reader*, Blackwell, Malden MA.

Eze, E.C. (2000) 'Hume, Race, and Human Nature', *Journal of the History of Ideas* 61(4): 691–8.

Fanon, F. (1967a [1952]) *Black Skin, White Masks*, Grove Press, New York.

Fanon, F. (1967b [1961]) *The Wretched of the Earth*, Penguin, Harmondsworth.

Farmer, P. (2005) *Pathologies of Power: Health, Human Rights and the New War on the Poor*, University of California Press, Berkeley.

Farmer, P. (2006) *AIDS and Accusation: Haiti and the Geography of Blame*, University of California Press, Berkeley.

Farmer, P., M. Connors and J. Simmons (1996) *Women, Poverty and AIDS: Sex, Drugs and Structural Violence*, Common Courage Press, Michigan.

Ferguson, J., and A. Gupta (2002) 'Spatializing States: Towards an Ethnography of Neo-liberal Governmentality', *American Ethnologist* 29(4): 981–1002.

Ferguson, N. (2003) *Empire: How Britain Made the Modern World*, Penguin, Harmondsworth.

Fick, C.E. (1990) *The Making of Haiti: The Saint Domingue Revolution from Below*, University of Tennessee Press, Knoxville.

Firth, J. (2012) 'Healthy Choices and Heavy Burdens: Race, Citizenship and Gender in the "Obesity Epidemic"', *Journal of International Women's Studies* 13(2): 33–50.

Foucault, M. (1979) *Discipline and Punish: The Birth of the Prison*, Penguin, Harmondsworth.

Foucault, M. (1980) *The History of Sexuality*, Vol. 1: *An Introduction*, Vintage, New York.

Fracchia, J. (2008) 'The Capitalist Labour-Process and the Body in Pain: The Corporeal Depths of Marx's Concept of Immiseration', *Historical Materialism* 16: 35–66.

Freedman, A. (1998) 'Two Americans Export Chemical Sterilization to the Third World', *Wall Street Journal*, 18 June.

Fremont-Barnes, G. (2007) *The Indian Mutiny 1857–58*, Osprey Publishing, Oxford.

Gathii, J.T. (1999) 'Representations of Africa in Good Governance Discourse: Policing and Containing Dissidence to Neo-liberalism', *Third World Legal Studies* 15(1): 65–108.

Gellman,B. (2000) 'The Belated Global Response to AIDS in Africa: World Shunned Signs of the Coming Plague', *Washington Post*, 5 July.

General Assembly of European NGOs (1989) 'Code of Conduct on Images and Messages Relating to the Third World', www.dgcd.be/documents/en/topics/european_conference_public_awareness/code_of_conduct.doc.

Gill, R. (2007) *Gender and the Media*, Polity Press, Cambridge.

Gill, R. (2012) 'As if Postfeminism Had Come True: The Turn to Agency in Cultural Studies of "Sexualisation"', in S. Madhok, A. Phillips and K. Wilson (eds), *Gender, Agency and Coercion*, Palgrave Macmillan, Basingstoke.

Gill, R., and O. Koffman, (2013) '"The revolution will be led by a 12 year old girl": Girl Power and Global Biopolitics', in D. Buckingham, S. Bragg, and M.J. Kehily (eds), *Youth Cultures in the Age of Global Media*, Palgrave Macmillan, Basingstoke.

Gilligan, A. (2007) 'The Rise and Rise of the Fundamentalist Father', *Evening Standard*, 11 June.

Gills, B., J. Rocamora and R. Wilson (eds) (1993) *Low Intensity Democracy: Political Power in the New World Order*, Pluto Press, London.

Gilman, S.L. (1985) 'Black Bodies, White Bodies: Toward an Iconography of Female Sexuality in Late Nineteenth-Century Art, Medicine, and Literature', *Critical Inquiry* 12(1): 204–42.

Gilmore, R.W. (2007) *Golden Gulag: Prisons, Surplus, Crisis, and Opposition in Globalizing California*, University of California Press, Berkeley.

Gilroy, P. (1993) *The Black Atlantic: Modernity and Double Consciousness*, Verso, London.

Goldberg, D.T. (1993) *Racist Culture: Philosophy and the Politics of Meaning*, Blackwell, London.

Goldberg, D.T. (2009) *The Threat of Race: Reflections on Racial Neoliberalism*, Wiley–Blackwell, Malden MA.

Golwalkar, M.S. (1944) *We, or Our Nationhood, Defined*, Bharat Publications, Nagpur.

Gordon, L. (1976) *Woman's Body, Woman's Right: A Social History of Birth Control in America*, Viking/Penguin, New York.

Gosine, A. (2006) '"Race", Culture, Power, Sex Desire, Love: Writing in "Men who have Sex with Men"', *IDS Bulletin* 37(5): 27–33.

Goudge, P. (2003) *The Whiteness of Power: Racism in Third World Development and Aid*, Lawrence & Wishart, London.

Gould, S.J. (1981) *The Mismeasure of Man*, Penguin, Harmondsworth.

Government of India (2009) *Committee on State Agrarian Relations and Unfinished Task of Land Reforms*, Vol. 1, draft report, Ministry of Rural Development, Government of India, New Delhi.

Gregory, D. (2006) 'Vanishing Points: Law, Violence and Exception in the Global War Prison', in D. Gregory and A. Pred (eds), *Violent Geographies: Fear, Terror and Political Violence*, Routledge, New York.

Greig, A. (2011) 'Anxious States and Directions for Masculinities Work with Men', in A. Cornwall, J. Edstrom and A. Greig (eds), *Men and Development: Politicizing Masculinities*, Zed Books, London.

Grosz, E. (1994) *Volatile Bodies: Toward a Corporeal Feminism*, Indiana University Press, Bloomington.

Grovogui, S.N. (2001) 'Come to Africa: A Hermeneutics of Race in International Theory', *Alternatives* 26: 425–48.

Grovogui, S.N. (2002) 'Regimes of Sovereignty: International Morality and the African Condition', *European Journal of International Relations* 8(3): 315–38.

Guha, S. (1998) 'Lower Strata, Older Races, and Aboriginal Peoples: Racial Anthropology and Mythical History Past and Present', *Journal of Asian Studies* 57(2): 423–41.

Gupta, A (2012) *Red Tape: Bureaucracy, Structural Violence, and Poverty in India*, Duke University Press, Durham NC.

Habib, I. (2007) 'Understanding 1857', *People's Democracy*, 13 May.

Hall, C. (2002) *Civilising Subjects: Colony and Metropole in the English Imagination, 1830–1867*, University of Chicago Press, Chicago.

Hall, D. (1999) 'Privatisation, Multinationals and Corruption', *Development in Practice* 9(5): 539–56.

Hall, S. (1978) *Policing the Crisis: Mugging, the State and Law and Order*, Palgrave Macmillan, Abingdon.

Hall, S. (1980) 'Race, Articulation and Societies Structured in Dominance', in *Sociological Theories – Race and Colonialism*, UNESCO, Paris.

Hall, S. (1986) 'Gramsci's Relevance for the Study of Race and Ethnicity', *Journal of Communication Inquiry* 10(2): 5–27.

Hall, S. (1997) 'The Spectacle of the "Other"', in S. Hall (ed.), *Representation: Cultural Representation: Cultural Representatives and Signifying Practices*, Sage, London.

Halperin, D.T., and H. Epstein (2004) 'Concurrent Sexual Partnerships Help to Explain Africa's High HIV Prevalence: Implications for Prevention', *Lancet* 364: 4–6.

Hammond, L., M. Awad, A. Ibrahim Dagane, P. Hansen, C. Horst, K. Menkhaus and L. Obare (2011) *Cash and Compassion: The Role of the Somali Diaspora in Relief, Development and Peace-building: Report of a Study Commissioned by UNDP Somalia*, Vol. 1, January, www.so.undp.org/docs/Cash%20and%20compassion.pdf.

Haritaworn, J., with T. Tauqir and E. Erdem (2008) 'Gay Imperialism: Gender and Sexuality Discourse in the "War on Terror"', in A. Kuntsman and E. Miyake (eds), *Out of Place: Interrogating Silences in Queerness/Raciality*, Raw Nerve Books, London.

Harrison, G. (2001) 'Post-Conditionality Politics and Administrative Reform: Reflections on the Cases of Uganda and Tanzania', *Development and Change* 32(4): 657–79.

Harrison, G. (2010) *Neoliberal Africa: The Impact of Global Social Engineering*, Zed Books, London.

Harrison, G., and C. Mercer (2010) 'Demanding Development', *Review of African Political Economy* 37(124): 119–21.

Hartmann, B. (1995) *Reproductive Rights and Wrongs: The Global Politics of Population Control*, South End Press, Boston MA.

Hartmann, B. (2009) 'The "New" Population Control Craze: Retro, Racist, Wrong Way to Go', *On the Issues*, Fall, www.ontheissuesmagazine. com/2009fall/2009fall_hartmann.php.

Hartmann, B., and H. Standing (1985) *Food, Saris and Sterilization: Population Control in Bangladesh*, Bangladesh International Action Group, London.

Harvey, D. (1998) 'The Body as an Accumulation Strategy', *Environment and Planning D: Society and Space* 16(4): 401–21.

Hearn, J. (2007) 'African NGOs: The New Compradors', *Development and Change* 38(6): 1095–110.

Heath, D., and C. Mathur (eds) (2011) *Communalism and Globalisation in South Asia and Its Diaspora*, Routledge, London.

Helman, G.B., and S.R. Ratner (1992–93) 'Saving Failed States', *Foreign Policy* 89, Winter: 3–20.

Hemmings, C. (2011) *Why Stories Matter: The Political Grammar of Feminist Theory*, Duke University Press, Durham NC.

Hendrixon, A. (2004) 'Angry Young Men, Veiled Young Women: Constructing a New Population Threat', *Corner House Briefing* 34, www.thecornerhouse. org.uk/resource/angry-young-men-veiled-young-women.

Hibbert, C. (1978) *The Great Mutiny: India 1857*, Penguin, Harmondsworth.

Hoad, N. (2007) *African Intimacies: Race, Homosexuality, and Globalization*, University of Minnesota Press, Minneapolis.

Hodgson, G. (2003) 'Walt Rostow: Cold War Liberal Adviser to President Kennedy Who Backed the Disastrous US Intervention in Vietnam', *Guardian*, 17 February.

Hodkinson, S. (2005) 'G8 – Africa Nil', *Red Pepper*, November, www.redpepper. org.uk/G8–Africa-nil.

Holslag, J. (2009) 'China's New Security Strategy for Africa', *Parameters*, Summer: 23–37.

hooks, b. (1982) *Ain't I a Woman: Black Women and Feminism*, Pluto Press, London.

Hulme, D., and J. Scott (2010) *The Political Economy of the MDGs: Retrospect and Prospect for the World's Biggest Promise*, BWPI Working Paper 110, Brooks World Poverty Institute, University of Manchester, Manchester.

Human Rights Watch (2008) '"Sodomy" Laws Show Survival of Colonial Injustice', 17 December, www.hrw.org/news/2008/12/17/sodomy-laws-show-survival-colonial-injustice.

Hunter, W.W. (1875) *A Statistical Account of Bengal*, Trubner, London.

Huntington, S.P. (1993) 'The Clash of Civilizations?', *Foreign Affairs* 72(3): 22–49.

IFPRI (2011) *Global Hunger Index 2011*, International Food Policy Research Institute, www.ifpri.org/publication/2011–global-hunger-index.

Ignatieff, M. (2003) *Empire Lite: Nation Building in Bosnia, Kosovo, Afghanistan*, Vintage, London.

INCITE! (2010) *INCITE! Women of Color Against Violence* website, www.incite-national.org; accessed 1 September 2010.

Iyayi, F. (1986) 'The Primitive Accumulation of Capital in a Neo-Colony: The Nigerian Case', *Review of African Political Economy* 13(35): 27–39.

Jackson, C. (1998) 'Rescuing Gender from the Poverty Trap', in C. Jackson and R. Pearson (eds), *Feminist Visions of Development: Gender Analysis and Policy*, Routledge, London.

Jacobs, S., R. Jacobson and J. Marchbank (2000) *States of Conflict: Gender, Violence and Resistance*, Zed Books, London.

Jaffrelot, C., and I. Therwath (2011) 'Western Hindutva: Hindu Nationalism in the United Kingdom and North America', in D. Heath and C. Mathur (eds), *Communalism and Globalisation in South Asia and its Diaspora*, Routledge, London.

Jaggar, A.M. (1988) *Feminist Politics and Human Nature*, Rowman & Littlefield, Totowa NJ.

James, C.L.R. (1938) *The Black Jacobins: Toussaint L'Ouverture and the San Domingo Revolution*, Secker & Warburg, London.

Kabeer, N. (1995) *Reversed Realities: Gender Hierarchies in Development Thought*, Kali for Women, Delhi.

Kaldor, M. (1999) *New and Old Wars: Organized Violence in a Global Era*, Polity Press, Cambridge.

Kalipeni, E., S. Craddock, J.R. Oppong and J. Ghosh (eds), *HIV and AIDS in Africa: Beyond Epidemiology*, Blackwell, Malden MA.

Kalpana, K. (2008) *The Vulnerability of 'Self-Help': Women and Micro-Finance in South India*, IDS Working Paper 303, Institute of Development Studies, Brighton.

Kalra, V., R. Kaur and J. Hutnyk (2005) *Diaspora and Hybridity*, Sage, London.

Kaoma, K. (2009) *Globalising the Culture Wars: U.S. Conservatives, African Churches, and Homophobia*, Political Research Associates, Somerville.

Kapila, S. (2007) 'Race Matters: Orientalism and Religion, India and Beyond c. 1770–1880', *Modern Asian Studies* 41(3): 471–513.

Kaplan, R.D. (1994) 'The Coming Anarchy', *The Atlantic Magazine*, February.

Kapoor, I. (2002) 'Capitalism, Culture, Agency: Dependency Versus Postcolonial Theory', *Third World Quarterly* 23(4): 647–64.

Kapoor, I. (2008) *The Postcolonial Politics of Development*, Routledge, London.

Karim, L. (2011) *Microfinance and Its Discontents: Women in Debt in Bangladesh*, University of Minnesota Press, Minneapolis.

Katz, A. (2003) 'AIDS in Africa', *Zmag*, September, http://zmagsite.zmag.org/Sept2003/katzpr0903.html.

Kelly, L. (2000) 'Wars against Women: Sexual Violence, Sexual Politics and the Militarised State', in S. Jacobs, R. Jacobson and J. Marchbank (eds), *States of Conflict: Gender, Violence and Resistance*, Zed Books, London.

khanna, a. (2011) 'Meyeli Chhele Becomes MSM: Transformation of Idioms of Sexualness into Epidemiological Forms in India', in A. Cornwall, J. Edstrom and A. Greig (eds), *Men and Development: Politicizing Masculinities*, Zed Books, London.

Kiely, R. (1999) 'The Last Refuge of the Noble Savage? A Critical Assessment of Post-Development Theory', *European Journal of Development Research* 11(1): 30–55.

Kinfu, Y., and J. Taylor (2005) 'On the Components of Indigenous Population Change', *Australian Geographer* 36(2): 233–55.

Klausen, S.M. (2004) *Race, Maternity and the Politics of Birth Control in South Africa, 1910–39*, Palgrave Macmillan, Basingstoke.

Kothari, U. (2005) 'From Colonial Administration to Development Studies: A Post-colonial Critique of the History of Development Studies', in U. Kothari (ed.), *A Radical History of Development Studies*, Zed Books, London.

Kothari, U. (2006) 'An Agenda for Thinking about "Race" in Development', *Progress in Development Studies* 6(1): 9–23.

Krishna, P. (2006) 'Who is Afraid of 1857', *Liberation* 12(8), December, www.cpiml.org/liberation/year_2006/December/1857_who_is_afraid.html.

Krishnan, K. (2007) 'Advani and Savarkar: The Sangh's Bid for Heroism via 1857', *Liberation*, June.

Kundnani, A. (2007) *The End of Tolerance: Racism in 21st Century Britain*, Pluto Press, London.

Lal, D. (1983) 'The Poverty of Development Economics', *Hobart Paper No. 16*, Institute of Economic Affairs, London.

Lentin, A., and G. Titley (2011) *The Crises of Multiculturalism: Racism in a Neoliberal Age*, Zed Books, London.

Lewis S. (2005) 'Africa's Children Left Out of HIV Treatment Breakthrough', *Sunday Independent*, 13 February.

Li, T.M. (2007) *The Will to Improve: Governmentality, Development, and the Practice of Politics*, Duke University Press, Durham NC.

Liberation (2011) 'Draft LARR Bill 2011: Seeking to Legalise Land Grab', October, www.cpiml.org/liberation/year_2011/oct_11/policy_watch.html.

Lidchi, H. (1999) 'Finding the Right Image: British Development NGOs and the Regulation of Imagery', in T. Skelton and T. Allen (eds), *Culture and Global Change,* Routledge, London.

Luke, N. (2005) 'Confronting the "Sugar Daddy" Stereotype: Age and Economic Asymmetries and Risky Sexual Behavior in Urban Kenya', *International Family Planning Perspectives* 31(1): 6–14.

Lurie, M., and S. Rosenthal (2009) 'Concurrent Partnerships as a Driver of HIV Epidemics in Sub-Saharan Africa: The Evidence is Limited', *AIDS and Behavior* 14(1): 17–24.

Macaulay, T.B. (1957 [1835]) 'Minute of 2 February 1835 on Indian Education', in *Macaulay, Prose and Poetry,* ed. G.M. Young, Harvard University Press, Cambridge MA.

Maclean, K. (2010) 'Capitalising on Women's Social Capital: Gender and Micro-finance in Bolivia', in S. Chant (ed.), *The International Handbook of Gender and Poverty: Concepts, Research, Policy,* Edward Elgar, Cheltenham.

Magubane, Z. (2001) 'Which Bodies Matter? Feminism, Poststructuralism, Race, and the Curious Theoretical Odyssey of the "Hottentot Venus"', *Gender and Society* 15(6): 816–34.

Magubane, Z. (2004) *Bringing the Empire Home: Race, Class, and Gender in Britain and Colonial South Africa,* Chicago University Press, Chicago.

Mah, T.L., and D.T. Halperin (2010) 'Concurrent Sexual Partnerships and the HIV Epidemics in Africa: Evidence to Move Forward', *AIDS and Behavior* 14(1): 11–14.

Malik, N. (2011) 'NGOs and their Position in the Global Administration of the Empire', South Asia Solidarity Group, www.southasiasolidarity.org/2011/08/13/ngos-and-their-position-in-the-global-administration-of-the-empire.

Malthus, T. (1798) *An Essay on the Principle of Population,* J. Johnson, London.

Mamdani, M. (1996) *Citizen and Subject: Contemporary Africa and the Legacy of Late Colonialism,* Princeton University Press, Princeton NJ.

Mamdani, M. (2001) *When Victims Become Killers: Colonialism, Nativism and the Genocide in Rwanda,* James Currey, Oxford.

Mani, L. (1987) 'Contentious Traditions: The Debate on Sati in Colonial India', *Cultural Critique* 7: 119–56.

Manji, F., and C. O'Coill (2002) 'The Missionary Position: NGOs and Development in Africa', *International Affairs* 78(3): 567–83.

Manzo, K. (1995) 'Black Consciousness and the Quest for a Counter-Modernist Development', in J. Crush (ed.), *Power of Development,* Routledge, London.

Manzo, K. (2008) 'Imaging Humanitarianism: NGO Identity and the Iconography of Childhood', *Antipode* 40(4): 632–57.

Marchand, M.H., and J.L. Parpart (eds) (1995) *Feminism/Postmodernism/Development,* Routledge, London.

Marx, K. (1976 [1873]) *Capital,* Vol. 1, Penguin, Harmondsworth.

Marx, K., and F. Engels (1959) *The First Indian War of Independence 1857–1859,* Foreign Languages Publishing House, Moscow.

Marx, K., and F. Engels (1974 [1846]) *The German Ideology*, Lawrence & Wishart, London.

Mass, B. (1976) *Population Target: The Political Economy of Population Control in Latin America*, Latin American Working Group, Toronto.

Mass, B. (1977) 'Puerto Rico: A Case Study of Population Control', *Latin American Perspectives* 4(4): 66–81.

Mbembe, A. (2001) *On the Postcolony*, University of California Press, Berkeley.

Mbembe, A. (2002) 'Africa in Motion: An Interview with the Post-colonialism Theoretician Achille Mbembe', by C. Höller, www.springerin.at.

Mbembe, A. (2003) 'Necropolitics', *Public Culture* 15(1): 11–40.

McClintock, A. (1995) *Imperial Leather: Race, Gender and Sexuality in the Colonial Contest*, Routledge, New York.

McEwan, C. (2001) 'Postcolonialism, Feminism and Development: Intersections and Dilemmas', *Progress in Development Studies* 1(2): 93–111.

Mehta, A.K., A. Shepherd, S. Bhide, A. Shah and A. Kumar (2011) *India Chronic Poverty Report: Towards Solutions and New Compacts in a Dynamic Context*, Indian Institute of Public Administration, Delhi.

Mehta, U. (1999) *Liberalism and Empire: A Study in Nineteenth Century British Liberal Thought*, University of Chicago Press, Chicago.

Mercia Group (2006) *Review of the Evidence Base on Faith Communities*, April, London, www.communities.gov.uk/documents/corporate/pdf/143816.pdf.

Mohanty, C.T. (1986) 'Under Western Eyes: Feminist Scholarship and Colonial Discourses', *Boundary 2*, 12(3): 333–58.

Mohanty C.T. (2003) '"Under Western Eyes" Revisited: Feminist Solidarity through Anticapitalist Struggles', *Signs: Journal of Women in Culture and Society* 28(2): 499–535.

Molyneux, M. (2008) 'The "Neoliberal Turn" and the New Social Policy in Latin America: How Neoliberal, How New?' *Development and Change* 39(5): 775–97.

Moore, D. (1999) '"Sail on, O Ship of State": Neo-liberalism, Globalisation and the Governance of Africa', *Journal of Peasant Studies* 27(1): 61–96.

Morton, A.L. (1938) *A People's History of England*, Victor Gollancz, London.

Mosse, D. (2005) *Cultivating Development: An Ethnography of Aid Policy and Practice*, Pluto Press, London.

Mukherjee, R. (1984) *Awadh in Revolt, 1857–1858: A Study in Popular Resistance*, Oxford University Press, Delhi.

Mukherjee, R. (1990) '"Satan Let Loose Upon Earth": The Kanpur Massacres in India in the Revolt of 1857', *Past and Present* 128: 92–116.

Mulinge, M.M., and G.N. Lesetedi (1998) 'Interrogating Our Past: Colonialism and Corruption in Sub-Saharan Africa', *African Journal of Political Science* 3(2): 15–28.

Musisi, N. (2002) 'The Politics of Perception or Perception as Politics? Colonial and Missionary Representations of Baganda Women, 1900–1945', in J. Altman, S. Geiger and N. Musisi (eds), *Women in African Colonial Histories*,

Indiana University Press, Bloomington.

Nair, S. (1989) *Imperialism and the Control of Women's Fertility: New Hormonal Contraceptives, Population Control and the WHO*, Campaign Against Long-Acting Hormonal Contraceptives, London and Amsterdam.

Nanda, M. (2003) *Prophets Facing Backward: Postmodern Critiques of Science and Hindu Nationalism in India*, Rutgers University Press, Piscataway NJ.

Narayan, U. (1997) *Dislocating Cultures: Identities, Traditions, and Third World Feminism*, Routledge, New York.

Nash, K. (2008) 'Global Citizenship as Show Business: The Cultural Politics of Make Poverty History', *Media Culture Society* 30(2): 167–81.

Nelson, R. (2006) 'AIDS Treatment Enters Its 25th Year', *Lancet* 6, August: 466–7.

New Internationalist (1992) 'In Black and White', *New Internationalist* 228.

Newland, K., with E. Patrick (2004) *Beyond Remittances: The Role of Diaspora in Poverty Reduction in their Countries of Origin. A Scoping Study by the Migration Policy Institute for the Department of International Development*, Migration Policy Institute, Washington DC.

Newsinger, J. (2006) *The Blood Never Dried: A People's History of the British Empire*, Bookmarks, London.

Nossel, S. (2004) 'Smart Power', *Foreign Affairs* 83(2): 131–42.

Noxolo, P. (2009) 'Freedom, Fear and NGOs: Balancing Discourses of Violence and Humanity in Securitising Times', in M. Duffield and V. Hewitt (eds), *Empire, Development & Colonialism: The Past in the Present*, James Currey, Oxford.

O'Brien, S. (2011) Speech on World Population Day to the All Party Parliamentary Group on Population, Development and Reproductive Health and International Planned Parenthood Federation, 11 July.

Omi, M., and H. Winant, (1986) *Racial Formation in the US: From the 1960s to the 1980s*, Routledge, New York.

Oppong, J., and E. Kalipeni (2004) 'Perceptions and Misperceptions of AIDS in Africa', in E. Kalipeni, S. Craddock, J.R. Oppong and J. Ghosh (eds), *HIV and AIDS in Africa: Beyond Epidemiology*, Blackwell, Malden MA.

Orzeck, R. (2007) 'What Does Not Kill You: Historical Materialism and the Body', *Environment and Planning D: Society and Space* 25: 496–514.

Osei, P.D. (2000) 'Political Liberalisation and the Effect of Value Added Tax in Ghana', *Journal of Modern African Studies* 38(2): 255–78.

Owusu, K., and F. Ng'ambi (2002) *Structural Damage: The Causes and Consequences of Malawi's Food Crisis*, World Development Movement, London.

Owusu, N. (2003) 'Pragmatism and the Gradual Shift from Dependency to Neoliberalism: The World Bank, African Leaders and Development Policy in Africa', *World Development* 31(10): 1655–72.

Oxfam (2008) 'Oxfam Unwrapped Raises £50 Million: 3 Million Life-changing Gifts in More Than 50 Countries', press release, 16 December, www.oxfam.org.uk/applications/blogs/pressoffice/?p=2739.

Packard R.M., and P. Epstein (1991) 'Epidemiologists, Social Scientists, and the Structure of Medical Research on AIDS in Africa', *Social Science and Medicine* 33(7): 771–94.

Padel, F., and S. Das (2010) *Out of this Earth: East India Adivasis and the Aluminium Cartel*, Orient Blackswan, Delhi.

Palme Dutt, R. (1970 [1947]) *India Today*, Manisha, Calcutta.

Parker, R. (2001) 'Sexuality, Culture, and Power in HIV/AIDS Research', *Annual Review of Anthropology* 30: 163–79.

Parpart, J.L. (2010) 'Choosing Silence: Rethinking Voice, Agency and Women's Empowerment', in R Ryan-Flood and R. Gill (eds), *Secrecy and Silence in the Research Process*, Routledge, London.

Parthasarathi, P. (1998) 'Rethinking Wages and Competitiveness in the Eighteenth Century: Britain and South India', *Past & Present* 158: 79–109.

Patnaik, U. (1972) 'Development of Capitalism in Agriculture', *Social Scientist* 1(2) and 1(3).

Patnaik, U. (2006) 'The Free Lunch – Transfers from the Tropical Colonies and their Role in Capital Formation in Britain during Industrial Revolution', in K.S. Jomo (ed.), *Globalization under Hegemony*, Oxford University Press, Delhi.

Patton, C. (1990) 'Inventing "African AIDS"', *New Formations* 10: 25–39.

Paxton, N. (1992) 'Mobilizing Chivalry: Rape in British Novels about the India Uprising of 1857', *Victorian Studies* 36(1): 5–30.

Pedwell, C. (2012) 'Affective (Self-)Transformations: Empathy, Neoliberalism and International Development', *Feminist Theory*, 13(2).

Petras, J. (1999) 'NGOs: In the Service of Imperialism', *Journal of Contemporary Asia* 29(4): 429–40.

Phillips, O. (2004) 'The Invisible Presence of Homosexuality: Implications for HIV/AIDS and Rights in Southern Africa', in E. Kalipeni, S. Craddock, J.R. Oppong and J. Ghosh (eds), *HIV and AIDS in Africa: Beyond Epidemiology*, Blackwell, Malden MA.

Pitts, J. (2006) *A Turn to Empire: The Rise of Imperial Liberalism in Britain and France*, Princeton University Press, Princeton NJ.

Ploch, L. (2011) 'Africa Command: U.S. Strategic Interests and the Role of the U.S. Military in Africa', Congressional Research Service, 22 July, www.fas.org/sgp/crs/natsec/RL34003.pdf.

Pomeranz, K. (2000) *The Great Divergence: China, Europe, and the Making of the Modern World Economy*, Princeton University Press, Princeton NJ.

Pool, I.S. (1967) 'The Public and the Polity', in I.S. Pool (ed.), *Contemporary Political Science: Toward Empirical Theory*, McGraw–Hill, New York.

Price, D. (2003) 'Subtle Means and Enticing Carrots: The Impact of Funding on American Cold War Anthropology', *Critique of Anthropology* 23:(4): 373–401.

Price, D. (2011) *Weaponizing Anthropology: Social Science in Service of the Military State*, AK/CounterPunch Books, Petrolia CA.

Prunier, G., (1997) *The Rwanda Crisis, 1959–1994: History of a Genocide*, C. Hurst, London.

Puar, J.K. (2004) 'Abu Ghraib: Arguing against Exceptionalism', *Feminist Studies* 30(2): 522–34.

Quinn, T.C., P. Piot, J.B. McCormick, F.M. Feinsod, H. Taelman, B. Kapita, W. Stevens and A.S. Fauci (1987) 'Serologic and Immunologic Studies in Patients with AIDS in North America and Africa: The Potential Role of Infectious Agents as Co-factors in Human Immunodeficiency Virus Infection', *Journal of the American Medical Association* 257(19): 2617–21.

Rahnema, M., and V. Bawtree (eds) (1997) *The Post-Development Reader*, Zed Books, London.

Ramamurthy, A. (2003) *Imperial Persuaders: Images of Africa and Asia in British Advertising*, Manchester University Press, Manchester.

Rankin, K. (2001) 'Governing Development: Neoliberalism, Microcredit, and Rational Economic Woman', *Economy and Society* 30(1): 18–37.

Rao, M. (1994) 'An Imagined Reality: Malthusianism, Neo-Malthusianism and Population Myth', *Economic and Political Weekly* 29(5), 29 January: PE40–PE52.

Ray, R.K. (2003) *The Felt Community: Commonality and Mentality before the Emergence of Indian Nationalism*, Oxford University Press, Delhi.

Razack, S. (1998) *Looking White People in the Eye: Gender, Race, and Culture in Courtrooms and Classrooms*, University of Toronto Press, Toronto.

Razack, S. (2004) *Dark Threats and White Knights: The Somalia Affair, Peacekeeping and the New Imperialism*, University of Toronto Press, Toronto.

Reverby, S.M. (2011) '"Normal Exposure" and Inoculation Syphilis: A PHS "Tuskegee" Doctor in Guatemala, 1946–48', *Journal of Policy History*, Special Issue on Human Subjects, January.

Roberts, A. (1998) 'More Refugees, Less Asylum: A Regime in Transformation', *Journal of Refugee Studies* 11: 375–96.

Robertson, D. (1997) *Killing the Black Body: Race, Reproduction and the Meaning of Liberty*, Pantheon Books, New York.

Robins, N. (2006) *The Corporation That Changed the World: How the East India Company Shaped the Modern Multinational*, Pluto Press, London.

Robinson, W.I. (1996) *Promoting Polyarchy: Globalization, US Intervention, and Hegemony*, Cambridge University Press, Cambridge.

Rodney, W. (1972) *How Europe Underdeveloped Africa*, Bogle-L'Ouverture Publications, London.

Roediger, D. (1999) *The Wages of Whiteness: Race and the Making of the American Working Class*, rev. edn, Verso, London.

Rogers, P. (2011) 'Libya and a Decade's War', *Open Democracy*, 1 April 2011, www.opendemocracy.net/paul-rogers/libya-and-decade's-war.

Rosenberg, A.P. (1993) 'Corruption as a Policy Issue', *Corruption and Reform* 7(3): 173–5.

Ross, E.B. (1998) *The Malthus Factor: Poverty, Politics and Population in Capitalist Development*, Zed Books, London.

Rostow, W.W. (1960) *The Stages of Economic Growth: A Non-Communist Manifesto*, Cambridge University Press, Cambridge.

Rowden, R. (2011) *The Deadly Ideas of Neoliberalism: How the IMF Has Undermined Public Health and the Fight Against AIDS*, Zed Books, London.

Roy, T. (1994) *The Politics of a Popular Uprising: Bundelkhand in 1857*, Oxford University Press, Delhi.

SAfAIDS (2011) 'ICASA 2011: Stephen Lewis Warns "Reckless" Donors: How Dare You Decide Whether Africans Live or Die?', www.safaids.net/content/icasa-2011–stephen-lewis-warns-%E2%80%98reckless%E2%80%99–donors-how-dare-you-decide-whether-africans-live-0.

Said, E. (1978) *Orientalism*, Penguin, London.

Saldanha, A. (2006) 'Reontologising Race: The Machinic Geography of Phenotype', *Environment and Planning D: Society and Space* 24(1): 9–24.

Sangari, K., and S. Vaid (eds) (1989) *Recasting Women: Essays in Colonial History*, Kali for Women, Delhi.

Sarkar, S. (1993) 'The Fascism of the Sangh Parivar', *Economic and Political Weekly*, 30 January: 163–7.

Sarkar, T. (2002) 'Semiotics of Terror: Muslim Women and Children in Hindu Rashtra', *Economic and Political Weekly*, 13 July: 2872–6.

Sarkar, T. (2011) 'Pragmatics of the Hindu Right: Globalisation and the Politics of Women's Organisations in India', in D. Heath and C. Mathur (eds), *Communalism and Globalisation in South Asia and Its Diaspora*, Routledge, London.

Saul, J.S. (1997) 'Liberal Democracy vs Popular Democracy in Southern Africa', *Review of African Political Economy* 24(72): 219–36.

Sawers, L., and E. Stillwaggon (2010) 'Concurrent Sexual Partnerships Do Not Explain the HIV Epidemics in Africa: A Systematic Review of the Evidence', *Journal of the International AIDS Society* 13(34), www.biomedcentral.com/1758–2652/content/13/1/34.

Schmidt, B. (1998) 'Forced Sterilization in Peru', *Political Environments* 6, Fall.

Searls, H. (1995) 'The NGO Revolution', unpublished discussion paper.

Sen, A. (1981) *Poverty and Famines: An Essay on Entitlement and Deprivation*, Oxford University Press, Oxford.

Sen, A. (1999) *Development as Freedom*, Oxford University Press, Oxford.

Sheller, M. (2000) *Democracy After Slavery: Black Publics and Peasant Radicalism in Haiti and Jamaica*, University Press of Florida, Gainesville.

Shilliam, R. (2008) 'What the Haitian Revolution Might Tell Us about Development, Security and the Politics of Race', *Comparative Studies in Society and History* 50(3): 778–808.

Shivji, I. (ed.) (1991) *State and Constitutionalism: An African Debate on Democracy*, SAPES, Harare.

Sinha, M. (1997) *Colonial Masculinity: The "Manly Englishman" and The "Effeminate Bengali" in the Late Nineteenth Century*, Manchester University Press, Manchester.

Sitze, A. (2004) 'Denialism', *South Atlantic Quarterly* 103(4): 769–811.

Sivanandan, A. (1985) 'RAT and the Degradation of Black Struggle', *Race and Class* 26(4): April.

Sivanandan, A. (2008 [1976]) 'Race, Class and the State', in *Catching History on the Wing: Race, Culture and Globalisation*, Pluto Press, London.

Smirl, L. (2008) 'Building the Other, Constructing Ourselves: Spatial Dimensions of International Humanitarian Response', *International Political Sociology* 2(3): 236–53.

South Asia Solidarity Group (2004) 'Campaigning against Hindutva Fascism in Britain – Stand Together against Communalism and War!', 31 March, www.southasiasolidarity.org.

South Asia Solidarity Group (2011) 'Strange Bedfellows for Action Aid', 13 August, www.southasiasolidarity.org/2011/08/13/strange-bedfellows-for-action-aid.

Spencer, H. (1895) *The Principles of Sociology*, D. Appleton, New York.

Spilsbury, J. (2007) *The Indian Mutiny*, Orion Publishing, London.

Spivak, G.C. (1988) 'Can the Subaltern Speak?', in C. Nelson and L. Grossberg (eds), *Marxism and the Interpretation of Culture*, University of Illinois Press, Urbana.

Spivak, G.C. (2003) A Conversation with Gayatri Chakravorty Spivak: Politics and the Imagination, interview by Jenny Sharpe, *Signs: Journal of Women in Culture and Society* 28(2): 609–24.

Srinivas, K.R., and K. Kanakamala (1992) 'Introducing Norplant: Politics of Coercion', *Economic and Political Weekly* 27(29): 1531–3.

Stiglitz, J. (1998) 'More Instruments and Broader Goals: Moving Toward the Post–Washington Consensus', 1998 WIDER Annual Lecture, Helsinki, 7 January.

Stillwaggon, E. (2002) 'HIV/AIDS in Africa: Fertile Terrain', *Journal of Development Studies* 38(6): 1–22.

Stillwaggon, E. (2003) 'Racial Metaphors: Interpreting Sex and AIDS in Africa', *Development and Change* 34:(5): 809–32.

Stillwaggon, E. (2006) *AIDS and the Ecology of Poverty*, Oxford University Press, New York.

Stockton, N. (1998) 'In Defence of Humanitarianism', *Disasters* 22(4): 352–60.

Stoler, A.L. (1995) *Race and the Education of Desire: Foucault's History of Sexuality and the Colonial Order of Things*, Duke University Press, Durham NC.

Stoler A.L. (2002) *Carnal Knowledge and Imperial Power: Race and the Intimate in Colonial Rule*, University of California Press, Berkeley.

Sundar, N. (1997) *Subalterns and Sovereigns: An Anthropological History of Bastar, 1854–1996*, Oxford University Press, New York.

Swanton, D. (2008) 'The Force of Race', *darkmatter*, February, www.darkmatter101.org/site/2008/02/23/the-force-of-race.

Sylvester, C. (1999) 'Development Studies and Postcolonial Studies: Disparate Tales of the "Third World"', *Third World Quarterly* 20(4): 703–21.

Szeftel, M. (1998) 'Misunderstanding African Politics: Corruption and the Governance Agenda', *Review of African Political Economy* 25(76): 221–40.

Tamale, S. (2006) 'Eroticism, Sexuality and "Women's Secrets" among the Baganda', *IDS Bulletin* 37(5): 89–97.

Tharu, S., and K. Lalita (1993) 'Empire, Nation and the Literary Text', in T. Niranha, P. Sudhir and V. Dhareshwar (eds), *Interrogating Modernity: Culture and Colonialism in India*, Seagull, Calcutta.

Third World (1977) '1865', *96 Degrees in the Shade*, Island Records, London.

Thoburn, N. (2003) *Deleuze, Marx and Politics*, Routledge, London.

Thompson, E.P. (1982) *The Making of the English Working Class*, Penguin, London.

Thornton, P., and S. Hext (2009) *Review of DFID's Work to Build Support for Development through work with Businesses, Trades Unions, Faith Communities, Black and Minority Ethnic Communities, and Diaspora Groups*, Final Report, July, Verulam Associates, Abingdon.

Trinh M.-H., (1989) *Woman, Native, Other: Writing Postcoloniality and Feminism*, Indiana University Press, Bloomington.

Trouillot, M.R. (1995) *Silencing the Past: Power and the Production of History*, Beacon Press, Boston MA.

Tsikata, D. (2004) 'The Rights-based Approach to Development: Potential for Change or More of the Same?' IDS Bulletin 35(4): 130–33.

UNAIDS (2010) *2010 Report on the Global AIDS Epidemic*, www.unaids.org/global-report/global_report.htm.

UNFPA (1999) *AIDS Update 1999*, United Nations Fund for Population Activities, New York.

US Joint Chiefs of Staff, Chairman (2008) Civil–Military Operations, Joint Publication (JP) 3–57, Washington DC: CJCS, 8 July: GL-6.

Van Allen, J. (1972) '"Sitting on a Man": Colonialism and the Lost Political Institutions of Igbo Women', *Canadian Journal of African Studies* 6(2): 165–81.

Vanita, R. (2002) *Queering India: Same-Sex Love and Eroticism in Indian Culture and Society*, Routledge, New York.

Wang, J. (2008) 'AIDS Denialism and "the Humanisation of the African"', *Race and Class* 49(3): 1–18.

Wangari, E. (2002) 'Reproductive Technologies – A Third World Feminist Perspective', in K. Saunders (ed.), *Feminist Post-Development Thought*, Zed Books, London.

Ware, V. (1992) *Beyond the Pale: White Women, Racism and History*, Verso, London.

Ware, V. (2011) 'The New Literary Front: Public Diplomacy and the Cultural Politics of Reading Arabic Fiction in Translation', *New Formations* 73: 56–77.

Wearing, S. (2012) 'Representing Agency and Coercion: Feminist Readings and

Postfeminist Media Fictions', in S. Madhok, A. Phillips and K. Wilson (eds), *Gender, Agency and Coercion*, Palgrave Macmillan, Basingstoke.

Whitcombe, E. (1995) 'The Environmental Costs of Irrigation in British India: Waterlogging, Salinity, Malaria', in D. Arnold and R. Guha (eds), *Nature, Culture, Imperialism: Essays on the Environmental History of South Asia*, Oxford University Press, Delhi.

White, S. (2002) 'Thinking Race, Thinking Development', *Third World Quarterly* 23(3): 407–19.

White, S. (2006) 'The "Gender Lens": A Racial Blinder?', *Progress in Development Studies* 6(1): 55–67.

Whitehead, A. (2001) 'Continuities and Discontinuities in Political Constructions of the Working Man in Rural Sub-Saharan Africa: The "Lazy Man" in African Agriculture', in C. Jackson (ed.), *Men at Work: Labour, Masculinities, Development*, Routledge, London.

WHO/UNAIDS/UNICEF (2011) 'Global HIV/AIDS Response: Epidemic Update and Health Sector Progress towards Universal Access 2011', www.unicef.org.uk/Latest/Publications/hiv-global-response.

Williams, D., and T. Young (2009) 'The International Politics of Social Trans-formation', in M. Duffield and V. Hewitt (eds), *Empire, Development & Colonialism: The Past in the Present*, James Currey, Oxford.

Williams, E. (1944) *Capitalism and Slavery*, University of North Carolina Press, Chapel Hill.

Wilson, A. (1983) *Black People and the Health Service: Some Developments since 1981*, Black Health Workers and Patients Group, London.

Wilson, A. (1989) *US Foreign Policy and Revolution: The Creation of Tanzania*, Pluto Press, London.

Wilson, A. (1994) 'New World Order and the West's War on Population', *Economic and Political Weekly* 29(34): 2201–4.

Wilson, A. (2006) *Dreams, Questions, Struggles: South Asian Women in Britain*, Pluto Press, London.

Wilson, A. (2007) 'The Forced Marriage Debate and the British State', *Race and Class* 49(1): 25–38.

Wilson, H.H., and J. Mill (1848) *The History of British India, from 1805 to 1835*, Vol. 1, James Madden, London.

Wilson, K. (1993) 'Globalisation and the "Muslim Belt": Reshaping of British Racism', *Economic and Political Weekly* 28(25), 19 June: 1288–90.

Wilson, K. (1999) 'Patterns of Accumulation and Struggles of Rural Labour: Some Aspects of Agrarian Change in Central Bihar', *Journal of Peasant Studies* 26(2): 316–54.

Wilson, K. (2007) 'Agency', in G. Blakeley and V. Bryson (eds), *The Impact of Feminism on Political Concepts and Debates*, Manchester University Press, Manchester.

Wilson, K. (2008) 'Reclaiming "Agency", Reasserting Resistance', *IDS Bulletin* 39(6): 83–91.

Wilson, K. (2012) 'Agency as "Smart Economics": Neoliberalism, Gender and Development', in S. Madhok, A. Phillips and K. Wilson (eds), *Gender, Agency and Coercion*, Palgrave Macmillan, Basingstoke.

Women for Women International (2011) www.womenforwomen.org/global-initiatives-helping-women/stories-women-afghanistan.php; accessed 1 March 2011.

World Bank (1989) *Sub-Saharan Africa: From Crisis to Sustainable Growth*, Oxford University Press, New York.

World Bank (1992) *Governance and Development*, World Bank, Washington DC.

World Bank (1997) *World Development Report 1997: The State in a Changing World*, World Bank, Washington DC.

World Bank (2010) *Africa Development Indicators 2010: Silent and Lethal: How Quiet Corruption Undermines Africa's Development Efforts*, World Bank, Washington DC.

World Bank (2011) *The World Development Report 2012: Gender Equality and Development*, World Bank, Washington DC.

World Bank/USAID (2010) 'Emerging Issues in Today's HIV Response Debate Series. Debate Six: Treatment as Prevention'www.aidstar-one.com/events/emerging_issues_todays_hiv_response_debate_series/debate_six_treatment_prevention.

Wright, C. (2004) 'Consuming Lives, Consuming Landscapes: Interpreting Advertisements for Cafedirect Coffees', *Journal of International Development* 16(5): 665–80.

Yadav, Anumeha (2011) 'Vibrant Gujarat? Your Coast Is Not Clear, Mr Adani', *Tehelka* magazine 8(8), 26 February, www.tehelka.com/story_main48.asp?filename=ne260211development_conflicts.asp.

Young, R.J.C. (1995) 'Foucault on Race and Colonialism', *New Formations* 25: 57–65.

Zack-Williams, A.B. (2001) 'No Democracy, No Development:Reflections on Democracy and Development in Africa', *Review of African Political Economy* 28(88): 213–23.

Index

About Zed Books

Zed Books is a critical and dynamic publisher, committed to increasing awareness of important international issues and to promoting diversity, alternative voices and progressive social change. We publish on politics, development, gender, the environment and economics for a global audience of students, academics, activist and general readers. Run as a co-operative, we aim to operate in an ethical and environmentally sustainable way.

Find out more at
www.zedbooks.co.uk

For up-to-date news, articles, reviews
and events information visit
http://zed-books.blogspot.com

To subscribe to the monthly Zed Books e-newsletter
send an email headed 'subscribe' to marketing@zedbooks.net

We can also be found on Facebook, ZNet,
Twitter and Library Thing.